PORTRAIT TO LANDSCAPE

A Landscape Strategy to Reframe Our Future

ALEXANDRA STEED

ALEXANDRA STEED
URBAN

ISBN: 978-1-7384204-1-4

For more information, email info@alexandrasteedurban.com

For my Angus and Johnny

Contents

Appendix

Introduction

Portrait to Landscape takes you on a captivating journey, inviting you to awaken to a profound new way of inhabiting our planet. In a world where humanity has lost touch with its essential nature—an inherent unity with all life—this book unveils a transformative path that awaits. With a gentle yet powerful shift in perspective from a narrow self-portrait focus to the expansive lens of a wide-angle landscape, we open our eyes to the marvellous community of life to which we belong. As the pages turn our gaze to the landscape, a radiant light is cast that makes visible a revolutionary and dynamic framework for living, guiding us towards a life brimming with joy, purpose and boundless possibilities.

The need for change reverberates throughout our world. Every day, we are inundated with news of historic environmental disasters—devastating floods and storms, rampant wildfires, unprecedented polar ice melt, species extinctions, water and food crises, and, of course, global pandemics. These crises are deeply interconnected, rooted in climate change, ecological collapse, and population expansion. Superficial solutions like switching to electric vehicles, eating dolphin-safe tuna, or replacing plastic with paper straws, while worthwhile, can feel like putting a band-aid on a bullet wound. Such measures merely address symptoms rather than the deeper root problem: our broken relationship with nature. It is in the landscape where this brokenness is most evident, but it is also the very place where healing can occur.

Humanity has been misguided, particularly in the Western world, to believe that we are separate from and dominant over the rest of nature. It is precisely this misperception of separateness that has led us to the challenges we face today. In an increasingly urbanised, industrialised, and technological world, the dualistic view of humans versus nature is easily accepted. Most people are physically and psychologically alienated from the natural world, forgetting that we are fundamentally dependent on the sun in the sky, the air around us, the soil below our feet, fresh water, and healthy plants as when Homo sapiens first appeared on earth. These life-giving elements allowed our species a chance of original evolution and survival. Relearning how to live in harmony with nature is essential to heal our fractured relationship with the living world.

Our society must undergo a transformative reorientation, moving away from an arrogant and self-centred portrait mentality towards an inclusive and holistic landscape mindset in order to instigate meaningful change. Consider an individual consumed by the act of incessantly taking selfies, their focus confined solely to themselves, oblivious to the awe-inspiring world surrounding them. This self-centred image mirrors the impoverished reality in which we currently reside. Only by redirecting our attention from a selfie-portrait orientation to a broader landscape lens can we truly grasp our place as integral members of a much grander living community.

However, making this shift can be challenging within our current culture. Those in power are often obsessed with perpetual economic growth and development, neglecting critical environmental and community health considerations. Our financial and political structures view nature merely as "resources" to be exploited, controlled, and commodified. The narrow metric of GDP as a measure of national prosperity further distorts our perception of value. This obliviousness to our interconnectedness with nature is most evident in our landscapes, especially urban landscapes, where nature is often treated as an intruder incompatible with the human habitat.

The exclusion of nature's presence and the dismissal of its gifts have led to polluted air, restricted availability of nourishing food, and a lack of opportunities for exercise, recreation, and green spaces. Lives are lived without the joy of birdsong, or even sufficient access to sunlight, or fresh water. However, integrating nature into our everyday lives is not only possible but essential for our health, well-being, and ability to thrive.

Our relationship with nature and the land, or the lack thereof, has become the defining feature of our era. The mindset of separation and dominion has led to severance and imbalance, physically manifesting in built-up areas and also in rural and wilderness landscapes. All landscapes are suffering under the weight of human-generated change, amplified by intense urbanisation, industrialisation, and technological advances.

Nature is saturated and can no longer hide or absorb the excesses we impose upon it. Greenhouse gas emissions, overfishing, pesticide use, plastic pollution, deforestation, and animal poaching —all of these human activities have had disastrous and incalculable effects on the global environment.

Yet, this is also an extraordinary time in history. We can now see and understand the consequences of destructive human forces on the planet, empowering global citizens to demand necessary change from world leaders and corporations responsible for much of the damage. Even more importantly, it allows us the opportunity to reimagine a world in which every person has the right to live as part of nature and not separate from it, to collaborate with nature rather than work against it, and to become caretakers of the planet, rather than its exploiters.

Humanity must collectively act from a place of wisdom. Mere attention to the symptoms of numerous crises falls short in its ability to usher in enduring planetary well-being and establish the groundwork for a regenerative future. To truly tackle the underlying issue, we must prioritise restoring our connection with nature while simultaneously offering immediate relief for the associated symptoms. The healing process begins by cultivating the essential conditions that foster recovery and equilibrium within the world's diverse landscapes.

Portrait to Landscape provides a framework to transform the state of the earth and the way we inhabit it. The book explains how turning your gaze from a portrait to a landscape perspective will open your eyes with wonder to the community of life all around. It reveals the challenges produced by a limited, human-centred perspective. It describes how embracing a broader landscape orientation liberates the creative intelligence of nature to address those challenges and heal the earth. Moreover, it details how the landscape—the physical expression of the human relationship with nature—is the sphere where healing can occur. It outlines a practical strategy for supporting regeneration through landscape protection, restoration, and long-term stewardship. This endeavour calls for the involvement of everyone, from policymakers to environmental charities, community activists, voters, and individuals like yourself. By embracing intelligent humility and respect for all of nature, we can become beneficial stewards and realise a better, resilient world for people and the environment.

I have spent over two decades working in the field of landscape architecture, spanning diverse locations and scales. From small urban roof gardens to expansive city masterplans and landscape strategies that encompass entire regions and countries, I have witnessed the transformative power of landscape first-hand. It is my firm belief that landscape, regardless of its context or size, has the profound ability to bring beauty and vitality into our lives.

Through my work and studies, I have come to recognise landscape as a living canvas where the past becomes visible, the present is cradled, and future possibilities unfold. It serves as the very foundation of life itself. By embracing landscape and engaging in collaborative efforts, we can forge new ways of relating to and coexisting with our planet. As a dynamic and adaptable infrastructure, landscape can be shaped to address monumental global challenges and restore the earth. It holds within it the promise of a thriving and regenerative future. Few fields can offer a more exhilarating prospect.

Over the course of the past twenty-five years, and with the hope of continuing for the next twenty-five, I have had the privilege of leading world-class design teams, overseeing complex multi-disciplinary projects, contributing to design review panels, teaching at universities, and participating in some of the most remarkable and strategic landscape endeavours worldwide. During my time as a graduate student at the University of British Columbia, I had the opportunity to collaborate with a research team in developing revolutionary models of sustainable development. These models operate in harmony with natural processes and systems, guided by principles that prioritise community and environmental well-being. I also worked with the newly established Vancouver Greenways department, a pioneering concept a quarter-century ago. Through this experience, I was able to contribute to the planning, design, and implementation of community and city-wide greenways, establishing an inclusive network of pedestrian and cycling routes.

For the past two decades, I have lived and worked in London. Partnering with leading design practices, I have been involved in projects spanning Europe, Asia, and the Middle East, where I have had the opportunity to develop innovative large-scale masterplans and strategies rooted in nature-based approaches. Working alongside experts in ecology, planning, engineering, architecture, art, economics, finance, and various other disciplines, I have gained invaluable insights. Additionally, I have been fortunate to learn from the communities I have served. Through my own observations, I have witnessed the remarkable capacity of landscape to foster community healing, both human and wild, through responsive and cooperative relationships. The landscape is co-created by the community, and in turn, it nurtures and strengthens the community.

A decade ago, I founded my own landscape architecture practice with a vision to bring joy to people's daily lives by forging fresh connections between people and nature. My aim with this book is to extend this vision directly to you. I want to remind you that you are an integral part of nature and, as such, play a vital role in the healing process. You possess agency and the power to effect change in the world. We do not need to rely solely on clever solutions or complex technological inventions. Instead of viewing nature as an obstacle to be conquered or controlled, let us adopt the mindset of loving and caring gardeners, tending to the earth with reverence and compassion.

Humanity stands at a crucial juncture, where embracing nature's intelligence and actively nurturing conditions for the earth's rejuvenation becomes paramount. Cultivating a regenerative mindset necessitates wisdom and humility, and it is a responsibility that falls upon each and every one of us—a responsibility we must wholeheartedly accept. This monumental task demands our unwavering attention. The pivotal realisation lies in our interconnectedness as global citizens, compelling us to care for our shared planetary home. The transformation we seek will permeate every level of society, involving politicians, corporations, entrepreneurs, charities, educators, community organisers, activists, voters, and students alike. Regardless of your background or role, it is my aim to share the knowledge and insights you need. Each of us plays a fundamental role in reshaping and re-establishing a harmonious relationship with nature in the landscape.

In this book, I have brought together a multitude of information, presenting it in a coherent and accessible manner. The narrative provides a comprehensive overview of the current state of the world's landscapes, the threats they face (which can sometimes appear overwhelming and gloomy, but remember, there is hope), the flawed thinking that has contributed to these threats, and a proposal for a new paradigm rooted in integration and inclusivity. Furthermore, I outline several critical moves that offer a way forward to restoring the earth. My hope is that this book will ignite your curiosity and inspire you to look deeper into the subject and become more actively engaged.

The book is structured as I best know how: as a landscape strategy, but this time at a global scale. It begins with an overarching vision, followed by an explanation of the baseline assessment of the physical and socio-economic context. The core themes of the evaluation are then outlined, along with overarching design principles that will guide our approach. I identify the key actions and moves required to realise our intended vision. Finally, the book describes how you can integrate a "Portrait to Landscape" approach into your own life.

Here is a snapshot of the major sections within the book.

Part 1: Vision. The first part of the book delves into the Portrait to Landscape concept which sets the tone for the entire journey. It establishes a framework for addressing global challenges by emphasising three key points. First, it acknowledges that the world's monumental problems stem from a delusion of separateness. Second, it highlights the imperative for humanity to free itself from this delusion. And finally, it underscores the necessity for humanity to embrace all of nature. The Portrait to Landscape framework serves as a guiding lens throughout the book, offering insights into the current state of affairs, altering the prevailing paradigm, and illuminating actionable steps that can be taken to restore the earth.

Part 2: The Big Picture. The second section provides a concise overview of significant environmental and socio-economic challenges, offering a comprehensive understanding of the present reality. It explores pressing issues such as climate change, ecological decline, and population expansion, emphasising the urgency for collective action. Moreover, it reveals how humanity arrived at this critical juncture and proposes that these formidable challenges can be transformed into inspiring opportunities by shifting our worldview from Portrait to Landscape. The section concludes with a tribute to the biosphere, highlighting its remarkable capacity to sustain life and reminding us of the profound interconnectedness of our global landscape.

Part 3: Defining Landscape. The term "landscape" encompasses multiple definitions, serving as both a noun and a verb, constantly evolving and reshaping. While it is often associated with the visible features and aesthetic appeal of a specific area, its true essence goes far beyond that. Landscape comprises layers, functions, processes, and systems of immeasurable value. This section explores landscapes at various scales, from the biosphere to backyard spaces, and across different types, such as forests and wetlands. It highlights the opportunity to transition from imbalance to equilibrium within each landscape. Part 3 concludes by distilling overarching design principles that prioritise creating healthy conditions for land—soil, water, and air—to design for the well-being of the entire community of life. Case studies demonstrate the tremendous benefits and absence of negative consequences when these land elements are considered at the forefront of the development process.

Part 4: Key Moves. Part 4 bridges the philosophical and practical aspects, outlining the essential steps to manifest an integrated, compassionate, and resilient approach to environmental restoration. The key moves identify policies, methods, and tools required to drive and support change, employing both top-down and ground-up approaches. The framework encompasses actions for governments, landowners, built environment experts, educators, students, and individuals. It proposes a comprehensive process involving investment, legislation supporting ecosystem protection and restoration, a landscape-led approach to development, a green curriculum in schools, and developing a workforce equipped with green skills. This section concludes with a series of proposals that provide a cross-section of actionable steps. By collectively pursuing these proposals, we can pave the way to a better world for all.

As the adage goes, "A picture paints a thousand words." As an artist by inclination and training, I tend to think more in images than words. Hence, graphics and illustrations are interspersed throughout the book, illuminating the concepts and ideas conveyed within these pages. I hope these visual elements bring the Portrait to Landscape vision to life for you.

This book is for those who want not only to survive but thrive. It is for those who have grown weary of the status quo and seek a new paradigm. It is for those who long for a fresh beginning, renewed hope, and a brighter tomorrow. It is for those who feel the stirring of awakening and are ready to undergo a profound transformation. It is for those who hold a deep love for this planet, and for those who are prepared to embrace the entire community of life, with its magnificent beauty and boundless wonders.

There is no time to waste. Humanity stands at the precipice. The scientific consensus unequivocally states that we must make radical changes within this decade to restore balance and health to our world. Failure to do so may trigger irreversible tipping points with far-reaching consequences. This is a call for everyone to become actively engaged.

Almost everyone I speak to yearns for a better world and carries grave concerns for the future of their children and the destiny of our species. The problems we face, stemming from historical colonisation, unbridled consumerism, corporate dominance, and a voracious greed economy, are so deeply entrenched in society that it can be challenging to envision an alternative path. The scale of the challenge is overwhelming, and feelings of helplessness and despair are understandable. I, too, have experienced these emotions, and I imagine you have as well. However, I firmly believe that reading this book will empower you and banish feelings of helplessness.

Hope can be found amidst this existential threat. It has sparked an awakening, an eco-consciousness that is propelling a fundamental reorientation reminding people of their inherent connection to nature rather than their separation from it. This inclusive ideology is gaining momentum, and by engaging with this book, you have become an integral part of this movement.

I felt compelled to share with you, and with anyone who will listen, one of the most promising approaches to address these existential challenges: the creative utilisation of landscape to reconnect people with nature and, in turn, with all life. In this book, my aim is to awaken people to a relational worldview and accelerate the transition toward a healthy and whole planet. *Portrait to Landscape* elucidates our current predicament, exposes the human-centred perspective that has contributed to it, and outlines a path to merge an awakening eco-consciousness with our physical environment within the landscape. It presents a clear strategy for a land-centred approach to sustainable development that places the entire community of life at its core. Specifically, it describes how a focus on rehabilitating global landscapes at every scale will foster thriving environments for all life—soils, waters, air, plants, animals, and humans alike. This transformative endeavour calls for grassroots healing initiatives involving each one of us, including you.

By unlocking the door to the extraordinary living world, liberating ourselves from the illusion of separateness, and harnessing the wisdom of nature, I invite you to imagine the possibilities of reorienting our perspective—from Portrait to Landscape—to compose a magnificent future together.

PART I

Vision

1

Embracing Landscape
SEPARATION TO INTEGRATION

"A human being is a part of a whole, called by us "Universe," a part limited in time and space. He experiences himself, his thoughts and feelings as something separated from the rest—a kind of optical delusion of his consciousness. This delusion is a kind of prison for us, restricting us to our personal desires and to affection for a few persons nearest to us. Our task must be to free ourselves from this prison by widening our circle of compassion to embrace all living creatures and the whole of nature in its beauty." [1]

—*Albert Einstein*

A FEW YEARS AGO, I came across this quote that had a profound impact on how I perceive the world. It contains a suggestion for a new vision and existential framework for humanity. Einstein, with his enduring insight, identifies our most significant problem as a delusion of separateness. His words provide a solution to liberate ourselves from self-imposed limitations by shifting our perspective from a narrow, individual focus to an all-encompassing community outlook—from Portrait to Landscape. This reframed worldview presents the possibility of a wholesome and regenerative future where we embrace the beauty of nature in its entirety.

Few people are gifted with the brilliance and insight that Einstein possessed. If Einstein tells us our task, we should sit up and listen. In one succinct paragraph, he reveals that our human plight is one of vision and consciousness: we are optically "deluded." This delusion—that we are "separated from the rest"—has confined us, obscured our understanding, and deprived us of fully experiencing life.

Thankfully, within that same paragraph, Einstein shows us how to break free from this predicament by "widening our circle of compassion to embrace all living creatures and the whole of nature in its beauty." We must transcend our individual selves, recognise our place as part of a greater whole, and reconnect with the natural world, assuming our responsibility to care for it.

In this chapter, I will utilise Einstein's quote as a framework to untangle the mess we have created as a species, and the misconception of separateness that has led to our current dilemma. I will explore how we can liberate ourselves from this mindset and underscore the importance of correcting our vision and thinking to genuinely restore our relationship with nature. A fundamental change is necessary, moving from a mindset of exclusion to one of inclusivity within the earth community, from separation to integration of all life. This internal shift becomes the catalyst for profound and lasting transformation in our external reality.

A Delusion of Separateness

Vision encompasses not only envisioning a different future but also perceiving the past and present with fresh eyes. To create a transformed future, it is crucial to understand how we arrived at the present moment. Therefore, let us begin by examining the prevailing worldview in Western thought. Einstein's quote illuminates the fact that humans are an integral part of a greater whole, and the notion of separation is merely an "optical delusion of consciousness." Despite our perception of being disconnected, this belief is unfounded. The dualistic framework that separates humans from nature serves as the foundation of much of our thinking and offers a simplified and coherent way of understanding the world. In many ways, viewing things in binary terms provides a convenient tool for the limitations of the human mind, allowing us to navigate and position ourselves in the world.

The world we inhabit is incredibly complex, and our minds naturally work to filter and make sense of the multitude of phenomena bombarding us from all directions. To process and organise this diverse information into something coherent, the human brain has developed systems that automatically organise inputs, bypassing processes that would otherwise require significant time, energy, and thought.

In an article titled "The Elusive Theory of Everything," physicists Stephen Hawking and Leonard Mlodinow recount an intriguing story about the City Council of Monza, Italy, banning round fishbowls to prevent cruelty towards goldfish. The reasoning behind the ban was that the curved glass distorted the fish's view of reality. This anecdote raises an important question: how can we be certain that our perception of reality is any less distorted than that of the fish? Hawking and Mlodinow propose, "For all we know, we, too, may spend our entire lives staring out at the world through a distorting lens."[2]

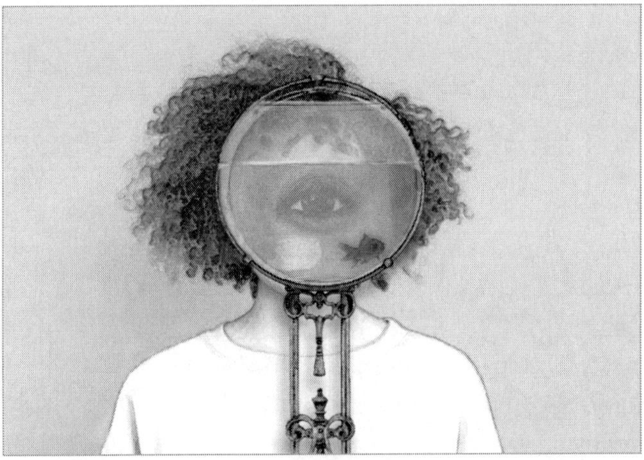

Figure 1.1 *– A Question of Perspective: How distorted is our version of reality compared to the view from inside a fishbowl? (© Alexandra Steed URBAN)*

3

Many people believe there is an objective reality and that our senses accurately represent the material world around us. However, this is not the case. Every day, our minds are busy constructing conscious and subconscious models for us to be able to interpret and understand the world. Hawking and Mlodinow explain, "There is no way to remove the observer—us—from our perception of the world, which is created through sensory processing and through the way we think and reason. Our perception—and hence the observations upon which our theories are based—is not direct, but rather is shaped by a kind of lens, the interpretive structure of our brain."[4] Each of us is constantly interpreting the signals we receive. What we perceive is shaped by how we understand ourselves in relation to the world around us, our paradigm, if you will.

Consider the intricate process of human vision as an illustration. As light enters the eye, it traverses the cornea and lens, converging onto the retina. The retina's photoreceptors then convert the incoming light into electrical signals. These signals travel along the optic nerve to the brain, where they undergo a remarkable transformation. The raw data is processed, refined, and woven together to construct a coherent and immersive three-dimensional model of the world.

Remarkably, there exists a noticeable gap in the incoming visual data where the optic nerve connects to the retina. Rather than perceiving black spots in our vision, our minds instinctively fill in these gaps, making assumptions and shaping our perceptions. It becomes apparent that the individual, the perceiver, is an active participant in constructing the image that is ultimately seen, just as much as the observed phenomena itself.[5]

This analogy of the human visual system serves as a compelling metaphor for our broader perception of reality. It highlights the fact that our interpretations and understanding of the world are not solely dictated by the objective stimuli we encounter but are also influenced by our active engagement with the information and the internal processes of our minds. Our perceptions are an intricate interplay between the external and internal, constantly shaping and constructing our understanding of the world.

Daniel Kahneman's pivotal book *Thinking Fast and Slow* provides excellent insight into the human mind, how we see ourselves, and how we understand the world around us. He explains "the notion of a *narrative fallacy* to describe how flawed stories of the past shape our views of the world and expectations for the future. Narrative fallacies arise inevitably from our continuous attempt to make sense of the world."[6] He explains that the most compelling stories are simple and concrete and that we more easily digest and wholeheartedly accept these stories when we are ignorant of a subject. If it is a good story, we believe it. "Paradoxically, it is easier to construct a coherent story when you know little, when there are fewer pieces to fit into the puzzle. Our comforting conviction that the world makes sense rests on a secure foundation: our almost unlimited ability to ignore our ignorance."[7]

Kahneman's insights shed light on the fact that what we consider to be true and knowable are often merely stories we tell ourselves. These narratives, though convenient, have been collectively constructed to simplify our understanding of the world. It is no wonder then that the notion of humans being separate from nature easily takes hold. Nature, in its essence, is unknowable, and our relationship with it appears abstract and distant. The concept of "us" humans versus "it" nature is a tangible and appealing concept for our limited minds, seeking simplicity in complexity.

Furthermore, there is a tendency to perceive ourselves as distinct and superior to other species. The prevailing narrative does not typically promote notions of separation and equality, separation and inferiority, or separation but complementarity. Rather, the dominant Western philosophy positions humans as independent entities exerting dominance over nature. This worldview is closely intertwined with Abrahamic religious beliefs which assert that humans are created "in the image of God."[8] Consequently, the narrative contends that humans stand at the pinnacle of creation, with nature existing solely for our domination and exploitation. Resources are often viewed as limitless, and humans are regarded as eternal rulers of the planet. This simplistic perspective holds great allure when attempting to comprehend ourselves, nature, life, and the future.

This construct of separateness and dominance is our inherited impairment, or as Einstein puts it, "a kind of prison for us." Its consequences are evident in the dysfunctional environment in which we find ourselves today. The natural world has been exploited to such an extent that entire ecosystems are collapsing. We have grown up in a world where this construct is perceived as reality, and we have been conditioned to turn a blind eye to the interconnected living communities around us.

Upon reflection, the illusion of separateness dissipates, revealing a profound truth. It becomes unmistakably clear that we not only depend on nature but are an inseparable part of it. The land, encompassing the air we breathe, the water we drink, and the food we consume, is the very foundation of our existence. It intertwines with every facet of our being, permeating each cell within us, just as we inhabit the land itself.

Our bodies, born from the earth, follow the inevitable path of returning to it through the cycle of decomposition. The land not only provides support and sustenance, but it is also intricately woven into the fabric of our essence. There exists no distinct boundary or separation between "us" and "it"; there is only "we." The relationship is boundless and indivisible, akin to the intimate connection between ourselves and our own physical forms.

To imagine that we stand apart from nature is as peculiar as envisioning ourselves detached from our very own existence. In truth, we are forever entwined, and recognising this profound unity is pivotal in fostering a harmonious relationship with the world around us.

The fallacy of constructed dualism has kept us trapped in ignorance for far too long. Now is the time to discard this narrative and embrace a new understanding of our place within the interconnected web of life.

Our Task is to Free Ourselves

Einstein's quote emphasises that "Our task must be to free ourselves from this prison."[9] His words paint a graphic picture: we have locked ourselves in a cage of self-absorption, isolating us from the world and confining us within our own desires. He notes that we have limited our experience to "our personal desires and to affection for a few persons nearest to us." In this self-inflicted incarceration, it is we humans who suffer the most. The responsibility falls upon us as individuals to break free from the illusion of separateness and embrace the oneness of life. No external force or entity can accomplish this for us; it is our personal journey of liberation.

Contemplating this concept, I began to perceive the stage of development in which humanity finds itself. As a species, Homo sapiens are still in their infancy, a fleeting moment in the grand timeline of our planet. According to Earth science, humans would only emerge in the final seconds if the planet's lifespan were condensed into a twelve-hour clock. Our rapid progress has propelled us from insignificant foragers to the dominant species, bypassing the graceful evolution and maturation that time typically affords. However, the powerful and elite among us, paradoxically, exhibit signs of immaturity. Driven by greed and self-centred desires, they remain stuck in an irresponsible stage of development. Like the mythical figure Narcissus, captivated by his own reflection, many world leaders exude narcissism, with their own image taking precedence over the well-being of their earth community and the things that truly matter.

Humanity must recognise that, akin to Narcissus, excessive self-obsession and a lack of concern for the world around us—the air we breathe, the water we drink, the life-giving soils, and the wondrous diversity of plants and animals—will inevitably lead to our downfall. Narcissus's story conveys the inseparable link between our fate and the attention we give to the natural world in which we reside.

Imagine replacing the narrow lens of a selfie portrait with a wide-angle lens capable of capturing vast landscapes and their full expanse. By adopting this different lens, our perspective shifts from focusing solely on ourselves to embracing the broader landscape. Similarly, adopting a landscape framework in our approach to growth and development reveals a relational perspective that positions us within our surroundings, recognising the interdependence of all living beings.

While humanity possesses abundant data, knowledge, and intelligence, we must rapidly evolve to cultivate the wisdom needed to integrate this information into a balanced way of coexisting with the earth. The fundamental requirement is to transform our thinking, enabling us to uncover innovative solutions. Additionally, we must seek out leaders and politicians who share a like-minded vision, replacing the narcissistic ones of today. By doing so, we empower society to make a developmental leap towards maturity, responsibility, and compassion, ultimately fostering an enhanced relationship with the world we inhabit.

Embrace the Whole of Nature

In his wisdom, Einstein urges us to break free from our delusions "by widening our circle of compassion to embrace all living creatures and the whole of nature in its beauty." This call to liberation not only offers an escape from our self-imposed prison but also paints a vivid and uplifting vision of a future where the richness and splendour of life hold us in a reciprocal embrace.

The journey of transformation begins with each of us as individuals. While we cannot compel others to awaken, we possess the power to change our own perceptions, consciousness, and way of existing in the world. As more individuals alter their worldview from a narrow focus on the individual to a broader perspective that encompasses nature, the movement gains momentum, strength, and influence.

Fortunately, this metamorphosis is already unfolding. The evolution towards a more inclusive view of the world is underway, with increasing numbers of people altering their perspectives to see themselves as interconnected participants in a vast, non-hierarchical, and interdependent community. This ecocentric mindset prioritises the well-being of all of nature and recognises the inherent value in every form of life. Embracing this open and inclusive worldview will accelerate humanity's journey towards maturity, wisdom, and a humble understanding of our place within the intricate tapestry of existence.

While anthropocentrism, a human-centred belief system that prioritises human value and experience, has long dominated our ideology, it is not the sole way of understanding the world. Throughout history, there have always been those who recognised our profound interconnectedness with all life. Indigenous cultures, religions, and philosophies, for instance, have articulated a similar understanding, emphasising the intrinsic value of plants, animals, organisms, water, air, and soil while de-emphasising human importance. Ecocentrism acknowledges the vitality of planet earth as a whole.

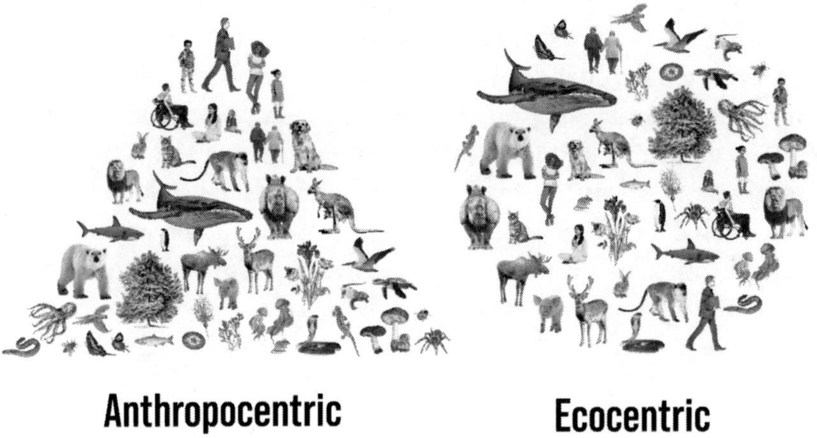

Figure 1.2 *– Anthropocentric to Ecocentric: Shifting from a human-focussed perspective to a nature-centred worldview is necessary to restore balance to the earth (© Alexandra Steed URBAN).*

10

This inclusive worldview is sometimes misconstrued as primitive. However, acknowledging our place within nature is not a regression to primordial ideas. Biologist and regenerative systems scholar

Daniel Christian Wahl explains, "Rather, it is a way of knowing that can be regarded as a dialectical synthesis of the long evolution from the primordial undifferentiated consciousness and the enchanted world of early humans when everything was sacred and alive, on to the dualistic alienation between self and world, mind and body, humanity and nature, to then arrive at a participatory worldview that embraces the paradox of being at one and the same time (seemingly) separate from and fundamentally interconnected with nature."[11]

Embracing this participatory worldview may present challenges, but it offers a much richer and more profound understanding than a simplistic "us versus it" dichotomy. We can view an ecocentric perspective as a synthesis of our deep union with nature and our modern dualistic view. Both ideas can coexist, as we simultaneously accept and embrace our oneness and individuality.

Richard Tarnas, in his book *The Passion of the Western Mind – Understanding the Ideas That Have Shaped Our World View*, elucidates the paradox further: "In this view, the essential reality of nature is not separate, self-contained, and complete in itself, so that the human mind can examine it "objectively" and register it from without. Rather, nature's unfolding truth emerges only with the active participation of the human mind. Nature's reality is not merely phenomenal nor independent and objective; rather, it comes into being through the very act of human cognition. Nature becomes intelligible to itself through the human mind. In this perspective, nature pervades everything, and the human mind in all its fullness is itself an expression of nature's essential being." [12]

One of the most remarkable aspects of the human mind is that it brings forth a perceiving consciousness to nature—we are eyes through which the living world sees itself. We have the capacity to observe and comprehend nature in a truly unique way. Embracing this paradox is vital for a transformative change in consciousness. What a marvellous privilege and joy it is for us as humans! Yet, this privilege must not be underestimated or squandered; it comes with great responsibility.

The Land Ethic

As individuals, we are not isolated entities but members of a community, and with that membership comes ethical responsibilities. In Western society, ethics have traditionally focused on relationships between individuals and between individuals and society, as seen in principles like the Ten Commandments or the Golden Rule. However, Aldo Leopold, in his influential work, *A Sand County Almanac*, published in 1949, pointed out that, "There is yet no ethic dealing with man's relation to land and to the animals and plants which grow upon it."[13] Writing from the perspective of an American citizen, Leopold asserts that the extension of ethics, as a third element, to the environment is "an evolutionary possibility and an ecological necessity."[14] Thus, he presented "the land ethic" as a means to expand our moral compass from humans to the entire land community.[15]

Leopold's message is as relevant today as it was when he first introduced it, despite initially going largely unnoticed.[16] (As I write this in my local coffee shop, with *A Sand County Almanac* lying on the table, someone taps me on the shoulder and says, "That is one of the most important books ever written." I couldn't agree more.) Considered the most influential conservationist of the twentieth century, Leopold's ideas resonate deeply with those who have encountered his work. His forward-thinking perspectives on the relationship between people and the land continue to inspire and guide environmental stewardship.

Leopold's legacy reflects his generosity of spirit and humble outlook. Throughout his career as a forester, ecologist, scientist, naturalist, conservationist, philosopher, and writer, he transformed society's understanding of the intricate connections between people and the land. His contributions range from establishing the world's first wilderness area in Gila, New Mexico, in 1924, to shaping the field of game management, emphasising habitat preservation, recognising the significance of watersheds for ecosystem health, and was very influential in bringing the subject of land restoration into the public consciousness.

While Leopold's early efforts focused on developing policies and regulations for land conservation, he later realised that enduring change in land management required more than administrative measures. He understood that a shared land ethic, upheld by the community, was essential. According to Leopold, ethical and aesthetic considerations should guide our decisions, with actions deemed right when they preserve the integrity, stability, and beauty of the biotic community, and wrong when they do otherwise.[17] Embracing a land ethic as part of our ethical framework naturally fosters an ecological conscience and makes each individual responsible for the health and self-renewal of the land community.[18]

With this revelation, Leopold dedicated himself to spreading his ideas far and wide. He engaged with diverse audiences, including landowners, farmers, hunters, students, businesspeople, and government officials, to communicate the importance of a land ethic. He also spent considerable time committing his ideas to paper, culminating in what many consider his greatest achievement—the development of the land ethic.

It was he who coined the term "ecocentric" to describe a paradigm that places value on the entire ecosphere. Leopold de-emphasises unique human importance and challenges the notion of humans as the sole arbiters of value and meaning, shifting focus to the significance of plants, animals, water, air, soil, and the holistic health of the earth. He writes:

> "The land ethic simply enlarges the boundaries of the community to include soils, waters, plants, and animals, or collectively: the land…A land ethic of course cannot prevent the alteration, management, and use of these 'resources,' but it does affirm their right to continued existence, and, at least in spots, their continued existence in a natural state. In short, a land ethic changes the role of Homo sapiens from conqueror of the land-community to plain member and citizen of it. It implies respect for his fellow-members, and also respect for the community as such."[19]

Leopold's land ethic explains the necessity of rising ecological consciousness. It provides humanity with a roadmap of how to move from separation to integration, from individual to community, and in Einstein's words, "to free ourselves from this prison by widening our circle of compassion to embrace all living creatures and the whole of nature in its beauty."[20]

Since Leopold's time, significant changes have occurred, and the extent of global land exploitation and degradation would likely shock him. The prevailing reductionist approach to economic development and growth has contributed to these challenges. Nevertheless, Leopold would recognise that altering the current system necessitates a shift in our thinking, perception, and understanding. The inherited visual impairment of society must be unlearned and rectified to attain a clearer vision of the world around us. External change is contingent upon internal transformation, as our thoughts and beliefs shape our actions.

Embarking on the journey towards a sustainable future demands embracing the entirety of nature's magnificence. We must re-establish our sense of belonging and interconnectedness with the natural world, forsaking the notion of separation. By infusing our psyche with a land ethic, we can unveil the beauty and intelligence inherent in nature. Rather than resisting it, we must rehabilitate our connection to the land. Such an open and harmonious relationship with the landscape unlocks boundless opportunities for creativity and regenerative thinking.

Now is the opportune moment to move from a limited portrait perspective to a more expansive landscape experience. By embracing the broader context, we gain a clearer understanding of the attitudes and actions that require rectification. Change is only possible as a reaction to the current state of things. Examining the present condition of the landscape and its most significant threats allows us to chart a course towards meaningful change. The subsequent chapter aims to provide an explanation of these aspects.

PART II

The Big Picture

2

The Current Landscape
CHALLENGE TO OPPORTUNITY

"We stand now where two roads diverge. But unlike the roads in Robert Frost's familiar poem, they are not equally fair. The road we have long been travelling is deceptively easy, a smooth superhighway on which we progress with great speed, but at its end lies disaster. The other fork of the road—the one 'less travelled by'—offers our last, our only chance to reach a destination that assures the preservation of the earth.

The choice, after all, is ours to make." [1]

—Rachel Carson

HUMANITY STANDS at a pivotal moment in its history, with scientists warning that we must urgently change our trajectory within this decade. Failure to do so will lead us blindly down a road towards a bleak and disastrous future. In the prevailing paradigm, the land is often viewed solely through an economic lens—as a problem to be solved, an obstacle to be overcome, and a resource to be exploited. It is seen as something to be controlled, manipulated, and subdued. However, there is an alternative road that is frequently overlooked—the scenic route. This route embraces the contours of the landscape, appreciates its intrinsic beauty, and harnesses its natural attributes. By taking the scenic route, we unlock vistas, discover the precious gifts of the land, and optimise the experience of our journey.

To make an informed choice about which road to take, we must have a clear understanding of both options. It is crucial to be well-informed about the facts and comprehend the advantages and disadvantages of each way. In order to assist you in this decision-making process, I will highlight the stark environmental challenges that have intensified since Rachel Carson's ground-breaking book, *Silent Spring*. These challenges include climate change, the alarming loss of biodiversity and ecosystems, and the mounting pressures of human population growth.

This chapter delves into the concept of planetary limits that must be upheld to ensure a safe and hospitable environment for human survival. Additionally, it introduces the potential of nature-based solutions as a means to address these pressing challenges. By harnessing the extraordinary capabilities of nature, humanity can choose to transform environmental crises into life-changing opportunities. As Carson aptly observed, "The choice, after all, is ours to make."[2]

Rachel Carson, a legendary nature writer, biologist, and conservationist, emerged as one of the first voices to inform the public about the harmful impact of human actions on the environment. In 1962, her seminal work *Silent Spring* shook the world by revealing the catastrophic consequences of our reckless and destructive behaviour towards nature. Moreover, Carson eloquently advocated for the preservation of the living world, stressing that the stewardship of nature's delicate balance is essential for human survival. *Silent Spring* quickly became a bestseller and sparked intense debate, earning its reputation as one of the most controversial books of its time. [3] It ignited a wave of discourse, underscoring the profound interdependence between humans and nature that unfolds in the landscapes we inhabit.

In the two decades leading up to the publication of *Silent Spring*, chemicals, such as DDT, were widely used to combat insect-borne diseases and protect crops from pests. DDT was hailed as a revolutionary discovery and celebrated as a miracle substance. Films from that time depict the indiscriminate spraying of DDT without considering its potential dangers.[4]

However, the dangers of this seemingly miraculous chemical soon came to light. Scientific studies began to show that DDT killed not only the intended pests but many other life forms and even entire ecosystems.[5] In 1958, one of Rachel Carson's friends, Olga Owens Huckins, owner of a bird sanctuary in Massachusetts, witnessed the poisoning of thousands of birds by planes indiscriminately spraying DDT over vast landscape areas. She was horrified that more spraying was planned and that she had no recourse to stop this senseless wildlife extermination. She asked Carson for help.[6]

Around the same time, Carson, working for the US Fish and Wildlife Service, came across a study titled "DDT: Its Effects on Fish and Wildlife," which she believed the public needed to know about.[7] Biologists within the field were aware of the dangerous effects of DDT and other new chemical substances being used, but this information wasn't reaching the wider public. Remembering her friend's words, Carson explains that the tragedy of "a spring without voices" moved her to action.[8]

Carson's message was one of caution. She brought attention to the need for a thoughtful approach to technological advancements. She highlighted the potential long-term effects of chemical substances on the natural world and eloquently described the intricate interdependencies between living organisms and their environment. As she had expected, once the public was aware, they sat up and listened. In fact, they did more than listen. A whole environmental movement began.

Unsurprisingly, Carson faced intense opposition and attempts to discredit her work. Detractors labelled her as a communist, a hysterical woman, a Luddite, unscientific, and a purveyor of distorted facts. Despite the backlash, Carson remained resolute and, though modest, would not be silenced.[9] She was determined, "The public must decide whether it wishes to continue on the present road, and it can do so only when in full possession of the facts." [10]

Carson's unwavering commitment to sharing the truth disrupted a human-centric worldview, illuminating the impact of human actions and our dependence on the delicate balance of nature. Had she been alive today, one can only imagine Carson's continued dedication to raising awareness about the escalating environmental crisis, including climate change, habitat loss, biodiversity decline, and the loss of birdsongs. The spectre of a silent spring grows ever closer.

Climate Change

Every day, the news brings us undeniable evidence of environmental decline. Climate change stories dominate the headlines, painting a grim picture of the current state of our planet. In 2022, the Intergovernmental Panel on Climate Change (IPCC), the United Nations' authoritative body on climate science, issued a Code Red for humanity, sounding the alarm on the urgent need for action.[11] The impact of climate change spares no one and no place.[12]

The effects of a warming climate, primarily caused by the accumulation of heat-trapping greenhouse gases like carbon dioxide (CO_2), have already made their mark on our lives. From the deepest oceans to the highest mountains, from the thawing Arctic to expanding deserts, and from rural landscapes to bustling cities, the consequences are evident. The scope and severity of climate change surpass even the predictions of climate scientists, with its rate of acceleration outpacing expectations.[13]

The catastrophic events of the past years have become impossible to ignore. Extreme heatwaves, droughts, and floods have inflicted profound damage worldwide. If greenhouse emissions are not halved by 2030, these events will only worsen. Nature and society are experiencing severe disruption, resulting in limited access to healthy food and clean water, compromised health and well-being, and the destruction of homes, livelihoods, and infrastructure.

Global climate changes exacerbate hazards and intensify the risk of extreme weather events. Over the past five decades, the number of weather-related disasters has increased fivefold, with droughts, floods, storms, and extreme temperatures causing significant human losses.[14] This decade has already witnessed some of the most devasting natural disasters on record.

One striking example is the monstrous floods in Pakistan, which submerged a third of the country—an area larger than the UK—in 2022. Approximately 33 million people were displaced.[15] One-seventh of the country's population became climate refugees overnight.[16] Like many other developing countries, Pakistan only contributes 0.9 percent of the world's carbon footprint, yet they bear the brunt of climate change.[17] The injustice of this situation will become evident as we explore the reasons behind it.

Similarly, South Asia's deadly floods and landslides have driven 12 million people from their homes in India, Nepal, and Bangladesh.[18] The flooding was so intense in Bangladesh in 2022 that a third of the country was underwater. While monsoons are a natural part of the local climate, they have been intensified by rising sea surface temperatures in South Asia.

In the Horn of Africa region, higher and more persistent sea temperatures, a consequence of climate change, have led to extreme heatwaves on land. As a result, the likelihood of drought has doubled, leading to severe and repeated droughts over the past decade. These droughts have devastated crops and livestock, leaving people without food and water and forcing millions to abandon their homes.[19]

The reality is that those who bear the tremendous burden of climate change are the least responsible. People in poorer countries, who are by far the lowest emitters of climate-changing carbon, are at least four times as likely to be displaced by extreme weather than those in rich countries.[20] Several factors contribute to this disparity. Firstly, low-income populations heavily rely on agriculture and natural resources, which are highly susceptible to changing weather patterns and ecosystem disruptions. Secondly, marginalised communities often reside in hazardous areas prone to flooding, landslides, and erosion. Thirdly, racial minorities, indigenous peoples, and women with fewer resources are disproportionately affected due to their exposure to health hazards and lack of resources for relocation. Finally, these communities lack the necessary emergency infrastructure to respond effectively to disasters, making recovery exceedingly difficult.[21] In all cases, the threats of climate change exacerbate existing vulnerabilities and further burden already stressed landscapes.

In Part 4 of this book, specifically Chapter 10, we explore ways to direct investments and support towards these nations, unlock funds for addressing loss and damages, and shift government subsidies from harmful activities to initiatives that combat climate change and restore landscapes. Additionally, Chapter 11 proposes practices to empower indigenous peoples and local communities to manage land using the wisdom of their traditions.

Integrated and long-term landscape strategies are imperative to address the threats of climate change globally. While poorer countries bear a more noticeable impact, wealthy nations are not immune to climate change and increasingly severe weather events. Australia, after experiencing its hottest year in 2020, faced its most devastating bushfire season, with fires engulfing 10 million hectares (approximately 25 million acres), displacing thousands of people, and decimating entire communities.[22] The fires also claimed the lives of over a billion native animals, leaving many species and ecosystems unable to recover.

My homeland, Canada, has also suffered. In 2021, we witnessed a record-breaking temperature of 49.6°C (121°F) in Lytton, British Columbia, concealed under an extreme heat dome. Tragically, a day after this scorching high, a devastating wildfire swept through the town, consuming it entirely. This heatwave, the deadliest in Canadian history, claimed the lives of over 600 people.[23] It resulted in the deaths of 650,000 farm animals, a billion seashore animals, and massive mortality among other marine life.[24] Thousands of birds faced dehydration and starvation while trees withered, crops failed, wildfires raged, and glaciers melted.[25]

During the same autumn, I received distressing messages from family and friends about severe storms, landslides, and extensive flooding in the Fraser River Valley of British Columbia. These calamities were intrinsically linked to the wildfires ignited by the heat dome, which destabilised soils and slopes months earlier. Once again, lives were lost, mass evacuations took place, and critical infrastructure and property were destroyed. The estimated cost of restoration is projected to reach $10 billion Canadian.[26] Just months prior, no one in the temperate Pacific Northwest could have fathomed such extreme weather events. Suddenly, the greater Vancouver region, often hailed as one of the most liveable places on earth, transformed into one of the most dangerous.

Even the polar regions are profoundly impacted. Antarctica and Greenland are losing ice mass at an alarming rate due to rising ocean and air temperatures. Many scientists view this ice loss as the most alarming consequence and a crucial element in the progression towards a hothouse earth.[27] The albedo effect, where ice and snow reflect sunlight and heat, plays a vital role in regulating our planet's temperature. However, as white ice and snow transform into blue water or brown earth, the ability to reflect light diminishes, leading to a positive feedback loop that drives escalating temperatures.[28] This cascade of events could easily tip the balance, causing irreversible changes such as ice-to-water transformation, loss of polar habitats, ocean and planetary warming, disruption of normal ocean circulation, rising sea levels, and inundation of vast productive lands, including numerous cities worldwide. Undoubtedly, melting polar ice poses one of the gravest threats to people and our planet.

Arctic ecosystems are also under severe threat, endangering indigenous species like seals, walruses, wolves, foxes, polar bears, and countless plants, lichens, and mosses that depend on stable sea ice platforms. However, with Arctic Sea ice declining by over 12 percent per decade, this fragile ecosystem is rapidly destabilising, and polar species are struggling to keep pace with the rapid changes and adaptation.[29]

No part of the globe remains untouched. From pole to pole and everywhere in between, our planet is undergoing climate-induced transformations.

This reality underscores the urgent need to improve land health and support natural processes and systems, enabling landscapes to withstand the increasing burden. By doing so, we can enhance the lives of both humans and nature. Part 4 of this book explores various nature-based solutions that can contribute to landscape mitigation strategies, climate adaptation, resilience improvement, and the prevention of vulnerability to the environmental changes we are already experiencing.

Before exploring solutions, it is crucial to examine the environmental challenges in greater detail, including global warming, ecological collapse, and population expansion. Understanding the scope of these challenges will illuminate the changes necessary for a sustainable future.

Global Warming

The earth has already experienced a warming of 1.1°C (2°F) above pre-industrial levels as of 2021, and this seemingly small increase has led to devastating consequences such as prolonged droughts, extreme heatwaves, and severe floods. The goal of the 2015 Paris Climate Accord was to limit global warming to 1.5°C (2.7°F), but at the current rate of acceleration, we are projected to reach this threshold by around 2040. However, even if we manage to meet this ambitious target, the impacts will still be significant, including the disappearance or significant loss of glaciers worldwide, increased water scarcity for millions of people, and a substantial risk of species extinction.[30]

The world is currently warming at an unprecedented rate, primarily due to the burning of fossil fuels in various sectors such as transportation, food and energy production, and industrial activities. These activities release greenhouse gas emissions, including carbon dioxide, methane, nitrous oxide, water vapour, and synthetic fluorinated gases, which accumulate in the atmosphere and trap heat from the sun and earth's surface. Normally, this heat would escape into space, but the presence of these long-lasting greenhouse gases causes the planet's temperature to rise, leading to the greenhouse effect.[31] To address global warming, a committed and integrated strategy encompassing both mitigation and adaptation measures is essential for long-term solutions.

It may be hard to comprehend how a relatively small temperature increase of 1.1°C (2 °F) can have such a profound impact. But if we consider the human body, we can understand its significance. We all know how unwell we feel when our body temperature deviates from the normal range of around 37°C (98.6 °F). A slight increase in temperature results in fever, signalling that something is amiss and we are in danger. Temperature fluctuations, whether too high or too low, can disrupt the delicate balance of our bodies and quickly lead to severe illness or even death if left untreated.

Similarly, the health of our planet and its natural systems is intricately connected. When the earth's temperature rises significantly, it experiences a kind of "fever," and life suffers as a consequence. Moreover, we humans have played a significant role in pushing the earth into a state of ill health. A concoction of poisons is incessantly spewed into the air, dumped into the soils, and spread in our waters, weakening the earth's stability. Polar ice caps continue to melt. Flood levels rise, hurricanes become stronger and more intense, droughts and heatwaves become more frequent and extreme, wildfire season is extended, and precipitation patterns become unpredictable.

The earth has not been given a chance to heal as harmful substances continue to be emitted or produced through many industrial and technological processes. While the planet feels the detrimental effects of these substances and the catastrophic consequences are evident all around us, we persist in the same destructive behaviours. Breaking free from economically profitable but harmful practices without clear alternatives is undoubtedly challenging. A global effort to rehabilitate the planet and adopt life-saving behaviours is urgently needed. Society must immediately abandon addiction to harmful substances and embrace a new way of living.

The world must take immediate action to address climate change. We must demand government legislation to control major polluters and enforce substantial reductions in emissions, particularly carbon dioxide (CO_2). Additionally, we can urge our governments to modify their investment approach by redirecting budgets and financial subsidies toward more sustainable forms of transportation, energy, food production systems, industry, and manufacturing.

Fortunately, countries worldwide have made formal commitments to reduce emissions by setting new standards and implementing policies to meet or surpass these standards. However, the not-so-good news is that progress is not happening fast enough, and many nations are falling short of their commitments. To avert the worst impacts of climate change, scientists emphasise the need to reduce global carbon emissions by as much as 40 percent by 2030 and achieve net zero by 2050.[32]

While reducing emissions is crucial, it is only one aspect of tackling climate change. A more promising and powerful solution lies in the radical transformation of vast landscapes worldwide.

Carbon Sinks

Nature provides us with a constellation of beneficial processes and systems that support life and regulate the planet. Part 3 of this book explores the attributes of landscapes that are freely provided by nature, often overlooked and taken for granted.

In today's world driven by economics and consumerism, these gifts of nature are primarily viewed in terms of their value and usefulness to humans, referred to as "ecosystem services." These services encompass various benefits such as food provision, fresh water, natural medicines, recreational opportunities, tourism, and inspiration. Nature's services also include vital functions like supporting healthy soils, decomposition, pollination, and regulatory effects that cleanse the air, manage floods, purify water, and sequester carbon.

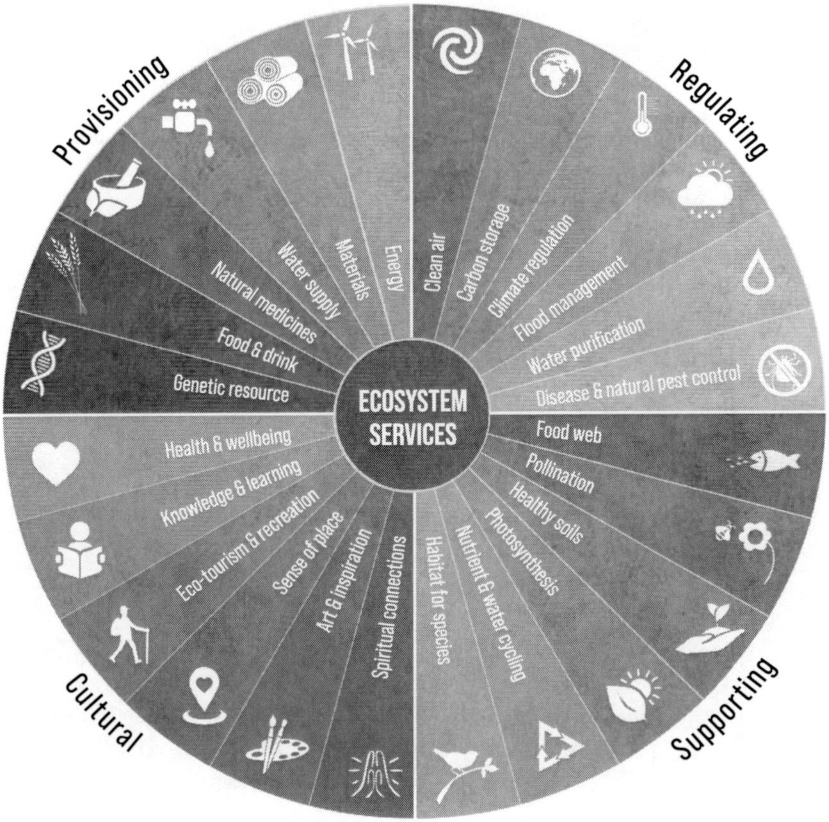

Figure 2.1 *– Unveiling Nature's Gifts: This ecosystem services wheel showcases the remarkable array of free services provided by nature, categorised by their provisioning, regulating, supporting, and cultural functions (© Alexandra Steed URBAN).*

33

These absorptive landscapes are often referred to as carbon sinks. Forests, soils, and oceans are the most significant carbon sinks, exerting a particularly effective regulatory influence on global temperatures. Their capacity to sequester vast amounts of carbon is truly remarkable. However, these carbon sinks face threats from human activities that alter land and sea use.[34]

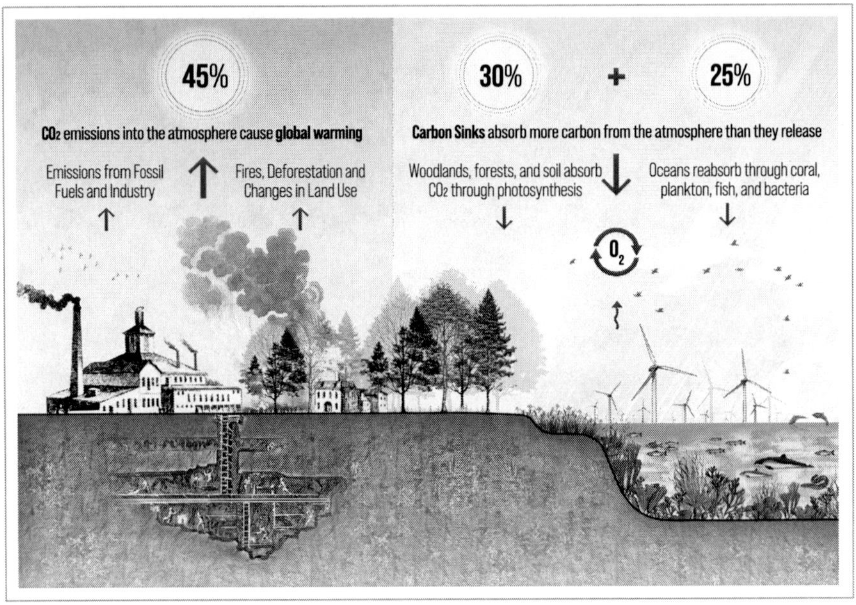

Figure 2.2 – *Carbon Sinks: Essential for combatting greenhouse gas emissions, plants, soils, and oceans serve as primary carbon sinks, absorbing and storing carbon from the atmosphere. (© Alexandra Steed URBAN).*

35

Soils, in particular, are unsung heroes in carbon capture, absorbing approximately a quarter of all carbon emissions each year and storing it underground for thousands of years while supporting a diverse population of microorganisms. Unfortunately, the widespread disruption of grasslands and forests, primarily for agricultural expansion, has the opposite effect, releasing carbon from the topsoil back into the atmosphere.[36]

Global forests absorb roughly 2.6 billion tonnes of carbon dioxide annually, with the Amazon Rainforest alone capturing a quarter of that total.[37] However, forests are lost at an alarming rate of one football pitch every second, jeopardising any progress in tackling climate change—and in fact, adding to the problem—while also threatening the survival of wildlife.

Trees are widely recognised for their remarkable ability to capture carbon, but there are other resilient ecosystems with significant carbon capture capabilities as well. Tundra, seagrass meadows, mangrove forests, and salt marshes are particularly effective in capturing carbon per unit area.[38] The concept of "blue carbon" refers to the carbon captured by ocean ecosystems, which can sequester and store carbon at a faster rate than forests.[39]

The ocean is so successful at absorbing carbon dioxide, capturing 90 percent of excess heat generated by these emissions, that it hid the effects of harmful emissions for many years. Like soil, it absorbs approximately one-quarter of all CO_2 and creates half of the oxygen in the atmosphere. These ocean ecosystems serve multiple functions, including coastal habitat protection and food security. However, if these ecosystems are degraded or damaged, a substantial amount of stored carbon is released back into the atmosphere. Unfortunately, warming, acidification, pollution, and other factors threaten the health of the world's oceans.[40]

To address global climate change, immediate action is needed to halt further destruction of these invaluable ecosystems and carbon sinks. We must harness the exceptional capacity of forests, soils, and oceans to pull CO_2 from the atmosphere. Moreover, we must protect, restore, and care for these landscapes at a historic scale and for the long term. Some practical ways to increase carbon storage include transitioning to sustainable forestry and agriculture, ecosystem restoration, and safeguarding intact wild places. The common thread linking all these effective solutions is their nature-based approach. They are measures that unleash the incredible processes of nature to correct the imbalances in the environment.

Part 4 of this book outlines precisely how we can enable nature to accomplish this feat when we collaborate, from governments to environmental organisations to individuals, by making a commitment to radical landscape rehabilitation and transformation.

Ecological Collapse

Climate change is only part of the world's environmental problems. Many scientists believe that ecological collapse is an even more significant threat. Despite receiving less attention in the news, the decline of biodiversity, erosion of habitats, and extinction of wildlife are occurring at an alarming rate. These impacts may not be readily visible in our urban lives, but the degradation of the natural world is unfolding in forests, soils, and oceans. Currently, species loss is accelerating, with approximately one million animal and plant species now under threat.[41]

While the Intergovernmental Panel on Climate Change (IPCC) addresses climate change, the Intergovernmental Science-Policy Platform on Biodiversity and Ecosystem Services (IPBES) provides scientifically credible assessments on biodiversity.[42] Comprised of nearly 140 member Governments, the IPBES offers an essential perspective on the current state of biodiversity. Their "Global Assessment of Biodiversity and Ecosystem Services" comes at a critical time, as in the last decade, there's been a significant increase in understanding biodiversity and ecosystems and their value to the quality of human life. This report is equally alarming as the IPCC's findings on climate change, as it highlights the worldwide deterioration of nature and ecosystems. According to the report, "The biosphere, upon which humanity as a whole depends, is being altered to an unparalleled degree across all spatial scales. Biodiversity—the diversity within species, between species, and of ecosystems—is declining faster than at any time in human history."[43]

Intense human landscape alteration and exploitation is the greatest threat to the earth's biodiversity. The IPBES has identified five critical human-induced triggers. [44] They include:

1. Changes in land use and sea use—any change in a species' environment caused by activities such as logging, unsustainable agriculture, infrastructure, mining, deforestation, and urbanisation resulting in habitat loss.

2. Species overexploitation—directly, when a specific species is targeted for sustenance or trade (for example, commercial fishing) or indirectly when a species is killed unintentionally as a by-product (i.e. catch from unsustainable fishing practices).

3. Invasive species and disease—native species are disrupted by invasive species that introduce disease, prey on native species, and take up space, food, and other resources.

4. Pollution—different forms of pollution have various deleterious effects on a species' environment; for instance, an oil spill has a sudden impact, whereas other pollutants, like microplastics, have a more gradual development.

5. Climate change—triggers irregular seasonal change, which confuses the natural order of phenomena such as migration and reproduction.

Figure 2.3 *– The Biggest Threats to Biodiversity: This curiosity box highlights the connection between damaging human enterprises and vulnerable species, juxtaposing items such as a heating planet, forest fires, industrial pollution, and marine plastic pollution with species at risk from climate change, over-fishing, invasive species, and changes to land and sea use (© Alexandra Steed URBAN).*

Threats to biodiversity and wilderness will be discussed in more detail in Chapter 8.

The World Wildlife Fund's "Living Planet Report" has similar findings to the IPBES report. Using data from over 4000 species, they track the number of mammals, birds, fish, reptiles, and amphibians across the globe and have found that from 1970 until 2016, there has been a dramatic decline globally.[46] Latin America and the Caribbean have seen the most significant reduction of 94 percent, with Africa at 66 percent, Asia Pacific at 55 percent, North America at 20 percent, and Europe and Central Asia at 18 percent.[47] Changes in land and sea use make up the largest percentage of the decline, with much of this loss being driven by the massive destruction of the earth's rainforests, which are especially important for biodiversity and carbon storage.[48]

The IPBES has issued a warning, emphasising that nearly one-fifth of the earth's surface faces a high risk of plant and animal invasion, particularly in biodiversity hotspots.[49] The movement of invasive alien species is significantly influenced by trade, as the introduction and spread of these species are often connected to the movement of people and goods. The consequences can be severe, with some invasive alien species leading to the decline of native populations on a regional scale.[50]

One example of the devastating impact of invasive alien species is the infectious fungal pathogen Batrachochytrium dendrobatidis, which has caused numerous amphibian extinctions. This pathogen has infected over 700 species worldwide, contributing to the decline of amphibian populations.[51] In the realm of agriculture, transboundary pests in the form of invasive alien species can have disastrous effects by decimating crops. Global crop losses of 20–30 percent occur annually due to these pests, posing a significant threat to food security.[52]

Scientists warn we may now be well into a sixth mass extinction event.[53] The fifth mass extinction, caused by a massive asteroid impact, ended the age of dinosaurs and obliterated 75 percent of all species on the planet at that time. In the 65 million years since, the natural world has been rebuilding, only now to be threatened, not by an alien invader, but by one of its own and most recent species—Homo sapiens. As part of the natural world, we are also a threat to ourselves. Human life is not a certainty, and our species is not exempt from the danger of extinction.

What are we doing about it? At COP15 in 2022, the UN biodiversity conference in Montreal, almost 200 countries agreed on goals and targets to halt and reverse biodiversity loss by 2030. The targets include conserving 30 percent of the world's lands, inland waters, coastal areas and oceans; restoring 30 percent of degraded terrestrial, inland waters, and coastal and marine ecosystems; reducing to near zero the loss of areas of high biodiversity importance; cutting food waste in half; raising financial flows for developed countries to deliver $30 billion for developing countries in the same timeframe.[54] These commitments are indeed profound and will be transformative if implemented. Chapter 10 considers these developments and the actions required in more detail.

The predictions from the IPCC are alarming, indicating that if we continue on our current path, climate change alone may jeopardise the existence of as many as one in every six species by the year 2100. However, certain vulnerable species, such as pollinators, face an even greater threat.[55] This issue becomes even more urgent when we consider the close connection between climate change and biodiversity decline, as highlighted by the IPBES. If we fail to address both these issues promptly and comprehensively, along with pollution and waste, we risk facing an imminent ecological collapse.

It has become evident that simply reducing greenhouse gas emissions will not be sufficient to tackle these global challenges. Fortunately, an equally effective approach lies in the protection and restoration of landscapes as carbon sinks, which can serve to regenerate ecosystems and reverse ecological decline. By adopting an integrated approach that addresses climate change and ecological collapse together, we can achieve synergistic and far-reaching benefits. This approach can be visualised and guided by the Ecosystem Services Wheel, which provides a framework for understanding the interconnectedness and interdependence of various ecosystem services. However, it is important to note that addressing climate change and ecological collapse represents only the initial steps in a much broader and more complex agenda.

Population Expansion

The relentless growth of the global population is placing unprecedented strain on our planet, exacerbating critical challenges such as climate change, ecological collapse, and a multitude of other issues. The rate at which humanity is expanding, both in terms of sheer numbers and the per capita exploitation of earth's resources, is staggering. In a remarkably short span of time, the human population has surged from approximately 1.25 billion in 1850 to 2.5 billion in 1950 and has now reached an astonishing 8 billion.[56]

According to the United Nations, this trajectory shows no signs of slowing down. By 2050, the world population is projected to reach around 10 billion, and it is anticipated to peak at nearly 11 billion by 2100.[57] These figures paint a concerning picture of the challenges we will face in managing resources, protecting ecosystems, and ensuring a sustainable future for all.

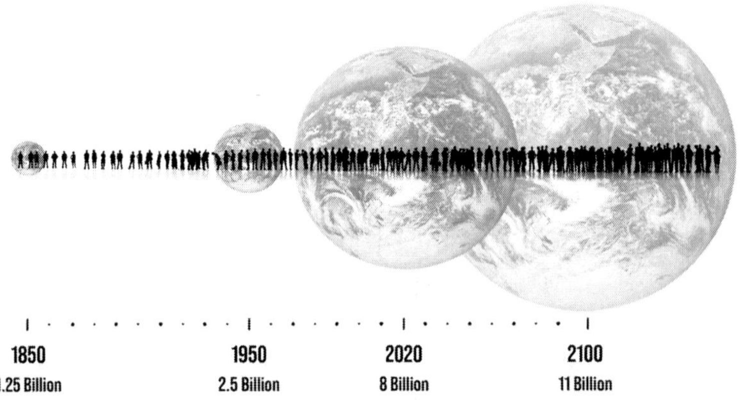

Figure 2.4 *– A Rapidly Expanding Human Population: Since 1850, the human population and its impact has radically grown, exerting tremendous pressure on the planet (© Alexandra Steed URBAN).*

[58]

However, the strain on our planet is not solely a result of the sheer number of people, but rather the insatiable greed and excessive consumption of the wealthiest nations and individuals who relentlessly pursue more—more power, more land, more resources, and more possessions. This unending quest for accumulation is placing an unprecedented burden on the earth, and the consequences of this overexploitation are far from equitable.

A prime example of this inequity is seen in the consumption of fossil fuels. The wealthiest countries, such as the United States, Canada, Japan, and much of Western Europe, account for only 12 percent of the global population, yet they are responsible for 50 percent of the greenhouse gases released from fossil fuels and industry since 1850.[59] Shockingly, the carbon emissions of the world's top 1 percent surpass those of the poorest 50 percent combined. The obscene excesses of the few are putting the whole world in peril.

Another striking illustration is the extreme increase in meat consumption, which demonstrates a clear bias towards the wealthiest nations while many of the world's poorest countries consume very little. The livestock industry has experienced explosive growth, with meat production surging by 600 percent since 1950. Presently, approximately 20 billion chickens, 1.5 billion cattle, and one billion pigs are raised for meat consumption annually.[60] Our unsustainable dietary habits have had catastrophic effects on wildlife, biodiversity, and our overall carbon footprint.

Livestock production methods are recognised as major contributors to environmental damage and climate change. They are directly linked to biodiversity loss through activities such as deforestation and land conversion to create more grazing space for commercial farming, as well as crop production for animal feed. Moreover, the use of harmful pesticides, insecticides, and fertilisers in these practices damages soil health and contaminates water systems, leading to adverse effects downstream.

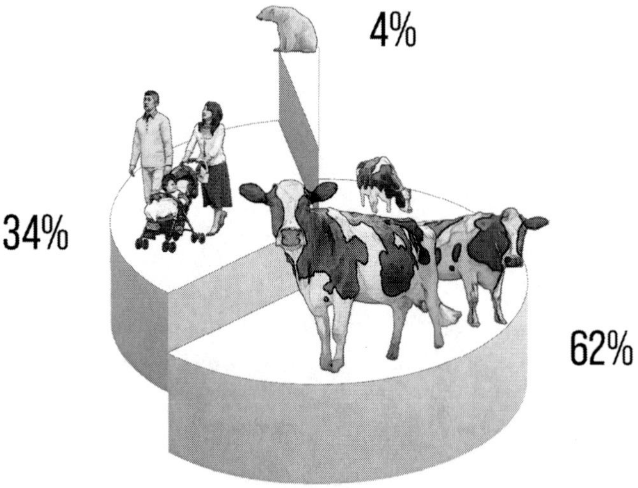

Figure 2.5 *– The Percentage Split of Mammals Globally: Wild animals comprise 4 percent of the world's mammals' biomass, with humans comprising 34 percent and livestock 62 percent (© Alexandra Steed URBAN).*

61

Figure 2.6 *– The Percentage Split of Birds Globally: Chickens and other farmed poultry comprise 70 percent biomass of all birds on the planet, with only 30 percent being wild (© Alexandra Steed URBAN).*

[62]

Astonishingly, wild animals comprise just 4 percent of the world's mammal biomass, with humans accounting for 34 percent and livestock dominating at 62 percent.[63] Chickens and other farmed poultry make up an astonishing 70 percent biomass of all birds on the planet, with only 30 percent being wild.[64] In North America alone, there has been a decline of approximately 3 billion birds from the abundance of fifty years ago.[65]

While the world's population has experienced exponential growth, the degradation of our planet has accelerated. However, it is important to recognise that not all global citizens apply equal pressure on the earth. Certain individuals in privileged positions, through their careless actions, have significantly compromised planetary health. The decline of the living world is a serious concern, and it begs the question: how much more pressure can the planet bear? What are its limits?

Planetary Boundaries

Johan Rockstrom, the former director of the Stockholm Resilience Centre, had a similar question. In 2009, he set out to explore and define what he referred to as, "the safe operating space for humanity."[66] Because, as he makes clear, the earth is not under threat, but the human species is in danger. He assembled a team of twenty-eight internationally renowned scientists to identify the processes that regulate the stability and resilience of the earth system. Their goal was to understand how the exponential growth of harmful human activities could potentially destabilise critical living systems and trigger abrupt or irreversible environmental changes that would be detrimental, or even catastrophic, to human well-being. They recognised, however, that the majority of society remains unaware of these risks.

Rockstrom asked, "What are the non-negotiable planetary preconditions that humanity needs to respect in order to avoid the risk of deleterious or even catastrophic environmental change at continental to global scales?"[67]

Noting that climate change and biodiversity loss are important issues that affect all others, Rockstrom's team identified nine quantitative planetary boundaries within which humanity can continue to develop and thrive for future generations. They include:

1. Climate Change
2. Biosphere Integrity
3. Nitrogen and Phosphorus Flows
4. Stratospheric Ozone Depletion
5. Ocean Acidification
6. Freshwater Use
7. Land System Change
8. Novel Entities and Chemical Pollution
9. Atmospheric Aerosol Loading

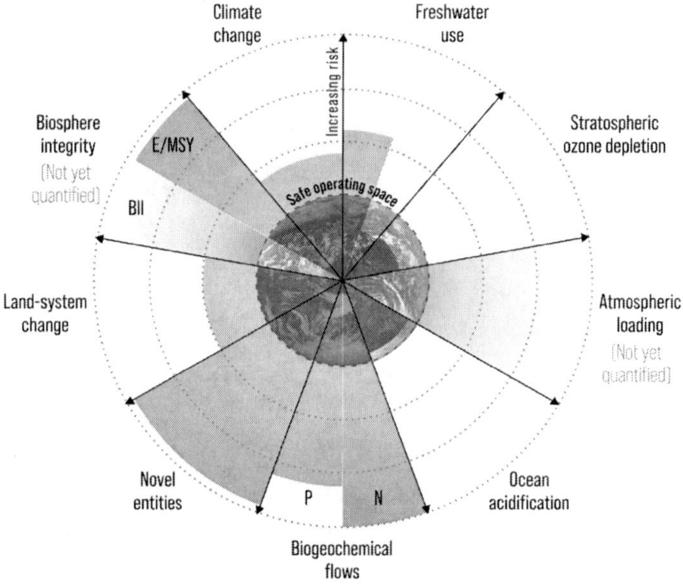

Figure 2.7 - *Navigating Planetary Boundaries: The concept of nine planetary boundaries defines the limits within which human development and prosperity can be sustained for future generations. This diagram illustrates the alarming extent to which humanity has already overshot many of these boundaries (© Alexandra Steed URBAN).*

(For more information, the boundaries are described in the Appendix. I urge you to watch any number of Johan Rockstrom's videos that clearly, succinctly, and visually drive the points home. The Stockholm Resilience Centre website, www.stockholmresilience.org, is also a great source of information.)

It is essential to understand that crossing any of these boundaries increases the risk of triggering large-scale abrupt or irreversible environmental changes. The transgression of one tipping point brings the earth's system closer to other tipping points. We have already witnessed this in the case of climate change, where the loss of polar sea ice due to global warming is almost certainly irreversible. This loss sets off a chain of consequences, such as rising sea levels, coastal erosion, the decline of Arctic wildlife leading to lower fish populations, more extreme weather events, thawing permafrost releasing methane and exacerbating planetary warming.

The behaviour of earth's systems is non-linear, and sudden shifts are not always predictable. Critical thresholds within the biosphere may become so weakened by significant pressures from various sources that they may fail, resulting in a cascade of catastrophic consequences that catch us off guard. Once tipping points have been exceeded, there is no simple way to reverse the damage. Research from the Stockholm Resilience Centre shows that society's activities have already transgressed the boundaries of climate change, biodiversity loss, changes in nutrient cycles, and land use, pushing them into unprecedented and unsafe territory. More recently, limitations related to freshwater use, environmental pollutants, and novel entities like plastics have also been surpassed.

If we continue to push the boundaries of our planetary home, conditions will worsen. The Amazon rainforest will be lost, Arctic ice will melt, coral reefs will perish in acidic oceans, fish populations will collapse, pollinating insects will disappear, and weather patterns will become more unpredictable and extreme. The consequences for humanity will be severe. All available data points to a code red situation for humankind unless we respond with transformative and holistic solutions. We have the opportunity and the knowledge to rectify our mistakes. That is why, in later chapters, this book lays out a framework to repair society's fractured relationship with nature.

Decade of Action

In 2015, the United Nations (UN) published "The 2030 Agenda for Sustainable Development," which was adopted by all member states and set a blueprint for peace and prosperity for people and the planet.[69] At its heart are seventeen Sustainable Development Goals (SDGs) that urge countries to collectively combat poverty, address social and economic inequalities, and tackle climate change and ecological collapse.[70] Recognising the urgency, the UN declared the following decade as "The Decade of Action" in 2019, aiming to accelerate progress towards the SDGs.[71]

Unfortunately, even before the COVID-19 pandemic, the implementation of the SDGs was already falling behind schedule. The pandemic further slowed down progress, making it clear that we are not on track to achieve the goals set in the Paris Climate Accord. Although there has been a notable increase in global political commitment to climate action, the scientific consensus is that immediate and coordinated action is crucial. Maintaining the status quo is inadequate, as the window of opportunity to address the urgent challenges facing our planet is rapidly closing. Delayed action would risk catastrophic consequences.

The upcoming years of this decade are pivotal, presenting a unique opportunity for transformative change. It is during this time that we must evolve our perspective from focusing solely on short-term gains to embracing a broader and more sustainable view. The looming reality of a silent spring grows closer with each passing day. The scientific data leaves no room for doubt, exposing the toll our relentless pursuit of economic and technological progress has taken on the natural world.

This era is the most critical in human history thus far; it could be the most tragic or the most revolutionary. Fortunately, as a species, we possess the capacity for self-awareness and introspection. We can acknowledge the consequences of exploiting and commodifying nature, but more importantly, we have the knowledge and power to change course. By cooperating with nature rather than acting violently towards it, we can seize this defining moment for humanity. This is an incredible opportunity to shift our perspective, embrace sustainable practices, and transform the world's greatest challenges into opportunities for positive change. Together, we can halt destructive behaviours and actively contribute to restoring the earth that sustains us.

While we now have a relatively good understanding of the physical processes that have led us to this critical juncture, it is equally important to examine the cultural conditions that have allowed us to harm the living world. How have we strayed so far from our own nature? This question warrants consideration as we navigate this seminal period. By reflecting on our actions and embracing a Portrait to Landscape mentality in our relationship with nature, we can forge a path towards a sustainable and harmonious future for all.

3

The Cultural Landscape

ANTHROPOCENTRIC TO ECOCENTRIC

"You are failing us. But the young people are starting to understand your betrayal. The eyes of all future generations are upon you. And if you choose to fail us, I say: We will never forgive you. We will not let you get away with this. Right here, right now, is where we draw the line. The world is waking up. And change is coming, whether you like it or not." [1]

—*Greta Thunberg*

WHETHER ONE AGREES with her methods and rhetoric or not, Greta Thunberg has become the embodiment of the voices of the next generation calling for radical change in our way of life and our relationship with the planet. At the age of fifteen, Thunberg took personal action against the climate crisis out of frustration with the inaction of her government. She had become deeply distressed and hopeless upon learning about the devastating consequences of climate change and was bewildered by the lack of response from society. How could people ignore the greatest threat humanity has ever faced? Why wasn't the climate emergency being treated just like that—an emergency?[2]

For some time, Thunberg withdrew in despair, feeling the weight of the world on her shoulders with no one to look to help bear the burden. She had been waiting for signs from world leaders, Swedish politicians, and grown-ups in general that they understood the severity of the climate emergency, the imminent danger it presented and that they were taking meaningful and immediate action to tackle this existential crisis. The signs never came.

Left with no other choice, Thunberg made a modest sign reading, "School Strike for Climate Action" (translated from Swedish) and sat in front of the Swedish parliament, armed with a fact sheet about the climate crisis. Her intention was to gather support for her cause before the national election. Although she did not achieve immediate success in influencing the government, Thunberg's unwavering determination, passion, and urgency have propelled her forward. She remains undeterred by the empty promises and eloquent words of politicians. Fearless and unconcerned with popularity, this young woman continues to hold world leaders accountable for their inaction in ensuring a sustainable planet and a future for our children.

In the years since, Thunberg's one voice has multiplied by the millions, and now children and young people from around the world stand beside her in the fight for climate justice.[3] For them, the issues are crystal clear. They can see how humans have wrecked the planet through a dysfunctional relationship with nature and the imminent doom that awaits us if transformative changes are not made immediately. Unlike many adults who cling to notions of endless economic growth and increasing GDP, these young individuals recognise that the pursuit of GDP at the expense of a liveable future is meaningless.

Our children, like us, have inherited a world with a broken relationship with nature—a relationship characterised by dominance, exploitation, arrogance, and disregard for other life forms. This dysfunction is evident in the state of our planet, marked by climate change, ecological collapse, and expanding human population. In recent decades, the impact of human activity has intensified to such a degree that we have entered the Anthropocene meaning the "recent age of man."

Nothing encapsulates the current state of our relationship with nature better than the term "Anthropocene," coined by ecologist Eugene Stoermer and popularised by chemist Paul Crutzen in 2000, to mark a fundamental change in the relationship between humans and the earth system.[4] It recognises that humans are now, irrefutably, the most influential species and force on the planet. Humans have significantly altered and harmed the earth's climate, land surface, water, flora, fauna, and atmosphere. The global environment is now shaped by humankind at every level. Never before have humans witnessed the advent of a new geological era, let alone been the physical force that, like asteroids and volcanoes before, abruptly redirected the context for life's evolution.

It wasn't always this way. Throughout most of human history, our activities had no greater impact than those of other living creatures. The stability of the planet began with the Holocene epoch, following the retreat of the last ice age approximately 12,000 years ago.[5] In this period, conditions radically stabilised, and humans enjoyed a relatively calm and gentle planet, with seasons that ebb and flow with a rhythm of predictability and reliability. With an average global temperature that did not waiver more than 1°C (1.8°F), a predictable and vital environment allowed our species to flourish. All life progressed and advanced in ways never before possible. Animated by a plethora of spectacular life forms exhibiting great complexity, the diversity seems to have created less chaotic conditions on the planet.

However, we have disrupted this stability and ventured into uncharted territory. As Thunberg rightly pointed out, our leaders have failed us. We can either continue down the path of business as usual, disregarding the warnings of visionaries like Einstein, Leopold, and Carson, and hastening our own demise, or we can unite with our children and demand revolutionary change from those in power. The choice is ours.

The Anthropocene

The concept of the Anthropocene, the era marked by significant human impact on the earth's systems and functioning, gained traction in the 1950s, commonly referred to as the "Great Acceleration."[6] This period has witnessed an unprecedented and exponential rise in the human impact on the environment, as indicated by various measurements and confirmed by independent scientists.[7] Regardless of the specific indicator observed, each graph depicts a consistent pattern—an initial period of relative stability followed by a sharp and steady increase resembling the blade of a hockey stick.[8]

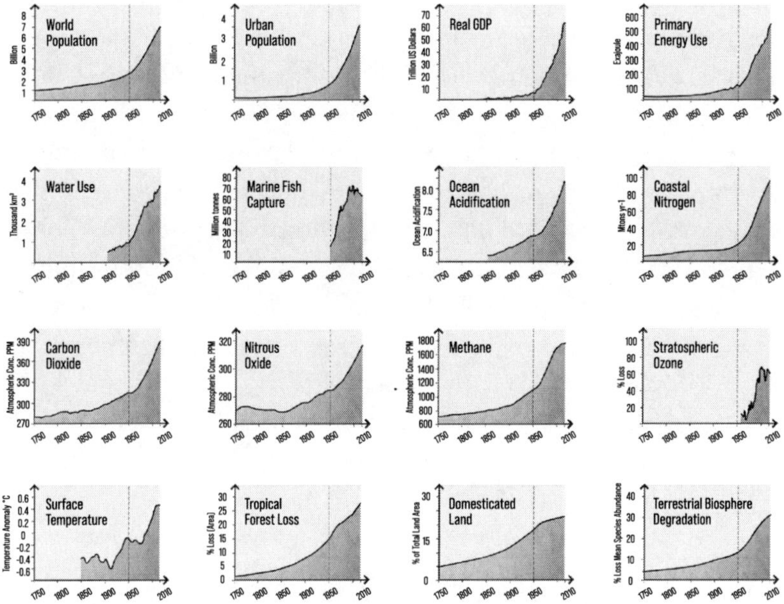

Figure 3.1 *– The Great Acceleration: This sombre collection of 'hockey stick' curves demonstrate human impact on the environment across multiple indicators. Despite variations in their shape, they all share a common upturn from around the 1950s, followed by a continuous spike (© Alexandra Steed URBAN).*

This pattern is evident across multiple indicators, such as population, GDP, energy use, water use, greenhouse gas concentrations, temperature, biodiversity loss, and more. From any perspective, the picture that emerges is deeply concerning, highlighting the magnitude of the escalating environmental crisis.

During this period, human exploitation of earth's resources has reached astonishing levels, leaving an undeniable and lasting imprint on the planet. The work of the international scientific community has allowed us to reflect on the effects of our actions in the past and project their potential consequences for the future if we continue on the same trajectory. However, in 1950, few people were aware that this curve of human impact would spike, nor were the terms "Great Acceleration" or "Anthropocene" even conceived.

At that time, the major concerns for humanity and the planet revolved around the risk of atomic war and the threats posed by the Cold War. Few imagined that "global warming," "climate change," and "ecological collapse" might one day be the outstanding issues of our time, nor would we have even understood the meaning or importance of those words. Concerns about the environment, which had their roots in the late nineteenth century, were still nascent, and the field of environmental history—the study of human's relationship to the natural world—was just beginning to emerge.

It wasn't until the release of Rachel Carson's ground-breaking book, *Silent Spring,* in 1962 that the field of environmental inquiry truly took off. As we know, the book stirred an enormous response. She questioned the inherent goodness of progress. She reminded us that the dualism between people and nature isn't real. Her well-researched and eloquently crafted arguments detailing the grave consequences of untested chemicals applied as pest and disease control inspired many sympathetic organisations and government agencies to action. The Environmental Movement experienced an eruption of activism and ecological consciousness. Organisations such as the World Conservation Union, World Wildlife Fund, Friends of the Earth, and Greenpeace started to take on powerful forces such as corporate pollution, rampant suburbanisation, and industrial agriculture. Nonetheless, even the most fervent environmental activists of the 1960s could not have anticipated the hyper rate of ecological decline that was already underway.

Man versus Nature

We are currently living in an era that the dominant ideology of Anthropocentrism has shaped. This worldview centres around human supremacy and considers nature solely in terms of its utility to us. This perspective has influenced and tainted our relationship with nature for centuries and is deeply ingrained in Western thought, including religious, philosophical, and scientific ideas. Aristotle wrote, "Nature has made all things specifically for the sake of man," thus, the value of non-human things is merely instrumental.[10] Descartes believed humans are "the masters and possessors of nature" and non-human animals are mindless machines without souls or consciousness to be manipulated at will.[11] Bacon proclaimed, "Let the human race recover that right over nature which belongs to it by divine bequest."[12] After all, in the Book of Genesis, doesn't God instruct man to, "Be fruitful and multiply, and fill the earth and subdue it; and have dominion over the fish of the sea and over the birds of the air and over every living thing that moves upon the earth."[13] When Adam and Eve are later expelled from the Garden of Eden, are they not faced with a harsh and hostile environment that must be subdued and controlled to survive nature's violent threats?

These religious and philosophical ideas fed directly into a scientific understanding of the world with an ideology of control and technological exploitation of nature. Even Darwin's evolutionary theory in *On the Origin of Species,* when misinterpreted, was used to assert human superiority over other species.[14]

This long-established and mainstream ideology persists today in Western consciousness, so entrenched that it is difficult for us to imagine a different order of things. The control of nature is an idea conceived in arrogance and ignorance, stemming from the belief that humans are separate from nature.

In this section titled "Man versus Nature," the deliberate use of the word "man" instead of "human" highlights the connection between the subduing of nature and the subjugation of the feminine principle, elevating the masculine. Western philosophical thought has suffered from an imbalance in this regard. The suppression of the feminine principle has contributed to a breakdown in the relationship between people and nature.

Examining the Chinese philosophical concept of yin and yang offers insights into the limitations of dominant Western thought. Yin and yang describe a universe of opposite and interconnected forces. It is a symbol that recognises the paradox of "an explicit duality expressing an implicit unity."[15] Yin and yang, black and white, chaos and order, soft and hard, feminine and masculine, earth and heaven, they are opposite but interconnected forces. One is only fully realised through the presence of the other. Their balance is essential to harmony and health on the planet.[16]

The concept of yin and yang deeply influenced the great Swiss psychologist Carl Jung. He introduced the terms *anima* and *animus* to represent the feminine in a man and the masculine in a woman, respectively.[17] Jung believed that a union of yin and yang exists within each person, two indivisible aspects of one body or one consciousness that must be nurtured.

The duality and unity depicted in the yin-yang symbol provide an alternative perspective on our current imbalanced predicament. Unfortunately, society tends to favour duality alone, neglecting the importance of unity. Furthermore, there is a prevailing overemphasis on the masculine principle of domination and conquest, while the feminine principle of creativity, empathy, and healing is undervalued. The suppression of the feminine has resulted in a weakened connection between humanity and the earth, diminishing our understanding of nature's sentience and intelligence.

In our imbalanced world, we are left with the consequences of these opposing forces—humans are seen as separate from nature instead of acknowledging the beautiful interconnectedness that unites us with the natural world. By rectifying this imbalance and equally valuing the feminine principle, we can shift our perspective toward a holistic understanding of the landscape community and celebrate our union with nature.

An Insignificant Species

Humans have not always viewed themselves as masters of the planet. In the grand timeline of earth's evolution, human existence is relatively insignificant. However, due to our limited memory and experience of the prehistoric era, it is challenging to conceive of life on earth being any different or potentially changing in the future. Throughout our known history, we have enjoyed a relatively stable and predictable climate, which has fostered the illusion that the future will continue along the same path. However, scientific evidence reminds us that life within the earth's biosphere is delicate and precarious. Over the course of the planet's 4.5-billion-year existence, there have been periods of turbulence, mass extinctions, and opportunities for new beginnings. Here are some of the highlights:

4.5 billion years ago. Planet Earth originated from a swirling cloud of dust and gas. Through the gradual accretion of particles and intense bombardment from asteroids, it began to take shape, marked by erupting volcanoes. However, at this early stage, earth was inhospitable and unsuitable for life.

4.0 billion years ago. The world's oceans and atmosphere formed as heavy elements and magma settled towards the planet's core. Simple life forms emerged within this still harsh environment, but survival remained challenging.

3.5 billion years ago. The biosphere came into existence, and life began to flourish in the oceans. The process of photosynthesis, which produced oxygen, improved the atmosphere and paved the way for the evolution of diverse and complex life forms. This period witnessed the birth of a self-sustaining and self-regulating ecosystem.

500 million years ago. The first plants appeared, followed by the emergence of animals. This further contributed to cooling the planet and increasing oxygen levels in the atmosphere, enabling the expansion of terrestrial animal life. However, over the next 500 million to 65 million years, the earth experienced five mass extinctions caused by factors such as global warming, cooling, and asteroid impacts.

65 million years ago. The last mass extinction occurred, wiping out 78 percent of species and bringing an end to the reign of the dinosaurs that lasted 175 million years. In the aftermath, nature embarked on the process of reconstructing the natural world, eventually leading to the introduction of the human species.

2.5 million years ago. The first humans evolved, appearing as latecomers to the planet. Initially, humans held little significance in the food chain, positioned somewhere between bears, raccoons, pigs, and anchovies. Various human species coexisted during this time.[18]

150,000 years ago. Homo sapiens emerged and joined other human species. At this stage, humans were still marginal creatures, with a global population likely not exceeding one million individuals. Harsh environmental conditions and fluctuating global temperatures posed challenges, with some estimates suggesting that the human population may have plummeted to only 20,000 survivors.[19] Ultimately, all other human species became extinct, leaving Homo sapiens as the sole surviving lineage.[20]

12,000 years ago. The Holocene epoch began, bringing a period of temperate climate stability, predictable seasons, and sea-level stabilisation. This era witnessed significant cultural progress, notably marked by the Agricultural Revolution, which transformed human life on earth. Prior to this revolution, humans had sustained themselves for over 2 million years through hunting and gathering, living in close harmony with the land and without dominance over other species.

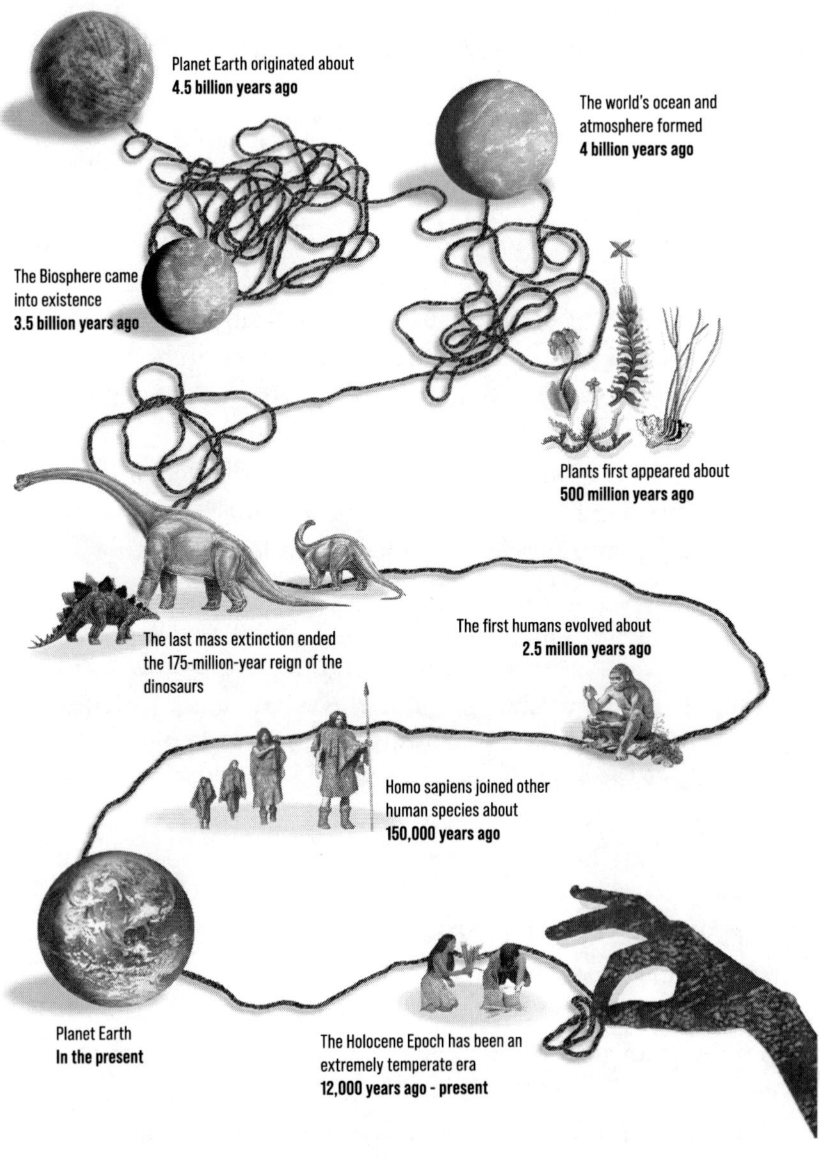

Figure 3.2 *– A Timeline of Human Life on Earth: Humans, notably Homo sapiens, made a relatively recent appearance on earth's timeline (© Alexandra Steed URBAN).*

21

For over 2 million years, humans sustained themselves through hunting and gathering, leading a lifestyle that was in harmony with nature and characterised by a light ecological footprint. In stark contrast to the notion of dominance over all other species, psychologist Carl Jung aptly observed that, "Primitive man…does not dream of regarding himself as lord of creation. His zoological classification does not culminate in homo sapiens but in the elephant."[22]

Our foraging ancestors possessed a profound knowledge of and reverence for the earth and its intricate workings. They developed exceptional skills in orienteering and navigation, becoming masters in the art of animal tracking and displaying an intimate familiarity with all plant species. They comprehended the benefits and risks associated with each plant, understood the nuances of weather patterns and seasonal variations, and they divined freshwater. As Yuval Harari highlights in *Sapiens: A Brief History of Humankind*, "At the individual level, ancient foragers were the most knowledgeable and skilful people in history."[23]

Our ancestors cultivated a deep connection to nature, a closeness that eludes us in the modern era. Regrettably, a significant portion of humanity has severed this vital bond with the earth, resulting in the loss of the wisdom and harmony that our foraging predecessors once embodied.

The Holocene

The Holocene, meaning "Recent Whole," is a period in earth's history where liveable conditions emerged. However, the exact factors contributing to its onset and the advancement of Homo sapiens remain uncertain. Nonetheless, evidence suggests that the proliferation and complexity of life within the biosphere, facilitated by the oxygen-producing process of photosynthesis, played a crucial role in stabilising the climate, and creating a favourable environment for human development.[24]

Taking advantage of these moderate conditions, humanity rapidly transitioned from insignificant cave-dwelling creatures to become the ascendant rulers of the planet. Anthropologist Donald

Henry explains, "After enjoying some 3 to 4 million years of success through foraging, the human species adopted a radically different adaptive strategy that within the last 10,000 years has replaced foraging in virtually every part of the world."[25] Across the globe, many humans put down their spears. They transitioned from spending their days gathering food to the demanding labour of tilling soil, sowing seeds, irrigating crops, and raising livestock.

Within a remarkably short span of 1,000 years, our ancestors initiated a profound transformation, exerting control over and manipulating nature on a large scale. They reshaped the land, altered natural processes, and introduced the concept of property and land ownership. These landscape modifications fundamentally redefined humanity's relationship with the natural world and set the stage for the events that have led us to the present day. The stability provided by the Holocene epoch enabled these changes to take place, making it the only known epoch to support human development.

Contrary to common belief, our dominance as a species does not stem from the size of our brains (as Neanderthals had larger brains) or some inherent greatness. Homo sapiens' long-term survival is not predetermined.[26] Rather, the progress we have achieved over the past 10,000 years is primarily attributable to the favourable climatic conditions of the Holocene, which facilitated reliable food production and the availability of freshwater. The major cultural milestones of the Holocene, including the Agricultural, Scientific, and Industrial Revolutions, were all made possible by the predictable, stable, and biodiverse environment. None of these transformative leaps could have occurred amidst constant climatic fluctuations or devastating natural disasters that could easily undo any infrastructural advances. In such challenging conditions, a large brain alone would offer limited benefits.

Maslow's "A Theory of Human Motivation" reminds us that individual and collective progress is impeded when basic physiological and safety needs are unmet.[27] A hungry person will be consumed with finding food. An unsafe person will be preoccupied with finding refuge. But a person who has their basic needs met can move beyond these and strive towards individual progress and transcendence. The same principle applies to the human race as a whole, where stability and security provide essential space for thought, organisation, and the development of structures that foster societal advancement. In essence, our remarkable expansion as a species has been entirely dependent on Homo sapiens' enjoyment of the moderate and stable climate conditions of the Holocene epoch, complemented by the support of productive and resilient ecosystems.

Change is Inevitable

Looking ahead 12,000 years from the onset of the Holocene, we find ourselves standing at the edge, witnessing the sunset on a stable and life-sustaining era. Beyond the horizon lies unexplored territory for which we are ill-prepared. Had it not been for the actions of humanity, scientists assert that under natural circumstances, earth would have likely remained in the mild Holocene period for an unusually extended period, possibly another 50,000 years.[28]

However, in recent decades, the rapid evolution of humankind, industrial agriculture, urbanisation, and technological advancements have caused such swift changes that nature struggles to keep pace. The impact of our collective actions on the natural world has become increasingly conspicuous and extreme. Whether society acknowledges it or not, humans are an integral part of the biosphere, interconnected with all other life forms. We depend on its functioning and life-sustaining processes while simultaneously influencing its shape and effectiveness. Undoubtedly, human expansion has had a profound impact, and an anthropocentric perspective has imposed immense pressures on the biosphere, constantly testing its boundaries.

Humanity may be in a state of denial, but we cannot feign ignorance as our predecessors did in the 1950s. Scientists are sounding the alarm with urgency. They warn us of the planetary boundaries that have already been breached and how these breaches can trigger a domino effect, resulting in dire and unforeseen consequences for humanity. Choosing to forsake a green and blue planet that has fostered humanity's achievements is a decision society is making. Civilisation must now re-establish its dependence and vital connection to the land, the very foundation upon which our success has been built.

Reflecting on human history, we can trace its course along a single line—a line that remained steady for thousands of years during the Holocene. Only recently have arrogant and uninformed human actions propelled us into the Anthropocene epoch, where one-way doors to an unknown future have opened. Yet, society continues with business as usual, arrogantly ignoring the mess before us. Erroneous omnipotence and a misguided sense of superiority have become deeply ingrained in the prevailing Western mindset, often fostering a belief in our immutability.

We have inherited this flawed worldview. But surely, it does not have to be our legacy.

The severity of the challenges we face may even be cause for celebration, as crises often precede an awakening of consciousness. Philosopher and spiritual teacher Eckhart Tolle reminds us in his book, *A New Earth,* "All life-forms need obstacles and challenges in order to evolve."[29] We are staring into the face of several epic obstacles and challenges that possess the potential to precipitate a necessary sea change. Let us heed the call of our children. Let us stoke the revolution, deconstruct the current paradigm, and recalibrate our approach to human progress and development through a transformative and regenerative framework.

Land is Not an Economic Problem

The notion that land is solely an economic matter must be transcended urgently, echoing Aldo Leopold's compelling call for a land ethic. The prevailing belief that land is property, nature is merely a resource, and Gross Domestic Product (GDP) is the sole measure of prosperity represents an antiquated and reductionist economic model. Regrettably, this outdated narrative has driven government agendas and individual pursuits for generations.

However, it is woefully inadequate to address the pressing challenges of the twenty-first century. We must seek a new model that is capable of tackling today's pertinent issues, one that incorporates a framework for sustainable land management and stewardship and can be translated into effective policies and regulations.

Kate Raworth presents a fresh economic model in her book *Doughnut Economics: Seven Ways to Think Like a 21st-Century Economist.*[30] Frustrated by the limited perspectives and unpreparedness of current economic approaches to tackle twenty-first-century challenges such as financial crises, extreme inequality, and environmental degradation, Raworth's model moves beyond the narrow focus on GDP and seeks to meet the needs of all while respecting the limits of the planet.

The celebrated progress of humanity has come at a significant cost, often at the expense of the living world. Relying on GDP as the sole economic metric to gauge a nation's prosperity provides an absurdly narrow lens and blunt tool when considering the multidimensional nature of life on earth. It is unsurprising that GDP follows the same hockey stick curve as other indicators of the Great Acceleration. In the absence of a land ethic, as GDP has risen, so has planetary destruction. Moreover, the land provides the resources that support economic growth, making economics inherently dependent on a healthy environment. Consequently, GDP must not be considered in isolation from other global community health and well-being indicators.

Raworth's doughnut model situates economic activity within a sphere of environmental and social responsibilities and establishes "A Safe and Just Space for Humanity."[31] This model consists of an inner circle that encompasses a social foundation inspired by the United Nations' Sustainable Development Goals (SDGs), including food, health, education, income and work, peace and justice, political voice, social equity, gender equality, housing, networks, energy, and water.

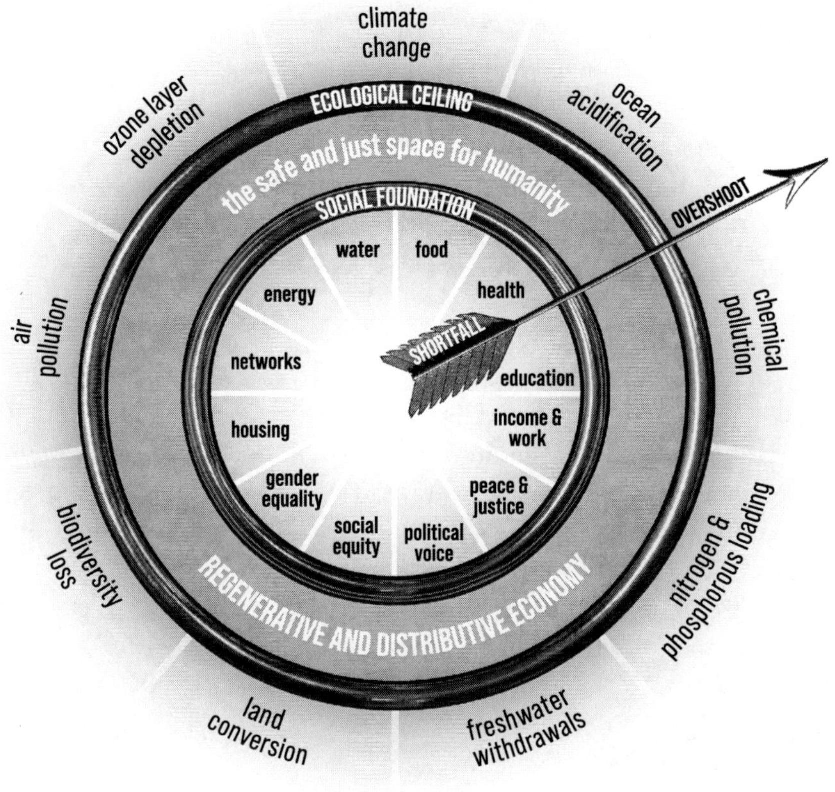

Figure 3.3 *– The Doughnut Model of Economics: This economic compass models a sustainable operating space for humanity in the sphere between the ecological ceiling and a social foundation of well-being (© Alexandra Steed URBAN).*

32

The outer ring overlays the nine planetary boundaries developed by Rockstrom's team, representing the ecological ceiling upon which life depends. The doughnut resides between these two circles, representing an enticingly good, safe, and just space for all.

Working within the economic dimension remains essential, particularly in this era where global decisions are predominantly made within this framework. However, as Kate Raworth demonstrates, society has the power to redefine the framework itself.

The outdated and one-dimensional GDP model, which lacks sophistication, can be replaced with a more inclusive and sustainable alternative. By embracing this new model and translating the principles of the doughnut into concrete policies and legislation, we can witness the possibility of improving the standard of living for human inhabitants while simultaneously prioritising the quality of the environment as a central component of economics. This transformative approach holds the potential to create a future where human prosperity and ecological well-being go hand in hand.

Earth Democracy

Earth Democracy, according to Indian scholar, environmental activist, and author Vandana Shiva, is a model that is founded on the concept of the earth family and advocates for the balance of economy, environment, and people to ensure sustainability. Shiva states, "As one family, all beings have equal rights to sustenance through the gifts of the earth. Its three components: economy, environment, and people, must be in balance to maintain sustainability."[33] This model clearly states the inherent value of all earth's inhabitants. Importantly, it takes us far beyond the notion of land as solely an economic problem.

Shiva's upbringing near the Himalayas and her personal experiences shaped her commitment to Earth Democracy. When she witnessed foreign logging companies threatening her favourite childhood forest, she joined a local women's movement to prevent its clearcutting. Through non-violent action and learning from these women, Shiva gained a deep love and appreciation for forests and the need for change. Others have noted that "Shiva was, literally, one of the early tree huggers."[34] She became a prominent advocate for the rights of nature and has since been recognised as a rockstar in the environmental and social justice movement.

The metaphor of the planet as a household is employed by authors like Raworth and Shiva. Raworth asserts, "This century we need some pretty insightful managers to guide our planetary household, and the ones who are ready to pay attention to the needs of all its inhabitants."[35] Shiva adds, "The terms "ecology" and "economics" both emerged from the same root in the Greek, oikos, meaning household. As long as economics was focused on the household, it recognised and respected its basis in natural resources, the limits of ecological renewal."[36] This metaphor serves as a reminder that the earth is our home, all its inhabitants are part of the same family, and the well-being of the environment and economy are closely intertwined. Each member has a responsibility towards others and a right to be cared for, loved, and respected.

Shiva teaches that protecting nature is not a luxury and that the foundation of every economic activity is the rivers, the land, the forests, and the biodiversity.[37] She recognises, "that we are members of an earth community, and have common responsibilities to protect the earth, and common rights to be sustained by her, for our food and water, our lives and livelihoods. We are living economies in which everyone participates, and no one is excluded."[38] Despite improvements in living conditions and access to clean drinking water, wealth distribution remains highly unequal, with the wealthiest 1 percent of the global population holding close to 50 percent of the world's wealth.[39] Disparities have deepened, and the COVID-19 pandemic and conflicts have further hindered progress.[40] Less developed nations will bear the brunt of climate change impacts caused by human exploitation of the land. This calls for a shift towards not only living within the earth's limits but also sharing its resources more equitably.[41]

Shiva's Earth Democracy presents a compelling challenge to the prevailing notion of the earth as private property by advocating for a perspective that views the planet as a commons and emphasises the importance of community and family.[42] This vision provides an alternative to a profit-driven world, prioritising ecological responsibility and economic justice.

At the heart of Earth Democracy lies the imperative for a fundamental change from an anthropocentric mindset, which places human interests at the forefront, to an ecocentric mindset that acknowledges the responsibility of individuals toward the entire community of life. This shift entails adopting an economic model that equally values social, environmental, and economic well-being.[43]

Embracing the role of caretakers for our earth represents the highest calling we can aspire to, and there is no better time than the present to assume this responsibility. To achieve this, we must unlearn the detrimental anthropocentric mindset and embrace an ecocentric worldview rooted in a robust land ethic and the principles of Earth Democracy. This revolutionary transformation will engender a deep recognition of our individual duty to the well-being of the entire community, supported by an economic model that considers social, environmental, and economic prosperity in equal measure.

Decades of destruction cannot be undone overnight. Reversing the impacts of massive worldwide devastation demands concerted and unwavering efforts from each and every individual. It requires taking corrective action in the landscape to heal our fractured relationship with nature. By engaging in landscape restoration, we can forge a promising path towards adapting to and mitigating the rapidly changing social and environmental conditions of our era.

The landscape holds the potential to establish a new equilibrium. Therefore, it is of utmost importance that we direct our attention towards the landscape and acknowledge its profound significance. The subsequent chapter will draw attention to the grandest landscape of all: the biosphere, offering further insights into its paramount importance.

4

The Grandest Landscape

IMBALANCE TO EQUILIBRIUM

"In this great chain of causes and effects, no single fact can be considered in isolation." [1]

—Alexander von Humboldt

AMIDST THE MULTITUDE of global challenges we face, it's natural to feel overwhelmed and despondent. However, it is essential to appreciate the potential for a revolutionary recovery. In this chapter, I invite you to pause and take a moment to consider the awe-inspiring world we inhabit, its marvellous capacity to sustain life, and, specifically, how interconnected and reliant you are on this extraordinary planet. It is worthy of utmost attention and care.

Humanity has a vital role in nurturing the planetary body and putting an end to destructive practices within each landscape. By creating conditions that allow nature to heal, we can contribute to the restoration of equilibrium in the biosphere, which is currently imbalanced. It's vital to remember that the living world, despite its fragility, possesses immense resilience and the capacity for self-renewal. Though under intense pressure, the world's landscapes, brought together as one in the biosphere, possess remarkable intelligence and wisdom that will guide us through these challenges.

The Biosphere

The world is covered in a tapestry of spectacular landscapes, each possessing unique beauty. The grandest landscape of all—the biosphere—elegantly weaves all landscapes into one colourful garment that gracefully adorns the earth. Though majestic, it is also fragile, and each thread, each landscape, within this garment is essential to the integrity of the full garment. Like the human body, the biosphere is one living system that relies on all parts to maintain a vital whole.

Naturalist and explorer Alexander von Humboldt introduced the world to the extraordinary vision that everything in nature is an interconnected web of life. Born in 1769, the same year as Napoleon, his profound insights into the natural world and extensive travels made Humboldt the most famous person on the planet in his time, aside from Napoleon himself. He was a person of insatiable curiosity, great intellect, and memory without equal. These gifts, among others, allowed him to make connections across temporal and spatial divides and to see the living world in a new way—as one living body.

At age twenty-nine, Humboldt departed from his native Germany on a five-year journey that would take him deep into Latin America. Along the way, he made astounding breakthroughs. He discovered the ocean current that now bears his name, pinpointed the magnetic equator, devised isotherms and isobars, and documented hundreds of unknown plant and animal species.

In 1800, Humboldt's travels brought him to the Aragua Valley in Venezuela.[2] Lake Valencia, in the heart of the valley, was surrounded by mountains. The locals complained to Humboldt that the lake's water levels were dropping rapidly. He soon discovered that as agriculture had expanded in the region, the clearing of the surrounding forests and diversion of watercourses for irrigation caused the lake to dry. Forest soils that had once retained water had become exposed and vulnerable. Consequently, agricultural soils were being washed away in heavy rainfall events. Humboldt could see the interconnectedness of the natural systems and began understanding that the effects of deforestation and farming techniques could have devastating consequences on the landscape. These human disturbances of land could become catastrophic if they continued so "brutally," as he noted. And so it was here at Lake Valencia that Humboldt developed the idea of human-induced climate change more than 200 years ago.[3]

Shortly after, in 1802, he arrived at Mount Chimborazo, in today's Ecuador. At the time, it was considered the highest peak in the world. As he and his companions climbed, Humboldt meticulously recorded any species he encountered. They ascended to more than 5,900 metres (precisely 19,413 feet) altitude, the highest climb ever recorded, giving them a view of the world not seen by others. From this vantage point, Humboldt looked down upon the landscapes below—vegetation zones stacked one on top of the other—and saw their structure and organisation in a whole new way. In her excellent book, *The Invention of Nature: The Adventures of Alexander von Humboldt*, Andrea Wulf explains Humboldt's epiphany when, "He saw the earth as one great living organism where everything was connected, conceiving a bold new vision of nature that still influences the way that we understand the natural world."[4]

Humboldt can be credited with many notable discoveries, but his most outstanding contribution to humanity was this miraculous insight he gained from the mountaintop: the wonderful web of life.

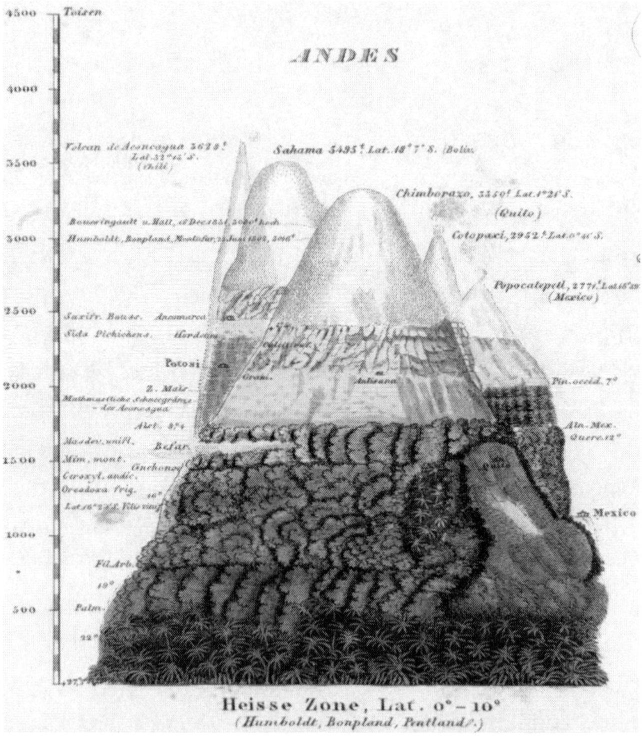

Figure 4.1 *– Alexander von Humboldt's Drawing of the Andes: This drawing is one of Humboldt's brilliant depictions of the mountain as one living system, drawn according to altitude and the corresponding vegetation zones, stacked one upon the other.*

5

Earth is largely a lifeless planet. But within a relatively thin skin, a cacophony of life exists. All the commotion takes place within the biosphere. It is the location of all life on the planet—on the ground, in the air, and the water—measuring only about twenty kilometres (about twelve miles) from top to bottom, where the total diameter of the earth is 12,756km (7,926 miles).[6] Life has flourished and evolved within this colourful wrap enveloping the globe. It is the only known location of all life on our planet, but also in our solar system, galaxy, and possibly our universe. Within this precious sphere, the glorious diversity of landscapes resides—from sculpted deserts and graceful plains to majestic mountain ranges and verdant forests to sparkling oceans and glowing polar regions—creating the most spectacular tapestry imaginable. The biosphere is our Garden of Eden, our Paradise.

Figure 4.2 *– The Biosphere: All life exists within a delicate and fragile skin surrounding the earth: on the ground, in the air and in the water (© Alexandra Steed URBAN).*

7

As Humboldt surveyed the earth from the mountaintop, he was overwhelmed by a transcendent experience of interconnectedness—a rare vision that only a few are privileged to witness. Astronauts, too, have encountered a similar phenomenon when beholding our planet from the vastness of space. They describe a profound opening of awareness known as the "Overview Effect," characterised by perceiving earth as, "a tiny, fragile ball of life," suspended in the infinite void of space.[8] Jim Lovell, Apollo 8 astronaut says, "The vast loneliness up here of the Moon is awe inspiring, and it makes you realize just what you have back there on Earth. The Earth from here is a grand oasis to the big vastness of space." Neil Armstrong of Apollo 11 said, "It suddenly struck me that that tiny pea, pretty and blue, was the Earth. I put up my thumb and shut one eye, and my thumb blotted out the planet Earth. I didn't feel like a giant. I felt very, very small." And Michael Collins of Apollo 11 observes, "The thing that really surprised me was that it [Earth] projected an air of fragility. And why, I don't know. I don't know to this day. I had a feeling it's tiny, it's shiny, it's beautiful, it's home, and it's fragile."[9] The encounter of witnessing the earth's fragility in such a manner is deeply transformative, evoking a sense of awe, humility, and reverence for life. It instils in individuals an intensified feeling of connection not only with fellow human beings but also with the entire planet.

Figure 4.3 – *Earth as Seen from Space: Astronauts often undergo a profound cognitive shift known as the "Overview Effect" when beholding the planet from outer space. This transformative experience grants them a fresh perspective, evoking a sense of awe and reverence while emphasising the delicate and invaluable nature of our precious planet.*

10

Take a moment to reflect on the captivating genesis of life on earth. While the precise details remain shrouded in mystery, one thing is clear: it began in close symbiosis with the sun, billions of years ago. Primitive cells dwelling within the vast oceans underwent a remarkable evolutionary journey, seizing the opportunity to harness the energy radiating from our star. This transformative and delicate dance, known as photosynthesis, adeptly converts sunlight, carbon dioxide, and water into life-sustaining sustenance, while generously releasing oxygen as a precious by-product. It is a process of exquisite intricacy that showcases the profound interplay between life and the creative energy of our celestial companion.[11]

Over millions of years, these primitive bacteria within the earth's oceans crept onto the land. By this point, the planet was already four billion years old and oceans that covered the majority of earth's surface were the primary location of organic life. The land was hostile. Dominated by volcanic activity, it was a violent and inhospitable environment—excruciatingly hot, charred, barren, and brutal, with a suffocating atmosphere of carbon dioxide.[12]

Somehow these pioneering organisms persisted. Through their photosynthetic process, through the cooling effect of oxygen in the atmosphere, the way was prepared for the eventual emergence of complex life on land. As the surface temperature cooled and the air sweetened with oxygen, a gradual evolution of flora and fauna radically changed the surface of our planet.[13] A tapestry of green clothed the land for the first time, generating an environment that supported the evolution of species from primitive bacteria in the ocean, to lush plants and trees, to a splendid diversity of fish, insects, amphibians, reptiles, and mammals, to spectacular birds, and a flush of breath-taking flowers. And eventually, to you and me.

Without this miraculous photosynthetic elixir, life on earth would not exist, and we certainly would not. During this process, plants, algae, and some bacteria take in carbon dioxide (CO_2) and water (H_2O) from the air and soil; water is transformed into oxygen and carbon dioxide into glucose; oxygen is released into the air; and energy is stored within the plant.[14] This energetic play between sunlight, plants, soil, air, and water has created a complex tapestry of landscapes within the biosphere that we call home.

The biosphere is the sum of myriad things yet performs as a whole moving in unison. From a lifeless planet eons ago, the biosphere emerged and evolved into a planetary domain teeming with a spectacular array of sentient and conscious life forms. Each supports the development of the other, gains meaning, and is enriched through their interconnection with the whole. As Alexander von Humboldt astutely observed, it is akin to an immense web, where every thread is interwoven, dependent on the vitality of all its parts. Mirroring the astronauts' experience of the Overview Effect, Wulf, in her book on Humboldt, reflects that, "When nature is perceived as a web, its vulnerability also becomes obvious. Everything hangs together. If one thread is pulled the whole tapestry may unravel."[15]

The Planetary Body

In understanding the biosphere, we must recognise that its parts are intricately interconnected, much like the components of a living organism. It cannot be disassembled and reconstructed like a mere building or machine. Any alteration or removal of its parts reverberates throughout the entire system. The whole shapes the parts, and the parts contribute to the whole. Similar to the human body, despite being composed of diverse elements, the biosphere operates as a unified and integrated entity.

When individual ecosystems or landscapes face pressures and reckless activities, they become susceptible to ailments. If such stress persists, it can initiate a chain reaction of detrimental consequences at the biosphere level. These cascading effects, as described in Chapter 2's concept of Planetary Boundaries, can destabilise the earth system swiftly, leading to calamitous outcomes.

I can relate. As a young woman, I had poor eating habits. I was one of those people who could eat anything and everything and never put on any weight. So, I did just that—ate loads of rubbish and carried on being skinny. Over time, even though I still looked fit and healthy, I began experiencing chronic health issues due to my reckless habits. The toxins accumulated within my system without adequate nourishment or exercise, causing discomfort, pains, and persistent ailments. However, I wasn't ready to change my lifestyle. Instead, I made some superficial changes—took some vitamins, had a healthy shake occasionally, and started jogging a bit—but unsurprisingly, it didn't help much.

Upon reaching my thirties, I felt so unwell that I knew a significant change was imperative. During this time, while house-sitting for a friend, I stumbled upon a book that caught my attention, *Eating Alive* by Dr John Matsen.[16] Although I didn't agree with every aspect, the book eloquently described the workings of the entire digestive system and how our choices impact our well-being. Furthermore, it explained that one must espouse a holistic and integrated approach to maintain health and homeostasis.[17] Fad diets, trendy supplements, and shortcuts never bring about sustained and deep health. What I needed was a complete lifestyle transformation—removing toxic foods from my diet, replacing those with nourishing whole foods, drinking plenty of clean water, having sufficient rest, and taking daily exercise. I finally accepted that a weekend detox or cleanse simply wasn't enough. A complete overhaul was necessary.

Matsen beautifully elucidates, "The incredible healing power within each of us is called homeostasis. It is the basic tenet of physiology that your body is a wise, self-adjusting organism capable of monitoring and correcting imbalances, fighting off invaders, and repairing damage. When homeostasis reigns, health is your natural state. Acute disease is your body's gathering of forces to throw off some outside interference, such as a viral infection. When the virus is defeated, the short-lived disease is over, and homeostasis returns your body to its normal, stable functioning. Chronic disease occurs when the body is unable to completely remove the outside influence—or fully correct damage from it—and the full return of homeostasis is thwarted."[18]

Everything that Matsen explains about how human health is predicated upon a state of homeostasis extends to the wellbeing of the biosphere. Both the human body and our planetary body possess inherent wisdom and regenerative capabilities. Yet, just as external forces can disrupt the balance within the human system, chronic stresses imposed on the planet disrupt the homeostasis of the earth system.

An elegant illustration of our relationship with nature can be found in Leonardo da Vinci's renowned drawing, the *Vitruvian Man.* The body depicted within it serves as an analogy for the workings of the universe, reflecting the harmony present in all things. The title of the drawing pays homage to Vitruvius Pollio, the author of an architectural treatise called *De architectura*, which extols the virtue of harmony through the perfect synthesis of strength, utility, and beauty.[19]

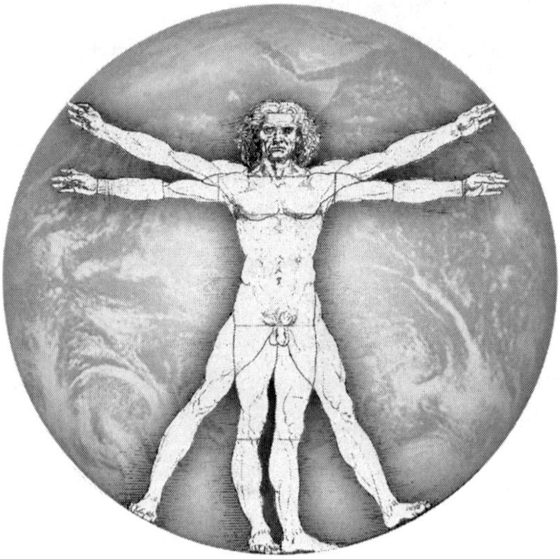

Figure 4.4 *– The Human Body, a Microcosm of the Planet: This captivating illustration compares Leonardo da Vinci's* Vitruvian Man *with a photograph of the earth from space. Da Vinci's insight into the interconnectedness of the planet and the human body reveals a profound analogy, showcasing the body as a microcosm mirroring the intricate workings of the universe (© Alexandra Steed URBAN).*

[20]

We can surmise that Da Vinci's drawing alludes to the profound significance of balance in all aspects—be it the human body, the planet, or the universe itself. In Chapter 12, we will consider Vitruvius's teachings and explore how landscape planning, design, and stewardship can help achieve the ideal of harmony on earth.

In his book, Matsen also explains how "pathology" is the study of the failure of homeostasis to return the body to normal physiology and how in modern healthcare, there is a tendency to focus on this pathology, or disease, rather than on the ability of the body to heal itself. Attention should be given to health improvement rather than the treatment of illness.[21] Supplements, medication, or minor surgery may allow us to continue our excesses and over-consumption in the short term, but it won't bring about sustained health.

While we urgently seek solutions for planetary health, it is important to understand that focusing solely on addressing symptomatic issues can divert attention from the chronic stresses our planet faces. Some individuals are seeking quick fixes or gimmicky solutions in an attempt to "fix" nature. However, such approaches often prove to be harmful or ineffective. For instance, mining for rare earth metals to produce electric car batteries presents its own set of problems. Similarly, seemingly nature-based solutions like planting monocultures of bioenergy crops can be both ineffective and harmful.

Quick fixes may appear harmless, but they can have disastrous consequences. Take for example, large-scale tree planting initiatives that focus on a single species or attempt to forest ecosystems where it is unsuitable can lead to dangerously negative outcomes.[22] To truly address the challenges at hand, we need substantial and integrated changes that address the root causes of the problem. It requires dedicated efforts to create conditions that support the healing of the planet as a whole. Anything less than a comprehensive overhaul of how we treat landscapes will be insufficient to address the living world's profound troubles.

The writer and environmental activist, Margaret Atwood, reminds us how vulnerable and dependent we are on a healthy functioning biosphere. "Three days without water and a human being is usually dead. The oxygen we breathe was not always such a large part of Earth's atmosphere as it is now: it was created by green plants, which continue to create it, so if we do away with all plants, we'd be gone. If Earth's temperature rises much higher, our planet will become uninhabitable—not by all life, perhaps—a few deep-ocean forms will surely survive, unless the ocean boils away—but certainly by us."[23]

Addressing the earth's health requires a radical shift, as the same thinking that led to harmful behaviours and disease symptoms cannot heal the planet. Instead, we must tap into the intelligence of nature and allow it to find its own balance and homeostasis. This transformation can occur within each landscape, regardless of its size, as every part is an integral thread within the intricate tapestry of the earth system. The future of the biosphere hinges on the evolution of human consciousness, moving beyond a limited perspective and embracing a broad landscape mindset that fosters integration with the natural world in every landscape.

While the complexity of the biosphere's workings may be overwhelming for the human mind to grasp in its entirety, we can start by focusing on the landscapes within our immediate view—our own backyards and neighbourhoods. By cultivating a personal connection with the world around us, we can re-establish rapport immediately and intimately. Therefore, at the landscape level, humanity can collectively begin repairing the harmful actions and interactions that have impacted the natural world.

Famously, Humboldt stated, "The most dangerous worldview is the view of those who have never looked at the world."[24] I firmly believe that we inhabit a world that has become blind to the awesomeness of nature, severed its vital connection to the land, and is not paying attention to humanity's reckless behaviours. Our world is in imminent danger. It is time to take heed.

In a society driven by progress and development, the significance of landscape is often overlooked, seen as non-essential, secondary to other concerns, or manipulated by humans with little thought, leading to devastating outcomes. This is a tragedy because landscape matters. Never before has the subject of landscape been more critical, and there is no more important subject than rehabilitating our relationship with all nature across all landscapes.

PART III

Landscape Matters

5

Defining Landscape

NON-ESSENTIAL TO NECESSARY

"To build, to plant, whatever you intend,
To rear the column, or the arch to bend,
To swell the terrace, or to sink the grot,
In all, let Nature never be forgot.
But treat the Goddess like a modest Fair,
Nor overdress, nor leave her wholly bare;
Let not each beauty everywhere be spied,
Where half the skill is decently to hide.
He gains all points who pleasingly confounds,
Surprises, varies, and conceals the bounds.
Consult the genius of the place in all." [1]
—Alexander Pope

OUR CONNECTION to life finds expression in our relationship with nature, and this bond unfolds within the realm of the landscape. It is the meeting point where humanity and the natural world converge, and it is precisely here that we can mend our disconnection from the earth. The landscape, when approached with the best interests of the full living community in mind, embodies its most exquisite and authentic form.

The landscape envelops us, an ever-present companion that shapes the context of our lives. Wherever we find ourselves, we are situated within a landscape. It is within this perpetual company that humans can collaborate with all nature to shape our shared future. This alone should serve as a compelling reason for us to care deeply.

In this chapter, I put landscape front and centre of our considerations when confronting the monumental environmental challenges faced by society. As Alexander Pope wisely reminds us, "In all, let Nature never be forgot." Neglecting to incorporate nature into our plans for growth and development leaves us a resulting environment that is surely bereft. Conversely, by honouring and embracing nature, the landscape becomes a canvas carefully sculpted into a beautiful, thriving, and regenerative form. Such landscapes offer extraordinary benefits to human life without any drawbacks, as demonstrated by the inspiring case studies described in the following pages.

Regrettably, the subject of landscape is often overlooked and does not receive the serious attention it deserves. Many fail to recognise that the landscape is subject to a variety of forces, both human and natural, but particularly influenced by our anthropocentric era. This chapter strives to elucidate how human modifications of the landscape can only become integrated and wholesome when we reorient our worldview from a narrow portrait frame to one refocused on the broader landscape community.

The Multi-Faceted Nature of Landscape

The term "landscape" encompasses a range of meanings, each carrying its own significance for different individuals. As a noun, it refers to the visible features of a land area, including rivers, hills, buildings, trees, plants, animals, and the sky, often appreciated for their aesthetic appeal. In the realm of art, a landscape refers to a painting or picture that captures the essence of the land within a framed view. Additionally, landscape can denote a specific area of activity, a context, or a scene, such as a political or cultural landscape. Despite these diverse definitions, they are interconnected, highlighting the relational aspect between the observer and the observed world. In landscapes, humans and nature are in constant relationship, both as active participants.

However, landscape is not only a noun but also a verb. The action of "landscaping" involves the human activity of shaping and enhancing an area of land. This concept reminds us that while the landscape provides us with a stable foundation and an appearance of timelessness, it is in a perpetual state of change. The landscape is ever-shifting, never the same, and subject to transformation even from one moment to the next. Humans play a critical role in this change-making.

Indeed, change is a fundamental characteristic of the landscape as a living system, making it captivating, fascinating, and invaluable. The earth's surface, the biosphere, undergoes constant modification through a series of processes that shape landscapes and alter our environment. Powerful geological forces such as tectonic uplift, subsidence, and volcanic activity have exerted their influence over vast periods. Other forces, visible in our daily lives, include the actions of water, ice, wind, fire, and the interactions among living organisms, such as worms, insects, birds, and beavers. Chemical reactions in soils and the gradual effects of gravity over time also contribute to landscape transformation. Even the sunlight or its absence can completely alter a landscape, not only in appearance but also in its photosynthetic interaction with plant life.

In recent times, human activity has emerged as the dominant force in shaping the land. Landscaping is often understood as minor human modifications to topography and vegetation within a defined area. As a landscape architect, I am familiar with this definition, but I am also aware of its superficiality and its potential to undermine the significance of such a monumental task. Remember, Einstein said, "Our task must be to free ourselves from this prison by widening our circle of compassion to embrace all living creatures and the whole of nature in its beauty."[2] Cooperating with nature to curate landscapes and shape the living world for the benefit of all is an exciting and purposeful pursuit, a great privilege and, one that I consider to be the most extraordinary art form.

Alexander Pope, in his famous essay, emphasises the importance of basing all human development on common sense, following nature, and aligning with the unique context of a place. Pope says:

> "That the first principle and foundation in this, as in every thing else, is Good Sense. The chief proof of it is to follow Nature, even in works of mere luxury and elegance. Instanced in Architecture and Gardening, where *all must be adapted to the genius and use of the place, and the beauties not forced into it, but resulting from it.* How men are disappointed in their most expensive undertakings for want of this true foundation, without which nothing can please long, if at all; and the best examples and rules will but be perverted into something burdensome and ridiculous."[3] (Italics mine.)

Pope argues that in architecture and gardening, all elements should be adapted to the genius and use of the site, with beauty emerging naturally from it. When we disregard this understanding and impose our constructions onto the landscape without considering its inherent intelligence, the result is not only ridiculous but even perverse.

However, in today's world, humans are "landscaping" entire ecosystems without proper knowledge, planning, design, or management strategies. In the following chapters, we will explore how changes in land use and other human activities across urban environments, farmland, and wilderness areas have led to widespread devastation. The climate crisis is poised to become the most significant driving force behind landscape change. While humans have set this process of climate change in motion, we have limited control over the resulting landscape outcomes shaped by the climate. Consequently, humanity is unwittingly landscaping the entire biosphere without fully realising the extent of our impact.

The EU Landscape Convention defines landscape as "an area, as perceived by people, whose character is the result of the action and interaction of natural and/or human factors."[4] This definition acknowledges that landscape is a manifestation of the interactions between humans and nature, reflecting people's values and beliefs about our relationship with the natural world. In this unique realm of communion, we have a remarkable opportunity to create a world of balance and harmony. However, the landscape often serves as a testament to humanity's failure, embodying a grave imbalance.

Unfortunately, we often shape the land thoughtlessly, leaving too much to chance and too little to intentional design. This ignorance leads to catastrophic effects on our biosphere, affecting both short-term and long-term human health and well-being. Nevertheless, it is possible to shape the landscape in ways that bring tremendous benefits when we rotate our approach from a narrow portrait frame to a broader landscape perspective.

In Chapter 2, we explored the concept of ecosystem services—nature's gifts that enhance our lives. These services represent only a fraction of the extraordinary benefits provided by nature. There is still much we do not fully understand. By working in harmony with the natural world, conscious landscape planning, design, and management can enhance environmental, social, and economic conditions. Some advantages include mitigating climate change, reducing flooding and air pollution, decomposing waste materials, increasing property values, attracting tourism, creating green jobs, and providing therapeutic and recreational opportunities that improve community health and well-being. Our actions in the landscape do not have to be negative; they can bring about positive changes when we embrace a shift from Portrait to Landscape.

Let's not forget that as much as we shape the landscape, the landscape shapes us. It can be felt at a spiritual and psychological level. When we are disassociated from the land and nature's beauty, it eats away at us and leaves us feeling empty, depleted, and alone. I—and many people worldwide—felt this despair and lack of connectedness during the COVID-19 epidemic. Numerous studies have demonstrated the positive mental health outcomes associated with feeling connected to the natural environment.[5] The lockdowns and isolation brought to public attention the significance of having daily access to landscapes to sustain overall well-being.

Even outside the pandemic, extensive research has shown the importance of integrating nature into our lives to improve mental health. Studies on "green therapy" reveal that hospital patients who can see greenery from their windows experience faster recovery times.[6] Similarly, just ten more trees in a city block can enhance an individual's health perception, making them feel seven years younger.[7]

The popular practice of "forest-bathing" has also shown significant benefits in reducing stress levels, as measured by lowered cortisol concentrations.[8]

Neglecting the essential connection with nature leads to suffering. Engaging with the natural world, whether through seaside visits, walks in the woods, cycling along greenways, swimming in natural bodies of water, tending to a garden, or simply smelling the roses, brings joy and well-being. An increasing body of evidence, coupled with personal testimonies, confirms the tremendous health benefits of integrating nature into our daily routines.

Introducing moments of connection with the natural world are genuinely fulfilling and restorative. Children experience these joys most profoundly. Their eyes are still open to the miracles of life around them. The simple joys of splashing in a puddle, discovering tadpoles in a tide pool, observing a caterpillar crawling on their fingers, or picking and savouring a juicy blackberry off a bramble bush are unparalleled. Children are naturally enchanted by nature, though sadly, all too often, many children only experience the abundance and delight of the living world through a screen.

This understanding motivated me to start my landscape practice —to bring joy to people's everyday lives by forging fresh connections between people and nature. So many individuals lack direct contact with the natural world, yet nothing brings greater delight than feeling the warmth of the sun on our face, gazing up at light filtering through the exquisite leaves of a tree, witnessing the blossoming of spring, waking up to the melodies of birds, feeling the grass beneath our toes, or swimming in the sea. Recently a butterfly landed on my hand and stayed with me for over half an hour. What a thrill!

Indeed, landscape is a rich, multi-dimensional, and interconnected entity that reflects the interactions between people and nature. While humans play a significant role in shaping the landscape, we must do so with knowledge, respect, and a deep understanding of the intelligence inherent in each unique environment. By adopting a landscape perspective and working in harmony with nature, we have the opportunity to create landscapes that bring about tremendous benefits for our environment, society, and personal well-being.

Landscape Benefits

In my project work, I often find it effective to visually present the many benefits that a restored landscape can bring to both human and wild communities. Similar to the Ecosystem Services Wheel, these benefits can be organised to showcase their interconnectedness and to make their value obvious at a glance. The circular nature of the wheel demonstrates how each benefit is related to the whole. An example of such a wheel is shown in the figure below, which was created for a regional landscape strategy discussed in Chapter 7.

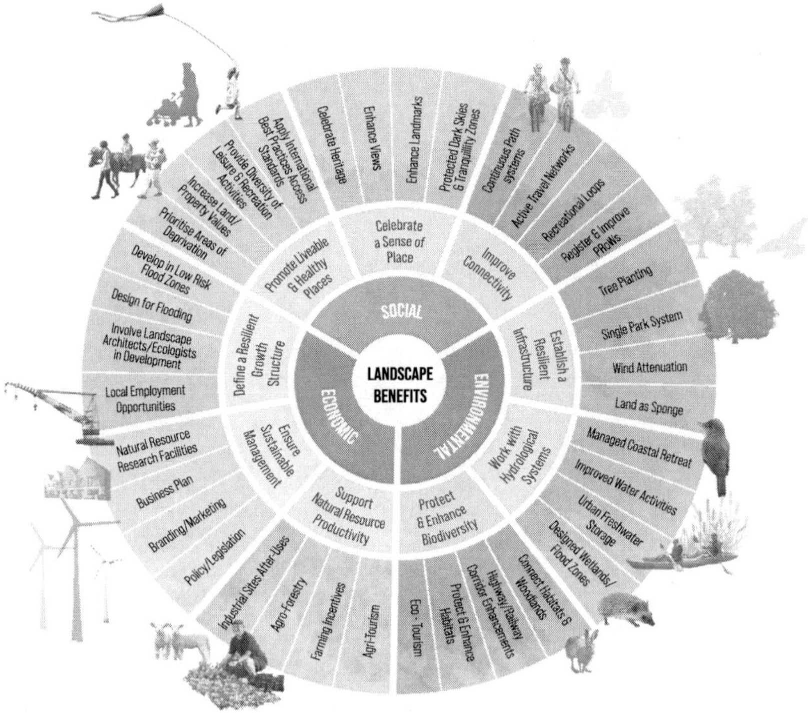

***Figure 5.1** – Landscape Benefits Wheel: This graphic presents some extraordinary advantages of implementing nature-guided landscape strategies. The benefits arise when the whole community of life is considered in landscape creation (© Alexandra Steed URBAN).*

9

While a table of benefits can be informative, examining a case study is often the most effective way to understand the concept in practice. It allows us to quickly grasp the value and benefits that well-planned, designed, and managed landscapes can provide in terms of social, environmental, and economic aspects. Let's take a closer look at one of the most renowned landscapes on the planet—Central Park in New York.

Central Park, New York

Can anyone imagine New York without Central Park? Designed by landscape architects Frederick Law Olmsted and Calvert Vaux, it first opened to the public in 1858. The park comprises 341 hectares (843 acres), extending from Midtown to Harlem, and contributing to the city's image, identity, beauty, and spirit.[10] It is one of the most known urban parks on the planet and the most filmed location in the world. I'm sure you too recognise it.

Figure 5.2 - *View of Central Park: This world-renowned park in the heart of New York City is unbelievably valuable, environmentally, socially and economically.*

[11]

Central Park performs on so many levels it is difficult to capture them all. Socially, it functions as the city's gathering place, offering opportunities for both active and passive recreation, cultural and entertainment activities, as well as informal social interactions. Moreover, the park acts as a magnet, attracting a significant number of tourists visiting New York City. With over forty million annual visits, the park welcomes an average of approximately 115,000 visitors per day.[12]

Ecologically, it is mainly self-sustaining and a source of biodiversity. The park is home to several species—from red-tail hawks and hundreds of migrating birds to the Gotham bee, goldfish, and largemouth bass—and interconnected ecosystems.[13] The land supports more than 20,000 trees of 174 species, 150 acres of water, and 80 acres of woodland, all of which provide habitats, improve air quality, absorb precipitation, and help to ease the urban heat island effect of New York.

Central Park is widely recognised for its social and ecological significance. However, the incredible economic benefits it generates are often overlooked. The park's contribution to property value and the overall economy is so substantial that its absence would significantly diminish the fiscal value of Manhattan as a whole.

Frederick Law Olmsted, the visionary behind Central Park, foresaw the tremendous increase in property values that would accompany the park's establishment. He meticulously documented the assessed land value of the three neighbouring wards in 1856, amounting to USD $26,429,565. Following the park's completion in 1873, the total value of those same areas skyrocketed to $236,081,515. In just seventeen years, the property values in those wards experienced a whopping tenfold increase, while other city wards not adjacent to Central Park only doubled in value.[14]

This effect is called the "Proximate Principle" where the capitalisation of parkland directly impacts the value of nearby properties.[15] As one might expect, property values are increased maximally closer to the park and decrease in value as they move away, usually dropping off after a few blocks.

Unsurprisingly, the most valuable properties in New York City are located in close proximity to Central Park or within a few blocks. The park's influence extends beyond property values, as it serves as a hub for cultural institutions and renowned hotels. Moreover, Central Park directly employs a significant number of individuals in various establishments such as restaurants, the zoo, kiosks, and venues, contributing well over USD $100 million to the local economy annually.[16] Annual maintenance and operation costs total $4.5 million. The value of Central Park alone today is $627 million per acre. However, if the land were to be developed, it would decrease economic gain across the entire city, significantly reducing the total commercial value of Manhattan's property.

The benefits observed in Central Park are not exclusive to this particular landscape. Urban parks worldwide have experienced similar effects, commonly referred to as the "edge effect." Extensive documentation demonstrates that investing in high-quality public spaces and landscapes is one of the most cost-effective means to enhance land values. Consequently, it is perplexing why well-designed landscapes and the public realm are often undervalued or considered merely optional in cities.

The High Line, New York

New York City, in recent years, has been creatively carving out more space for people and nature within its dense urban fabric. Many streets have repurposed existing parking spaces to create spill-out areas for outdoor seating and greenery adjacent to cafes. Former industrial sites along the waterfront have been transformed into public green spaces, featuring miles of improved promenades, parks, playgrounds, and nature areas, including captivating temporary street installations.

One of the most exciting and successful landscape projects to date has been the transformation of a disused railway viaduct into a community-driven greenway known as The High Line.[17] Once considered an eyesore by many, community members, who had grown to love this nature-colonised piece of infrastructure, founded Friends of The High Line to advocate for its preservation and repurpose it as a public park. (It was inspired by the linear park Coulee Verte in Paris, which traverses through the heart of Paris on an old railway line.[18]) The High Line gained strong support from the City, leading to a design competition. Landscape architect James Corner Field Operations and their team were selected as the winning designers.

Friends of The High Line proudly report, "The High Line is now one, continuous, 1.45-mile-long (2.3km) greenway featuring 500+ species of plants and trees. Friends of the High Line maintain, operate, and program the park in partnership with the NYC Department of Parks and Recreation. On top of public space and gardens, The High Line is home to a diverse suite of public programs, community and teen engagement, and world-class artwork and performances, free and open to all."[19]

Figure 5.3 *- View of The High Line: An elevated and linear park that offers a contemporary New York City landscape imaginatively constructed atop a disused railway viaduct.*

20

Since its opening, this innovative elevated linear park has gained international recognition and has become a renowned tourist destination, attracting over eight million visitors annually. Similar to the impact of Central Park over a century earlier, The High Line has become an emblem of American landscape architecture, catalysing real estate developments in adjacent neighbourhoods and significantly increasing property values along its route. It serves as a testament to the power of community agency in improving their environments and shaping urban landscapes.

The benefits of embracing nature in human communities are boundless, regardless of perspective. It is illogical to overlook the opportunity to integrate the living world into our cities. Other built structures and infrastructures, such as paved roads, industrial buildings, skyscrapers, or large office blocks, often create adverse conditions, including increased flooding, elevated air pollution, wind tunnels, and fragmented communities. Conversely, the creation of a healthy landscape holds no downsides. The absence of disbenefits is a compelling indicator of its inherent value. These benefits encompass protecting buildings and infrastructure from flooding, providing habitats for struggling wildlife, producing nourishing food, sequestering carbon, improving air quality, promoting health and well-being while reducing healthcare costs, offering safe and delightful spaces for children's play, bringing joy and beauty into our daily lives, and even generating economic prosperity. Considering these generous, life-giving and life-sustaining contributions, one would expect landscapes worldwide to inspire awe, respect, and unwavering care, regardless of their scale. If only that were the case.

In my work, I often find frustration in the lack of attention paid to landscapes and the limited understanding surrounding their significance. Those involved in development and real estate frequently prioritise buildings over the landscape, relegating the latter to a secondary, peripheral consideration. It is common to refer to urban landscapes as the "space between buildings," "leftover spaces," "bits of green around the edges," "non-essential," or a "nice-to-have." However, nothing could be further from the truth. The landscape endures and its healthy functioning remains critical. It persists long after buildings have crumbled and faded into the ground.

Previous civilisations comprehended the vital connection with the landscape. Geographer and earth scientist Suzanne Leroy, in her study "Natural Hazards, Landscapes and Civilisations" found that, "The role of landscape was paramount in the initial development of civilisations, with a clear influence on the emergence of agriculture and of cities. Ancient cities are closely inscribed in a landscape."[21] Leroy explains that settlements were strategically located based on access to fresh water for drinking and irrigation, fertile soils for agriculture, waterways for transportation and communication, and secure positions for safety and protection. Our ancestors did not disregard the landscape; rather, their cities evolved harmoniously with it, carefully chosen to support human habitation. They also recognised the catastrophic consequences of selecting an unsuitable location.

This chapter began with a quote from Alexander Pope. He asserts, "That the first principle and foundation in this, as in every thing else, is Good Sense. The chief proof of it is to follow Nature, even in works of mere luxury and elegance. Instanced in

Architecture and Gardening, where *all must be adapted to the genius and use of the place, and the beauties not forced into it, but resulting from it.*"[22] Pope further contends that working without a clear understanding of the genius and purpose of a place or without respecting the unique landscape conditions will result in absurdity. We currently inhabit a world teetering on the edge of collapse, and now we understand why.

We have missed the mark in our approach to growth and land development. The resulting urban, industrial, and agricultural landscapes are most often distorted, almost mocking nature's inherent wisdom.

By embracing the beauty and significance of our immediate landscapes, including those of our homes and neighbourhoods, we glean a valuable lesson in cultivating love and care for all environments. Failing to appreciate and nurture the surroundings that envelop us raises the question: how can we possibly extend our concern to the vast rural and wilderness landscapes beyond our immediate sight? However, when we reset our perspective and recognise the inherent value of landscapes within our human habitats, a more inclusive worldview naturally emerges. This evolution in mindset enables urban populations to develop a deeper appreciation for the living world that extends far beyond their immediate surroundings. Living authentically and harmoniously with nature unlocks far-reaching benefits that manifest in beauty, utility, and a profound sense of delight across all landscapes.

The subsequent chapters will begin by zooming in on urban landscapes before gradually expanding to peri-urban areas and eventually encompassing rural and wilderness landscapes. In each context, we will uncover the human imprint on these landscapes, ranging from the smallest to the grandest, from the most immediate to the most remote.

6

Urban Landscapes

EXCLUSIVE TO INCLUSIVE

"Slowly but surely water has created most of the landscapes we inhabit. It erodes mountains, carves valleys, and meanders at will across plains. While sculpting the form of the land from the raw material of geology, water also makes settlement possible in the landscape it creates. Fresh water for drinking and irrigation, combined with coastal and river transport, has determined the location of most towns and cities. London is a perfect example." [1]

—*Kim Wilkie*

LET'S focus our attention on the primary human habitat: urban landscapes. Within cities, the intricate bond between humanity and nature is visibly severed, a consequence of our dichotomous worldview. These landscapes, once adorned with fresh streams and fertile soils that enticed early settlers, now lie hidden beneath layers of buildings and infrastructure, burdened by contamination.

As rural dwellers worldwide migrate to city centres, the strain on urban landscapes grows more acute. The cities become denser, and these new city-dwellers, displaced from their homelands, struggle to establish roots in their unfamiliar urban surroundings. They long for connection, community, and an improved quality of life.[2] Yet, access to vital landscapes, exemplified by Central Park or The High Line as discussed in the previous chapter, becomes increasingly critical, and at the same time, more elusive.

But we cannot afford to ignore this challenge, for the well-being of both people and the planet demands our attention. We must recognise that the revitalisation of the connection between people and environment in cities cannot be achieved through the same dualistic thinking that led to their estrangement.

With this in mind, we must ask ourselves: How can we rekindle the relationship between people and nature within these constrained cityscapes? Is it possible to carve out space for nature within the urban fabric? Can we uncover the inherent beauty of the landscapes upon which cities were originally built? In this chapter, we embark on a journey to find the answers. Through the lens of London, we examine how human interaction with the landscape has shaped our cities. We witness the promise of the past erode with time. However, we also uncover how an exclusive portrait mindset can be transformed into an inclusive landscape perspective, allowing us to rectify past mistakes and cultivate more liveable spaces for all urban inhabitants, both human and wild.

Let us begin our exploration in the vibrant city of London, where I am among the nine million residents who call it home. London stands as a global metropolis with a rich history that stretches back centuries, predating even the Roman establishment of Londinium in the first century AD. The Romans were drawn to this area precisely due to its enchanting landscape, appealing geographical location, and the presence of a thriving river. One cannot overlook the allure of this city, nestled in a landscape that has captivated inhabitants for generations. At the heart of London's charm lies the River Thames, a vital lifeline that courses through the city. This iconic waterway has left an indelible mark, sculpting the land, shaping its banks, and depositing fertile sediments along its terraces.

In his delightful book, *Led by the Land*, landscape architect Kim Wilkie eloquently describes the river's multifaceted role. It serves not only as a conduit for water but also as a carrier of light, space, rhythm, change, and wildlife. It breathes vitality into the heart of the city, both along its banks and within its waters.[3] Beyond its poetic allure, the river serves the practical purpose of efficiently transporting goods and materials for human consumption, ensuring the smooth functioning of London's bustling existence.

The Romans had a history of selecting accessible sites located at fordable points: where a river was narrow enough to build a bridge but deep enough to allow marine vessels passage. In London, they chose to settle on the northern bank, located on the current site of the City of London. In his insightful book, *Shaping London*, architect and planner Terry Farrell explains that a combination of landscape attributes informed the Roman settler's decision. "Such simple matters of natural terrain and geography, and the effect of the forces of nature working together – meant London was founded here, just where it is."[4] Its fertile, south-facing and sunny slopes, fordable position on the river, location on the bank that allowed easy moorage, deeper channel, and defensible position made it an optimal spot to settle.

Centuries later, long after the departure of the Romans, the Royal Parks—still one of London's most exceptional features—were originally established as royal hunting grounds along many tributaries feeding the Thames. Settlements also began to spring up along the streams, and the industrial revolution brought increasing flow and pollution levels to the Thames and its tributaries: factories, slaughterhouses, tanneries, and mills, all depositing their putrid waste into the waterways. With rapid population growth in the Victorian era—from about one million people in 1800 to well over five million in 1900—the waste problem was exacerbated.[5] The River Thames, used as a dumping ground for the capitol's waste for centuries, could no longer hide the effects. Solid waste often found its way into the city streets, then the tributaries, and ultimately flushed into the Thames. Poor sanitation led to cholera and typhoid outbreaks, resulting in millions dying. A scorching summer in 1858 brought the problem to a head in what is known as "The Great Stink;" centuries of waste in the Thames began to ferment. Repulsed by the smell and concerned about the health effects, a plan was finally implemented to deal with the sewage.[6]

Chief Engineer, Joseph Bazalgette, was made responsible for delivering a new system that would carry wastewater underground in a series of interconnecting sewers—including all of London's original tributaries—whisking sewage away from the centres and out eastward into the Thames Estuary, where the effluent would be dispatched on the outgoing tide.[7]

London still operates on the same Bazalgette infrastructure (though it is currently undergoing renewal and expansion into a "super-sewer").[8] While the Thames no longer emits the same repulsive smell, it is still the receptacle of a massive amount of our waste. During extreme storm events, which the city is experiencing more frequently, sewage pipes become overwhelmed. Though illegal, the excess water and waste overflow into the river to prevent the sewer network from backing up and flooding local homes and properties. For example, in a 2022 storm event, over two billion litres of raw sewage were dumped into the Thames in only two days.[9]

The mighty River Thames, rejuvenating tributaries and favourable landscape conditions attracted humans to settle here in the first place. However, in a twist of irony, the processes of urbanisation have transformed the once cherished attributes that attracted early settlers—the life-giving watercourses and soils—into repositories for our waste and have subjected them to degradation under layers of infrastructure. London is not alone in this predicament. The originally beautiful and productive landscapes of numerous cities worldwide have suffered a similarly unfortunate fate.

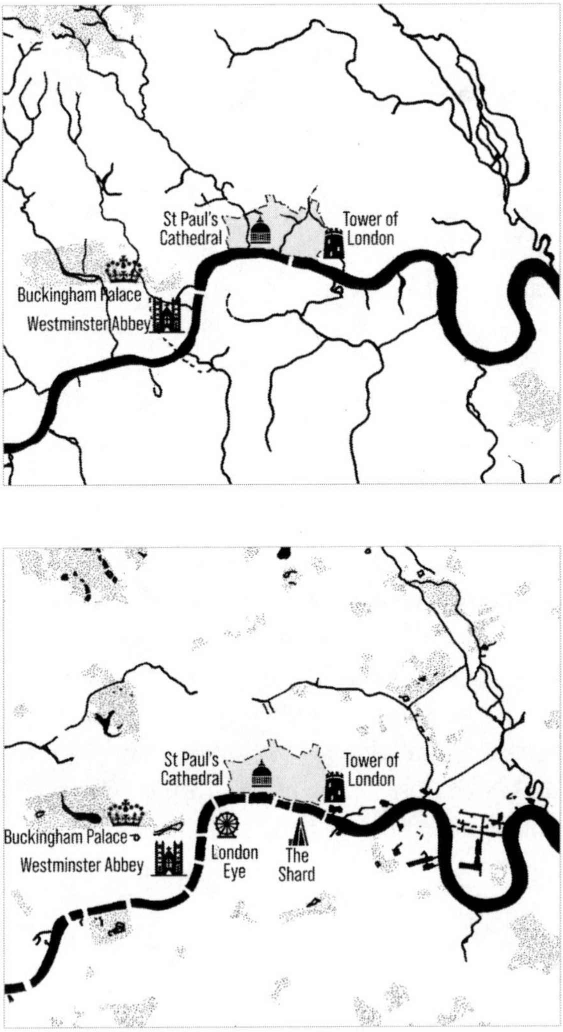

Figure 6.1 *– London's Lost Streams: Most of London's tributaries have been contaminated and buried below the surface. The top image reveals the former watercourses in London, and the bottom illustrates those remaining, including introduced canals (© Alexandra Steed URBAN).*

Straining Urban Landscapes

The transformation of landscapes into bustling urban centres has resulted in some of the most degraded ecosystems on our planet, where the natural environment is often overshadowed and obscured by layers of human infrastructure. It is within these urban environments that the pressures of human population growth against the earth become most apparent and concentrated. Rivers, once sources of vitality, become contaminated; fertile soils are buried beneath concrete; the air becomes polluted, and wildlife is displaced. As the urban population continues to grow, these assaults on urban nature only intensify, placing even greater strain on the delicate balance between human development and the natural world.

In recent decades, most population environmentsgrowth has been geographically focused on cities. Only 3 percent of the earth's surface area is urban,[11] yet 56 percent of the human population resides in these urban centres.[12] Census data presents a dramatic sweep from 1950, when circa 750 million people lived in cities, to 4.2 billion today.[13] The density of cities continues to rise as our population increases and as people continue to migrate from rural to urban areas. Since the 1990s, more than 75 percent of the US population has lived in cities, and by 2000, France, Spain, the UK, Mexico, Korea, Australia, and Brazil had followed suit.[14] Around the world, every other country is following the same trend. The United Nations tells us that by 2050, the projected world population will be circa ten billion, with 68 percent of those living in cities.[15]

As populations soar, urban environments face immense pressure. Increasing demands for housing, commerce, infrastructure, and services such as transportation, energy, technology, water, and sewage compound the strain. These urban pressures extend beyond city limits, causing far-reaching environmental repercussions.

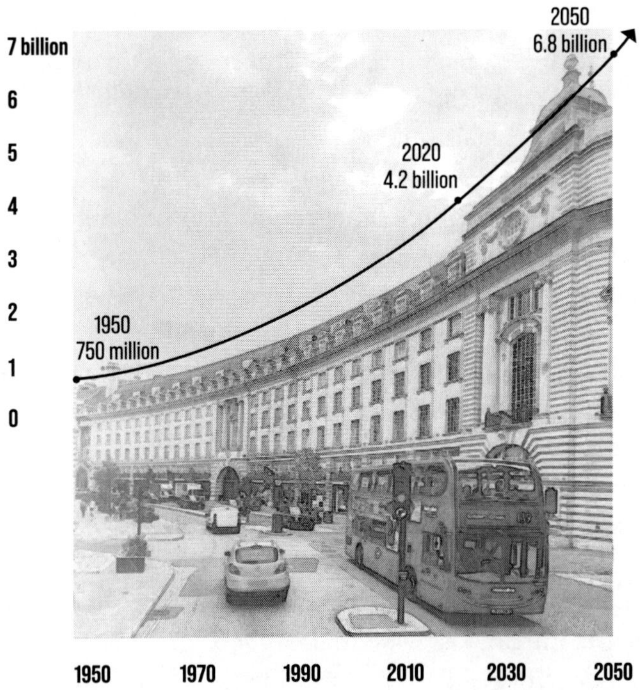

Figure 6.2 *– The Rise of Cities: Since 1950, the human population in cities has radically increased from 750 million to approximately 4.2 billion today (© Alexandra Steed URBAN).*

16

Human Habitats

Urban landscapes have emerged as the primary human habitat, where our interaction with the natural world is most intense. This interaction reflects the significance we attribute to nature. However, the resulting fusion often manifests as the complete subjugation of nature. In many cities, the once-vibrant tapestry of the living world is extinguished, replaced by isolated pockets of greenery, painting a mournful picture that has become the norm. Layers of lifeless asphalt and concrete stifle and regulate nature's presence. Urban streams, once teeming with life, are now channelled and shrouded, overwhelmed by sewage and stormwater. Soils are excavated or buried deep underground. The polluted air suffocates the cityscape. Trees and plants are mercilessly uprooted to make way for development. Local wildlife is displaced or labelled as pests. We have grown so accustomed to suppressing nature in urban environments that we may believe nature and cities are incompatible, deeming their integration impossible or unnecessary. If we were to view urbanity's treatment of nature as a personal relationship, it would be recognised as severely dysfunctional.

In the relentless pursuit of development, the space for nature to breathe has dwindled, leaving us with little room for the landscape to thrive. Those in positions of power have prioritised maximising development area, property values, and technological efficiency, often at the expense of the natural world. In this quest for perceived security and low risk, urban landscapes have been severely compromised, unable to fulfil the diverse functions and ecosystem services that are vital for human survival. As previously discussed, these services encompass essential aspects such as fresh air, clean water, temperature regulation, waste decomposition, and even food production. This dysfunctional treatment of urban landscapes not only harms the environment but also inflicts suffering upon people.

To ensure the well-being and health of urban dwellers in crowded cities, a complete transformation in our relationship with city nature is imperative. As responsible citizens, we bear the responsibility of urging city officials to prioritise the protection and restoration of urban landscapes. It is essential to enact legislation and enforce regulations that mandate thoughtful consideration, meticulous planning, effective design, and proper maintenance of external spaces. Streets, rooftops, waterways, parks, natural areas, or private gardens are all important components of urban landscapes. While the current reality may fall short of these ideals, there is a gradual global improvement taking place, offering a glimmer of hope for a more harmonious coexistence between humans and nature.

Rethinking Streetscapes

Streetscapes, the dominant feature of urban landscapes, serve as a prime example of underperforming spaces. In cities like London, approximately 25 percent of urban land is dedicated to roads—a statistic mirrored in many cities worldwide.[17] Despite occupying a significant portion of public land, streets have been designed in a way that squanders a critical opportunity.

Roads have been engineered primarily for efficient vehicular movement and parking, neglecting other essential considerations. These routes are paved with impermeable concrete or asphalt surfaces that sever the connection between the earth below and the air above, forming a complete barrier above the ground—limiting the landscape's ability to breathe.

Within this sealed urban street environment, the only openings are the drains that swiftly flush rainwater into an underground pipe network, mixing it with wastewater and sewage during storm overflow situations. This rainwater, once a source of replenishment for groundwater, streams, and vegetation, now combines with vehicle oil and petrol, losing its ability to perform beneficial functions. Tragically, even urban streams are incorporated into this culverted sub-ground network, deprived of their life-supporting functions for waterside plant life and aquatic creatures.

The only other opening in this impermeable urban street environment is sometimes a tree "pit"—an apt name for urban trees' homes—squeezed in amongst a mess of underground infrastructure and incarcerated within a "root barrier" to keep its roots away from our precious utilities. These once majestic life forms are imprisoned in a small cell measuring about $1m^3$ (circa 35 ft3) and expected to survive the pollution, wind, heat, and drought conditions of a city street environment. What a tragic life sentence.

Figure 6.3 **-** *Conditions Below Urban Streets: A spaghetti jumble of utilities exists under the surface level of roads. It is difficult for trees, plants, soils, or other life forms to survive in these cluttered and uncoordinated corridors.*

18

Wildlife surviving such conditions tend to be those most adaptable and resilient to harsh environments and scavenging—rats, mice, and pigeons—while once common creatures like badgers, hedgehogs, and songbirds are scarce.

Air quality within these street corridors is compromised by the endless traffic, emitting toxic gases and fine particulate matter that pose health risks to residents. Those breathing it in daily are slowly poisoned. In many cities, including London, air quality is so unhealthy that the UN considers it "illegal."[19] In cities around the world, including London, air pollution has reached alarming levels, causing premature deaths, stunted lung growth in children, and various respiratory, and cardiovascular diseases, and dementia.[20] The environmental impact of road transportation extends beyond the local urban environment, contributing to CO_2 emissions, with wide-reaching and long-lasting effects, lingering for years or even decades to come.[21]

Contrary to the assumption that nature finds refuge elsewhere in public lands, the reality is different. The London Plan notes, "The public realm includes all publicly-accessible space between buildings, whether public or privately owned, from alleyways and streets to squares and open spaces, including the Thames and London's waterways."[22] That sounds like an awful lot of space. But here's the clincher. It goes on to say, "Streets account for 80% of London's public spaces."[23] This staggering figure is reflective of many urban areas worldwide.

Thus, transforming streetscapes into healthy and functioning ecosystems is vital for the well-being of urban inhabitants. They don't have to remain entirely paved and vehicle-dominated; with visionary leadership and citizen engagement, streets can become resilient, vibrant, and joyful environments. Landscape architects have long advocated for sustainable and green street design, which involves reducing impervious surfaces, incorporating swales for natural stormwater drainage and pollutant filtration, planting trees and native vegetation, and prioritising pedestrian and cyclist-friendly spaces.

***Figure 6.4** – View of a Living Street: Streets are a significant component of the urban environment and can be multi-dimensional corridors, serving people, birds, bees, other local wildlife, soil, water, and air (© Alexandra Steed URBAN).*

24

Furthermore, it is paramount to rethink the design of underground services, coordinating and confining utilities within trenches, allowing streets to accommodate nature and creating a network of living infrastructure.

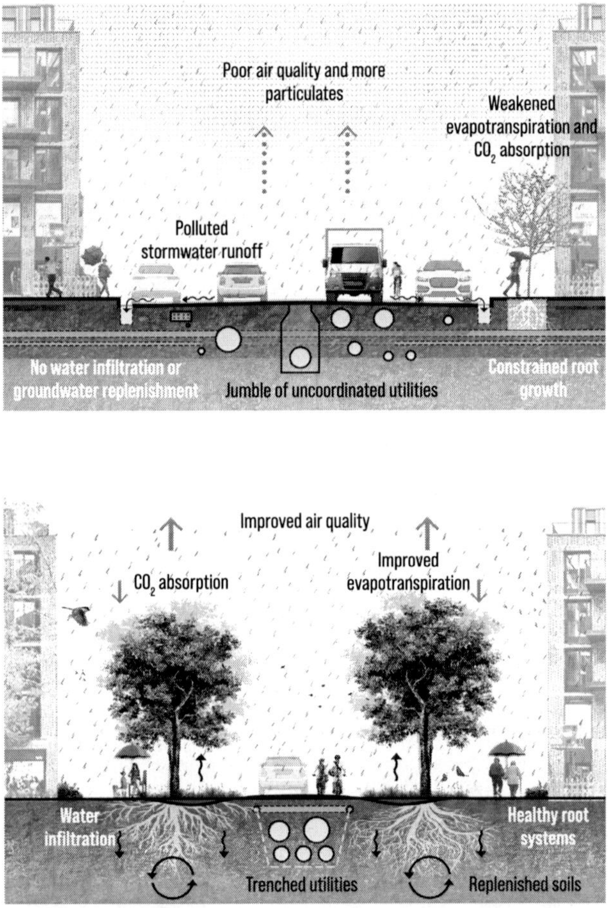

***Figure 6.5** – Enhancing City Nature Through Street Design: The design and use of streets are too often squandered. The top image portrays a conventional street, while the lower image exemplifies a sustainable street approach (© Alexandra Steed URBAN).*

25

As part of nature, we depend on the healthy functioning of ecosystems in our cities. Therefore, integrating green and blue infrastructure—comprising streets, parks, gardens, green roofs, living walls, streams, ponds, and more—is essential. Sustainable streetscapes serve as excellent examples of green and blue infrastructure, showcasing the integration of urban culture with nature, resilience in the face of climate change, and support for the health and well-being of urban populations.

The table of Green and Blue Infrastructure Functions presents a comprehensive range of effective measures available:

GBI Functions	Description
Temperature control	Regulates temperatures in urban areas by providing shade and cooling, reducing the urban heat island effect
Carbon storage and sequestration	Absorbs and stores carbon dioxide from the atmosphere in the water, trees, and soil, - mitigating climate change effects.
Storm damage control	Absorbs and slows rainwater runoff, reduces the risk of flooding and minimises storm damage in urban areas.
Regulation of flows	Helps to manage water flows, prevents erosion, reduces runoff, and improves water management in urban environments.
Water purification	Filters and purifies stormwater, enhances water quality and reduces pollution.
Freshwater storage	Stores and retains water, replenishes groundwater supplies and maintains water availability during dry periods.
Soil fertility	Contributes to the fertility of urban soils by providing organic matter and supporting beneficial soil microorganisms.
Habitats	Creates a diverse ecosystem that supports a variety of plant and animal species, promotes biodiversity and ecological balance in urban areas.
Biological control	Provides habitats for beneficial insects and birds, helps control pests naturally, reducing the need for pesticides.
Air quality	Assists with absorbing pollutants, filters particulate matter, and releases oxygen, improving air quality and reducing the negative impacts of urban pollution.
Noise regulation	Acts as natural sound barriers, absorbing and reducing noise levels, creating a more peaceful urban environment.
Image enhancement	Enhances the aesthetic appeal of urban areas, making them visually attractive and inviting.
Tourism	Parks and natural areas can attract tourists, contributing to the local economy and promoting recreational activities.

Table 6.1 *–Green and Blue Infrastructure (GBI) Functions.*

26

By placing a strong emphasis on the redesign of streetscapes and supporting the integration of green and blue infrastructure, we can shape urban environments that embrace and foster nature, while promoting the health and well-being of all residents.

To truly grasp the extraordinary gifts that nature graciously provides, let's now turn our attention to a few case studies that exemplify the transformative potential of these approaches. These real-life examples shed light on how urban landscapes can be reimagined to prioritise nature, enhance public health, and improve the overall well-being of all city residents.

The Value of London's Parks

Having made London my home two decades ago, I've had the privilege of immersing myself in the vibrant tapestry of green parks, gardens, and squares that intertwine with the city's villages. London boasts a rich and storied history of urban parks, eloquently described by Farrell as "trapped pieces of countryside" caught within a great metropolis.[27]

Figure 6.6 *– London Park Life: Parks are a critical component of London's life, design and spirit.*

28

The quality, character and distribution of London's parks are one of the primary reasons I decided to make London my abode. I am not alone. These green spaces are as deeply rooted in the psyche of the Londoner as they are entrenched in the city's fabric. Seeing people flocking into these well-used communal gardens the moment the sun appears is heartening.

The stark contrast in the provision and distribution of green spaces between London's affluent areas and the East End is a well-known reality, perhaps familiar to those who have watched the series *Call the Midwife*. This disparity, unfortunately, echoes a common pattern found in many cities, where neighbourhoods with greater wealth enjoy better access to parks, gardens, and other natural sites. The proximity to such green spaces often translates directly into higher property values. Just like the renowned Central Park in New York, the highest property values in London can be found adjacent to Hyde Park in the affluent borough of Westminster.

However, the hosting of the 2012 Olympic Games provided a revolutionary possibility for London, particularly in the regeneration of the vast East London area. At the heart of the winning Olympic Masterplan was the proposal put forth by visionary landscape architect and master planner Jason Prior with the design practice EDAW.[29] They recognised a unique opportunity to restore the River Lea (one of London's many polluted waterways) and to create the Queen Elizabeth Olympic Park, including circa 100 hectares (250 acres) of open space along the river valley and anchored by parks at either end. The landscape-driven plan used the opportunity to develop an inspiring setting for the Games and simultaneously build a resilient landscape. The scheme remediated a once-contaminated river valley. It took on future rising water levels, flood attenuation, and enhanced biodiversity while providing access to a new "green lung" for East London and its many inhabitants.[30]

***Figure 6.7** – A New Park for London: Queen Elizabeth Park restores the River Lea Valley in East London and is an essential new piece of London's long-established park network.*

31

London's parks give heart and soul to the city. In 2019, a grassroots movement led London to become the first National Park City to, "improve life in London by enjoying being outdoors more and making the city greener, healthier and wilder."[32] Those involved celebrate the city's green and blue spaces—parks, gardens, allotments, rivers, and canals—and recognise that London's inhabitants include more than humans, with 15,000 identified species, over eight million trees, and dozens of protected habitats. National Park City is a community-led initiative that advocates the coming together of people and nature in the city, recognising the many benefits of including nature in city life.

London's parks have not only captured the hearts of its residents but have also garnered attention for their substantial economic contributions. Recognising the need to articulate the often intangible and challenging-to-quantify value of these green spaces, London embarked on a "natural capital account"—a way to value nature's resources and ecosystems economically. The aim was to shed light on the economic worth of parks and justify their protection and maintenance. The comprehensive report analysed various aspects of natural capital services, including tourism, recreation, physical health, property premiums, stormwater management, air quality, and temperature regulation. Astonishingly, the findings revealed that "London's parks have a gross asset value in excess of £91 billion."[33]

The benefits extend far beyond financial figures alone. The report highlighted the significant reduction in healthcare costs attributable to the natural capital provided by these green spaces, estimating a remarkable annual savings of £950 million. Such quantifiable advantages, coupled with the immeasurable social and environmental benefits, underscore the critical role played by London's network of parks, gardens, squares, and green spaces. Together, they elevate the quality of life for all inhabitants, enhancing the economic, social, and environmental fabric of the city.

Reviving Urban Liveability

The quest for liveability has become a defining factor in the appeal of cities. Across the globe, urban centres vie for top rankings in renowned liveability tables, such as those curated by the Economist and Mercer.[34] Stability, healthcare, culture and environment, education, and infrastructure all contribute to the evaluation of a city's quality of living. Remarkably, the cities that consistently score the highest tend to possess exceptional settings, exemplified by Vienna, Copenhagen, Vancouver, Melbourne, and Osaka. These cities boast a seamless integration of high-quality green spaces, sustainable transportation, and safe, comfortable environments.

Recent times have witnessed a renewed interest in urban green spaces, catalysed by the implementation of social distancing measures to combat the spread of COVID-19. The pandemic underscored the profound reliance humans have on the natural world, as the denial of access to nature during lockdowns highlighted its vital importance. The yearning to venture outdoors, breathe fresh air, bask in the warmth of the sun, listen to birdsong, and immerse oneself in nature's beauty became palpable. This awakening shed light on the crucial role played by accessible, high-quality green and blue spaces to improve human health and well-being.

Nature is not only compatible with city life; it is essential to it. While the benefits of open spaces on human health and well-being have long been appreciated, the lockdown laid bare the stark disparity in people's experiences. Some enjoy abundant access to green open spaces, while others, particularly those residing in less affluent areas of densely populated cities, lack such opportunities.

Regrettably, dwindling local budgets and austere conditions worldwide have left precious public parks and open spaces increasingly underfunded.[35] Some have fallen victim to privatisation, consumed by large development companies.[36] It is imperative that we implore our governments to halt the sale and loss of public land whenever possible and reclaim it for the public domain. Urban areas should adopt governance models that safeguard landscapes from detrimental development practices, restore compromised landscapes, and identify new nature spaces that blend with the built environment to benefit the extended community.

Just like the earliest settlers, individuals are drawn to beautiful landscapes and aspire to reside in environments where they can thrive. This attraction should come as no surprise. What is truly disheartening is that many cities have neglected nature, resulting in planned and developed spaces that are devoid of life and beauty. A new paradigm of coexistence and collaboration is urgently needed.

Indeed, our appreciation for landscape and our relationship with nature must be rekindled within our human habitats and cities. It is imperative to revive the interconnectedness between urban areas, the home of humanity, and the natural world. By revitalising the relationship with nature in urban environments, we can unlock expansive benefits.

The concluding chapters of Part 3 delve into the far-reaching effects of human economic growth, development, and resource consumption on broader landscapes. We examine the detrimental impact of city enterprises on peri-urban areas and reflect on the widespread degradation of wilderness caused by human encroachment into rural lands. We present regenerative models in each chapter that embrace natural processes and systems. These solutions offer a beacon of hope, revealing the transformative power of adopting a landscape-centric approach. If only we have the eyes to see them, they hold the potential to address monumental environmental challenges and provide holistic remedies for a sustainable future.

7

Peri-Urban Landscapes

MANAGING RESOURCES TO MANAGING OURSELVES

"The ecosphere is where we live, humanity is dependent on nature, not the reverse. Sustainability requires that our emphasis shift from "managing resources" to managing ourselves, that we learn to live as part of nature. Economics at last becomes human ecology." [1]

—Mathis Wackernagel and William Rees

WHILE URBAN AREAS occupy just 3 percent of the world's land surface area, their imprint on the planet is nearly all-encompassing. As the human population rapidly expands, we witness not only an increase in sheer numbers but also a notable surge in per capita exploitation of earth's resources. Over the past half-century, energy and material consumption per person have skyrocketed at a rate surpassing population growth.[2] In this context, the concept of "ecological footprints" emerges as a vital measure, quantifying the burden imposed by a given population on nature and revealing the extent of humanity's influence on the planet. It is imperative for society to assume responsibility for its impact and shift from the outdated notion of exploiting natural resources to managing ourselves. This revolutionary change can only occur when our worldview transitions from a self-focussed perspective to an expansive landscape vision. Within this reorientated paradigm, the human enterprise is seen as one subsystem within many other equally vital earth systems.[3]

Continuing our exploration of London, this chapter breathes life into the concept of ecological footprints by focusing on peri-urban environments. Often marginalised and solely considered for their utility to the city, landscapes at the urban edges bear the brunt of thoughtless development. Taking a deeper dive into London's surroundings as a case study, we confront the devastating effects of haphazard suburban expansion. However, amid this disheartening effect, there lies an opportunity to transform the outlook for peri-urban areas and foster a resilient perspective for the future.

Through a compelling case study, we present a landscape strategy that transcends the constraints of traditional development. This visionary model limits harm, restores landscapes, and establishes an adaptable and resilient framework for communities within and surrounding cities. By highlighting the potential of this approach, we illuminate a path towards sustainable coexistence between urban and peri-urban environments, nurturing landscapes that respond to the needs of both culture and nature.

As we navigate the concept of ecological footprints, we gain a deeper understanding of the urgent need for transformative action. By embracing a landscape mindset, we can establish a new relationship with our surroundings, fostering balance and resilience while preserving the precious resources of our planet.

Ecological Footprints

Planners Mathis Wackernagel and William Rees introduced the ground-breaking concept of the ecological footprint, which serves as a powerful metric to gauge our impact on the planet. They define it as "the land area necessary to sustain current levels of resource consumption and waste discharge by that population."[4] This concept illuminates the intricate relationship between human progress and the natural world, reminding us of our deep dependence on the biosphere for our very existence. The biosphere generously provides us with essential elements of life: food, water, fuel, timber, energy, clean air, and waste assimilation.[5]

Despite this inherent interdependence, our experience of nature within cities often becomes limited to viewing it solely as a source of goods and services, rather than recognising it as our extended family, community, and life-support system. Consequently, humanity's demands on the earth continue to escalate, depleting its resources at an alarming rate. As Wackernagel and Rees assert, "Through the economic production-consumption-pollution cycle, humankind has become a major—and often the dominant—species in virtually every ecosystem on the planet."[6]

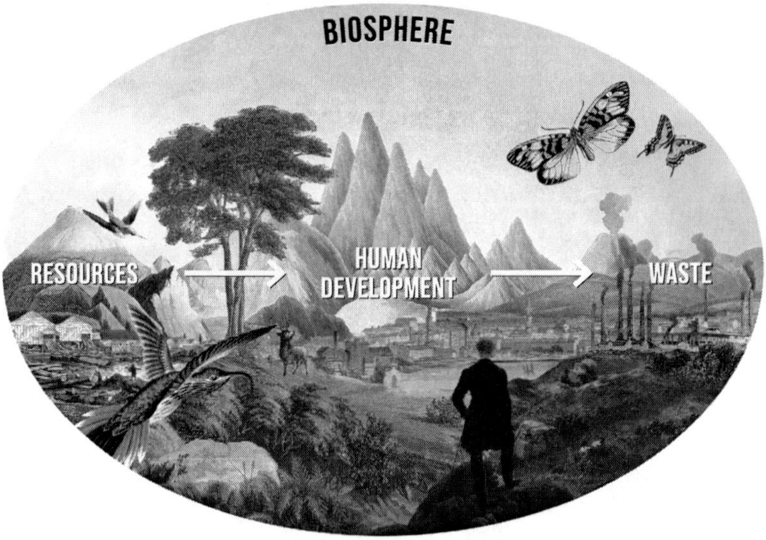

Figure 7.1 *– Our Ecological Footprint: Humans have left a significant imprint on the planet. The ecological footprint measures the land area needed to sustain current human resource consumption and waste discharge, revealing the scale of our impact on the environment (© Alexandra Steed URBAN).*

7

Acknowledging that our role as a dominant species carries immense responsibility is critical. By embracing the concept of the ecological footprint, we gain a profound understanding of the urgent need to rebalance our relationship with the natural world. We must transcend our current perspective of exploitation and depletion to reach towards one of stewardship and preservation. Only then can we hope to ensure the sustainable coexistence of humanity and the planet, recognising that our choices and actions ripple through ecosystems, affecting not only ourselves but also the intricate web of life that sustains us.

London's Impact

Drawing upon London as a case study, Wackernagel and Rees reveal a staggering reality—the ecological footprint of the city is approximately 120 times larger than its physical land area.[8] This profound disparity exposes the deep entanglement between global power dynamics, resource exploitation, and the consequences felt by countries worldwide.

As the leading world power for many years, Britain possessed the ability to assert its authority over colonies spread across the globe. In the pursuit of resources, materials, and natural wealth, they engaged in unprecedented levels of plundering. The repercussions of this resource drain were acutely felt by the nations affected, with far-reaching consequences on their populations and environments.

George Orwell, in his classic work *The Road to Wigan Pier*, poignantly captured this harsh reality. He articulated that for England to maintain its comparative comfort, a hundred million Indians had to endure lives teetering on the brink of starvation. This distressing state of affairs is a sobering reminder of the hidden costs we unwittingly perpetuate when we indulge in the luxuries of modern life.[9]

Britain's exploitation of other territories' natural resources is as entrenched as ever, importing everything from bananas to cotton to timber. Its consumption of forest product imports may be the most significant. Britain's impact on the world forest is estimated to be approximately 6.4 million hectares (15.8 million acres). To provide wood products for the UK, an additional circa 67,000 hectares

(165,500 acres) are deforested each year, 75 percent of which come from developing countries.[10] Only a quarter or less of the productive forest upon which Britain depends is in the UK. However, the numbers don't account for the entire forest area required for Britain's other requirements, including carbon sequestration (to make up for its fossil fuel emissions), biodiversity net gain, etc. It would undoubtedly be far more than three times its forest area.

The connection between London's ecological footprint and the global exploitation it represents demands our attention. It compels us to question the sustainability of our current systems and the ethical implications of our choices. Acknowledging these interconnections is the first step towards reshaping our relationship with the natural world, seeking equitable solutions that transcend borders and ensure the well-being of all.

The Local Consequences

The far-reaching impact of London's ecological footprint has global and local repercussions. Its effects are starkly visible in the immediate surroundings, where suburban sprawl, agricultural practices, expansive landfills, mining activities, bustling ports, and other industries have shaped the landscape. Nowhere is this more evident than in Essex County, located east of the city and nestled within the Thames Estuary.

For centuries, Essex County has been London's dumping ground. The once-vital marshland, tragically dismissed as mere wasteland, has been swollen with the accumulation of rubbish. Mucking Marsh, a site that now stands as one of Western Europe's largest landfills, bears witness to this ecological burden. Year after year, it receives a staggering 660,000 tons of waste from London, transported downriver by barge.[11]

Numerous other landfills spoil the banks of the Thames—at Rainham, East Tilbury, Pitsea, Two Tree Island—and their pernicious concoctions will seep into the soils, waters, and winds for years to come. The air quality is some of the most toxic in the country, polluted with an array of chemicals pumped out from the concentration of factories here.[12]

Tragically, Essex's once wild and stunning marshlands have been filled with London's waste, industry, and agriculture over the last four hundred years, reducing 30,000 hectares (74,000 acres) of thriving intertidal salt marsh to a struggling 2,500 hectares (6,200 acres), a colossal loss on many counts. [13]

Unfortunately, the beauty and value of these messy coastal habitats have been and still are, misunderstood. Not only are they a haven for wildlife—teeming with a myriad of species within their thick herbaceous vegetation, mud, and waters—but a source of livelihood and food for local communities. Importantly, they are incredibly effective carbon sinks—soaking up our excessive emissions—and robust and adaptable flood barriers. They protect the land like an absorptive cushion from the wave action of increasing storm surges and flooding.

In Essex, sea level rise threatens the remaining intertidal salt marshes. Surrounding development encroaches and prevents the wetlands from having the ability to migrate inland to avoid inundation. "Coastal squeeze" is an appropriate name given to this constraining predicament.

Not only is this a disastrous situation for the wildlife of the marshlands, but for the life of everyone they once protected. Due to the loss of these absorptive coastal cushions, or sponges, flooding threatens all development within reach of the River Thames. Current projections show that sea level rise in the Thames will increase between 20 cm (nearly 8 inches) and 90 cm (about 35 inches) by 2100. Although due to uncertainty over polar ice melt, it could increase to 2 metres (circa 6.5 feet).[14]

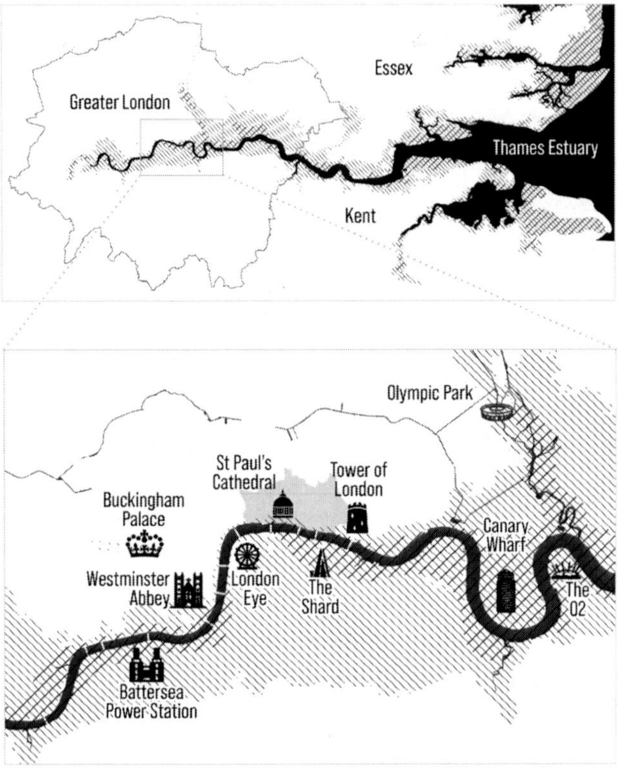

Figure 7.2 *– Thames Estuary Flooding 2100: These diagrams depict projected flood zones in London and its surrounding region by 2100. Without adequate measures to mitigate sea level rise and storm surges, these hatched areas are at risk of being submerged (© Alexandra Steed URBAN).*

15

North Sea storm surges swept into the mouth of the estuary are also a significant threat. The increasing intensity and frequency of storms, combined with sea level rise, could one day overwhelm the Thames Barrier—one of the most significant moveable barriers in the world, and designed to prevent London from flooding due to tidal surges—and flood a massive area of London. The River Thames has overflowed its banks before, and it will happen again.

Figure 7.3 *- The Thames Barrier: Located on London's River Thames, it is a massive movable flood barrier. Protecting a significant portion of the city from flooding, it faces the risk of being overwhelmed by the rising intensity of storm surges and sea levels, potentially leading to extensive flooding in London.*

16

The challenges faced by London are not unique; they echo across cities worldwide. Urban sprawl and the exploitation of surrounding landscapes are pervasive phenomena, leading to the destruction of precious habitats in the process. Estuaries, in particular, stand as one of the most vulnerable ecosystems, yet they are the very foundations upon which many cities have thrived. Twenty-two of the thirty-two most prominent cities in the world are in estuaries.[17] From Tokyo and Hong Kong to Jakarta, New York, San Francisco, and Rio de Janeiro, these cities have witnessed a significant decline in their estuary environments due to urban activities. The consequences of this degradation are especially concerning in the face of climate change, with rising sea levels and intensified storms posing existential threats to coastal cities. The United Nations even warns that many cities will be underwater soon.[18]

Mathis Wackernagel and William Rees assert the undeniable link between human enterprise and the natural world, challenging the prevailing belief in separation. They advocate for a profound shift in policy and mindset, urging us to embrace a holistic approach to planning and development, with nature always in mind. Merely addressing environmental symptoms through controls and protections is insufficient, as it fails to address the root cause of the issue—a misguided worldview of separation. Instead, we must view the landscape as more than a mere backdrop; it is the very essence of our existence. The landscape "becomes the play itself."[19] In this context, the landscape is the play in which humankind can initiate the rehabilitation of its relationship with all life.

This transformative perspective is slowly gaining traction in cities around the globe, particularly those compelled to confront the urgent realities of climate change, rising sea levels, and the looming spectre of flooding. Strategic thinkers are embracing and integrating nature into their urban plans, recognising the power of nature-based solutions. These solutions, often referred to as green and blue infrastructure, encompass a range of approaches outlined in Chapter 6. From stormwater management and climate adaptation to biodiversity enhancement, heat stress reduction, and improved air and water quality, this integrated and sustainable approach offers a light touch to address the multifaceted challenges cities face.

To exemplify the potential of nature-based solutions, we turn our attention to the South Essex Green and Blue Infrastructure (SEGBI) Study. Commissioned by the Association of South Essex Local Authorities (ASELA), this innovative strategy represents a revolutionary transformation in the region's approach to growth and development. The SEGBI study harnesses the influence of regional green and blue infrastructure, emphasising the interdependence of landscapes and communities. By reframing our perspective towards the landscape, we can restore degraded environments and create thriving communities that embrace and support the diversity of life.

South Essex Green and Blue Infrastructure (SEGBI) Study

In response to the complex challenges posed by rapid urban development, environmental concerns, and the pressing need for resilience, ASELA has demonstrated its commitment to a comprehensive and holistic approach. With a focus on meeting the demands of residential, commercial, and industrial growth while addressing critical issues such as sea level rise and flooding, ASELA commissioned the SEGBI as a key program within their joint strategic framework plan. Situated as the gateway to London, the region faces unprecedented growth pressures and has been identified as a national priority for regeneration and expansion. The SEGBI Study embodies ASELA's visionary efforts to create a flourishing and resilient community that cooperates with the natural environment, setting an exemplary precedent for future urban development.

The Thames Estuary 2050 Growth Commission Vision states, "The Thames Estuary area provides the long-term solution to managing the impacts of sea-level rise on London. If appropriately planned, opportunities including maximising flood attenuation and improving air quality should be pursued alongside provision and replacement of habitats and improved access for recreation and leisure (as promoted in the Thames Estuary 2100 Plan)."[20] With plans to deliver thousands of new homes and jobs, tackle flood risk and preserve internationally important nature sites, the region requires a bold vision and an integrated approach.

A fundamental rethinking of growth and development was necessary to address these complex challenges. The SEGBI proposed a landscape-led approach that positioned all development within a comprehensive and living framework. This paradigm shift required moving away from the prevailing anthropocentric view of urban development, which exploits and dominates nature, and embracing an ecocentric perspective that recognises our interrelation with the natural world.

The team sought to answer the questions: How can we unlock the intelligence of nature to create a new sustainable planning and development model? And how can green and blue infrastructure create thriving places for the whole community of life?

Figure 7.4 *– South Essex Estuary Park: A visionary depiction of a resilient and adaptable landscape that addresses the needs of the community. It showcases a harmonious coexistence between humans and nature, fostering balanced and thriving communities (© Alexandra Steed URBAN).*

21

The SEGBI study employed a land-based methodology, drawing from landscape and ecological planning research.[22] Works by academics such as Pierre Belanger, *Landscape as Infrastructure*,[23] Carl Steinitz, *A Framework for Geodesign*,[24] and Ian McHarg's classic *Design with Nature*,[25] were notably instructional. The study identified challenges and opportunities for landscape transformation through comprehensive analysis and mapping of environmental and social information. Essential themes such as climate change, water management, connectivity, sustainability, health, and growth emerged from this analysis, highlighting conflicts and synergies between various elements. For example, mapping flood risks, nature reserves, and green spaces revealed habitat losses, inadequate access to nature for low-income communities, and restricted waterfront access.

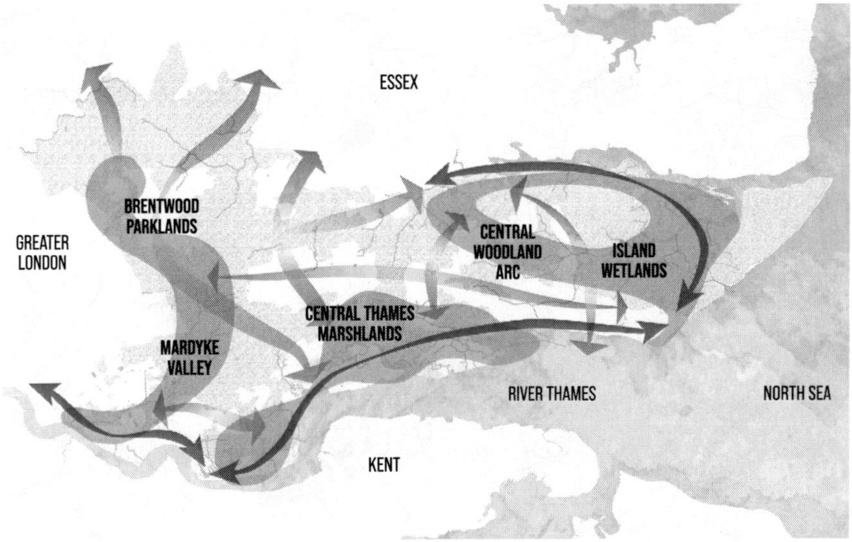

Figure 7.5 - *Landscape Strategy Diagram: The SEGBI offers a comprehensive framework that encompasses the entire region, featuring five distinct landscapes and well-defined green and blue corridors connecting them (© Alexandra Steed URBAN).*

26

The SEGBI study demonstrated how this radical change in thinking can be applied to the planning and development process. Through landscape-led strategies, comprehensive analysis, bold vision, and long-term stewardship, healthy communities can be created while restoring balance to our cities and planet. By integrating natural systems, the built environment, and social equity, the SEGBI approach not only promotes sustainability but also strives for regeneration. In Chapter 12, we uncover this landscape-led approach in detail.

The six key moves identified in the SEGBI strategy are essential tools for addressing climate change, ecological collapse, and community health and well-being while also providing suitable locations for development. These moves, applicable to many peri-urban environments, are as follows:

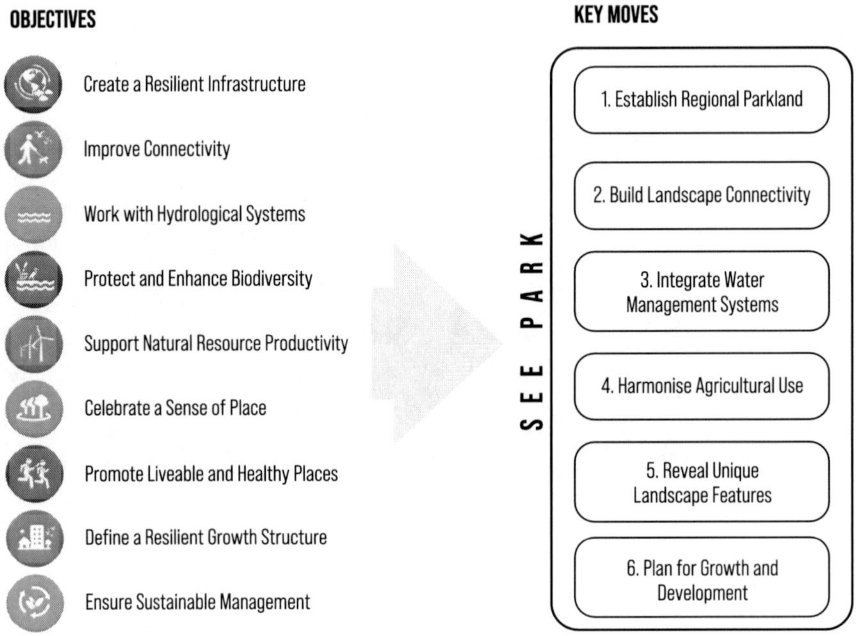

Table 7.1 *– Objectives and Key Moves: Well-defined Objectives for South Essex were formulated based on thorough site analysis. These objectives were translated into strategic Key Moves, forming a robust and comprehensive plan for the region (© Alexandra Steed URBAN).*

27

1. *Establish Regional Parkland:* Safeguarding and restoring 30 percent of the land area through a network of significant landscapes, including challenging sites like former landfill or industrial zones, floodplains, waterfronts, existing nature reserves, public parks, and marginalised farmlands. This robust landscape framework enhances biodiversity, restores carbon sinks, and provides flood mitigation. The overarching landscape framework, composed of five major sites, is shown in the figure below.

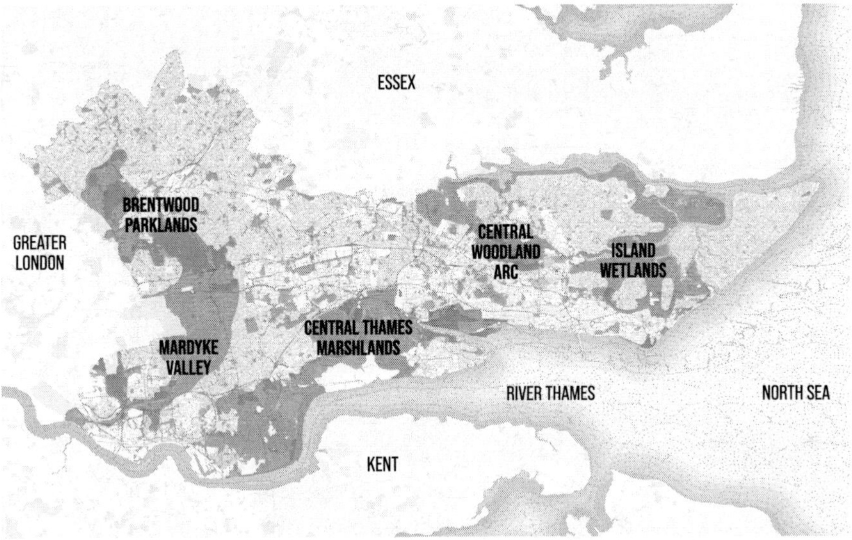

Figure 7.6 – *Establish Regional Parkland: The South Essex Green and Blue Infrastructure Study outlines the identification of five major landscapes, serving as a robust and resilient framework to enhance the quality of life in the region (© Alexandra Steed URBAN).*

28

2. *Build Landscape Connectivity:* Creating a complete network of green and blue corridors that connect urban and rural areas, enabling the healthy movement of people and wildlife. These corridors provide accessible, safe, and beautiful routes for pedestrians and cyclists while supporting wildlife movement through various habitats.

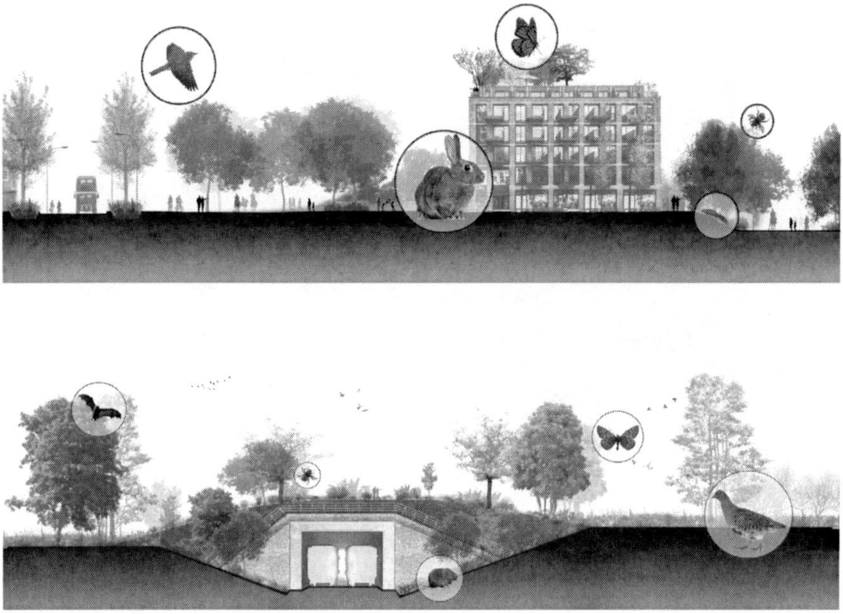

Figure 7.7 *– Build Landscape Connectivity: These cross-sections vividly illustrate the fundamental importance of connectivity within the landscape strategy. They showcase the inclusion of designated routes for pedestrians and cyclists, as well as habitat connectors designed to facilitate the movement of local wildlife (© Alexandra Steed URBAN).*

29

3. *Integrate Water Management Systems:* Taking a coordinated approach to water management at a regional watershed scale, which in South Essex includes shoreline realignment, coastal access, marine conservation, restoration of rivers, flood storage, and integration of water management into urban infrastructure.

Figure 7. 8 *- Integrate Water Management Systems: By synergistically harnessing multiple "blue assets" such as swales, ponds, and rivers, this approach effectively captures and manages groundwater, while also enhancing ecosystems and providing recreational opportunities for the community (© Alexandra Steed URBAN).*

30

4. *Harmonise Agricultural Use:* Integrating nature conservation with farmlands, considering climate change, biodiversity, water, and food production. This approach aligns with government programs and incentives, promotes flooding plans for vulnerable areas, and incorporates agri-tourism to support farmers and educate the public.

Figure 7.9 *– Harmonise Agricultural Use: An integrated approach combines nature conservation with farmlands, addressing climate change, biodiversity, water, and food production. It aligns with government programs, supports farmers, and promotes agri-tourism for public education and engagement (© Alexandra Steed URBAN).*

31

5. *Reveal Unique Landscape Features:* Celebrating and enhancing the distinctiveness and beauty of South Essex's landscapes, such as ancient woodlands, historic parks, river valleys, and coastal marshes. These features provide essential ecological services, recreational opportunities, and cultural heritage benefits.

6. *Plan for Growth and Development:* Designating suitable areas for new development, ensuring that they align with the SEGBI strategy, and providing affordable housing, job opportunities, and improved access to green and blue spaces for all communities. Development

plans incorporate principles of sustainability, biodiversity, and resilience.

These moves provide a spatial framework for ongoing investment, conservation, management, and development, promoting green and blue infrastructure across South Essex.

Implementation of the SEGBI study promises numerous benefits, including natural flood management, biodiversity net gain, improved active travel networks, enhanced urban open spaces, community facilities within nature areas, regeneration of industrial sites, climate change mitigation, collaboration across authorities, economic growth, and attracting investments. (A preliminary natural capital account was undertaken as an extension of the study and estimated a total value of £7.2 billion of existing natural capital in the region.)

To create a sustainable future, we must recognise our interdependence with the natural world and reframe our focus from resource exploitation to managing ourselves within the landscape. The SEGBI study sets an inspiring example, demonstrating how the liberation of nature's intelligence can guide sustainable development even in peri-urban environments under intense urban pressures. By integrating natural systems, the built environment, and social equity, we can build a cohesive relationship with nature and create a greener and healthier future.

The active engagement of communities holds utmost significance in this process. Merely depending on governmental bodies and professionals in the planning and design fields is insufficient to drive the necessary changes. True transformation will be realised through the proactive efforts of communities and individuals, as they actively advocate for change.

The benefits are endless. Indeed, we must not consider human development in isolation from the natural world. We depend on nature and must shift our focus to living lightly within the landscape, from managing resources to managing ourselves. Humanity has not been paying attention to the impact of our reckless behaviours, and our footprints are now visible everywhere.

8

Rural and Wilderness Landscapes

DEVASTATION TO REGENERATION

"We have replaced the wild with the tame. We regard the Earth as our planet, run by humankind for humankind. There is little rest for the living world. The truly wild world—that non-human world—has gone. We have overrun the Earth."[1]

—Sir David Attenborough

VERY LITTLE WILDERNESS remains on earth. What remains is declining. As human lives expand, the living world fades. Human activity has been so disruptive on our planet that no place is untouched. Urbanisation, expansive industrial agriculture, and technological and mechanical advances have altered environmental conditions so rapidly and radically that nature can't keep up.

Among the myriad threats, the impact of food production looms large as it drives significant land and sea changes. Landscapes once teeming with life in forests, grasslands, and wetlands are sacrificed to make way for croplands, even before the actual process of food production begins. Meanwhile, the oceans, often overlooked as wilderness, bear the weight of rampant overfishing, pollution and waste, pushing their delicate ecosystems to the brink. It is clear that the food industry, particularly farming and its practices, requires a creative restructuring to instigate a vast revitalisation of wilderness areas. The pursuit of food security must not come at the expense of nature; instead, adopting a Portrait to Landscape perspective reveals that nature conservation and agriculture can coexist symbiotically, yielding synergistic effects. Embracing a regenerative approach to land use in all its forms holds the key to ensuring the long-term well-being of all life.

Wilderness Loss

David Attenborough, broadcaster and naturalist, is nearing a century on this planet. He has witnessed the decline with his own eyes. You may have seen his film, *A Life on Our Planet.* At times it's troubling to watch as he mourns the thriving, dynamic, and diverse natural world he once knew, now devastated by poor human planning and development. Attenborough says, "Since the 1950s, on average, wild animal populations have more than halved."[2] Providing example after example of devastated ecosystems—from the Amazon Rainforest to the Great Barrier Reef, to our world's soils, and the Arctic regions—he calls the destruction of the living world, "Our greatest mistake."[3] And rightly so.

In a mere three decades, wilderness areas equivalent to the mass of India have vanished.[4] Most countries have no wild places at all, so severe is the impact of human activity and industry. The world's remaining wilderness (excluding the high seas and Antarctica) is in just five countries—Russia, Canada, Australia, the United States, and Brazil—and even these remote places have been affected by humankind.[5] The IPBES 2020 report on the status and trends of nature identifies that the world's urban and agricultural lands now account for more than 30 percent of the terrestrial surface.[6] True wilderness areas comprise only 23 percent of land and 13 percent of oceans, often confined to remote and marginal landscapes like tundra.

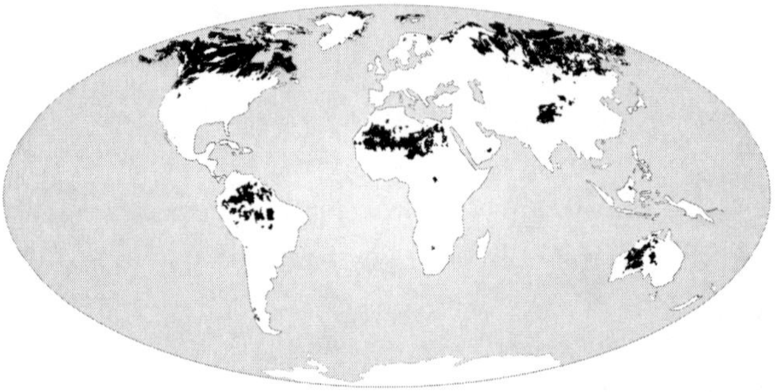

Figure 8.1- *Map of Remaining Wilderness Locations (© Alexandra Steed URBAN).*

7

Land-use changes driven by agriculture represent the most significant driver of negative impacts on land and freshwater, while overfishing has wreaked havoc on marine environments. Collectively, global food systems emerge as the primary catalyst for biodiversity loss, demanding urgent action to reverse these alarming trends.

Global Food Production

A host of problems are related to the global food system. Natural habitats and ecosystems are destroyed and cleared, leading to species loss and sometimes extinction. Once removed, the land is primed to grow food with large amounts of artificial herbicides and fertilisers, often toxic to organisms, including damage to human health. These chemicals also escape into the air as harmful pollutants and into the water system, polluting soils, watercourses, and ecosystems and poisoning other organisms.

Food production is a key contributor to greenhouse gas emissions. The fertilisers and pesticides used are energy-intensive to produce. Fossil fuels are also used to fuel farm equipment, like tractors, graders, and combines, and of course, to transport food to the consumer. Even packaging, especially for products including wine and beer, is a major contributor to emissions. The Food and Agriculture Organization of the United Nations (FAO) reports that methane accounts for about 35 percent of food system emissions, mainly from livestock raising and rice cultivation.[8] Refrigeration is also a primary culprit, increasing fluorinated greenhouse gas emissions and amplifying global warming.

An immense strain is placed on potable water resources. Crop irrigation is intense, and livestock requires copious amounts of water, draining freshwater supplies at a tremendous rate. Soils are also degraded and depleted through conventional farming methods, especially monoculture farming, which leaves the earth barren after tilling and harvesting.

Finally, the amount of food waste is alarming. It happens at every stage of the food production cycle—from crop growth to harvesting, transport, supermarket screening, household preparation, and consumption. The UN provides the following food waste facts:

- Around 14 percent of food produced is lost between harvest and retail. Significant quantities are also wasted in retail and at the consumption level.
- An estimated 17 percent of global food production is wasted (11 percent in households, 5 per cent in food service and 2 percent in retail).
- Food that is lost and wasted accounts for 38 percent of total energy usage in the global food system.

Paradoxically, our global food production methods threaten global food security rather than ensure it and simultaneously destroy the world's wilderness habitats and ecosystems on which life depends.

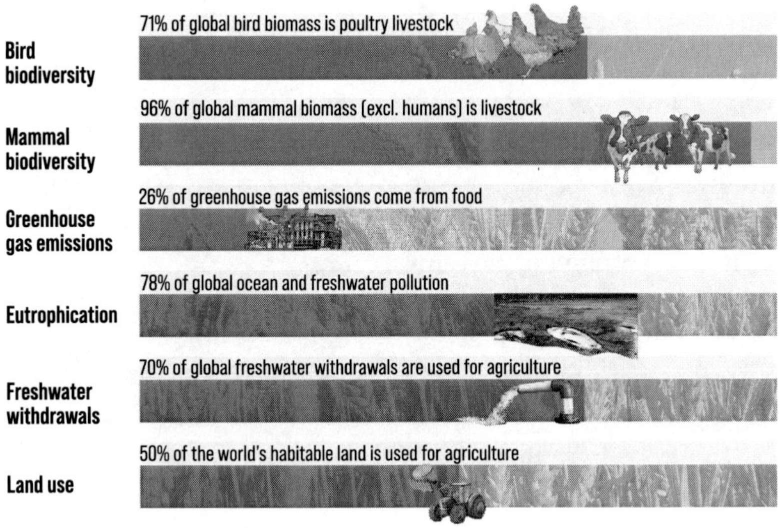

***Figure 8.2** - The Environmental Cost of Food Production (© Alexandra Steed URBAN).*

9

Humanity must urgently reassess its relationship with food, recognising the significant impact of our food choices and production methods on critical environmental challenges such as water stress, pollution, climate change, land restoration, and wildlife conservation.

Agricultural Expansion

The expansion of agriculture on a global scale is undeniable, with farmland now covering a staggering 38 percent of the earth's land surface.[10] Furthermore, agriculture employs nearly one-third of the world's labour force, highlighting its essential role in sustaining human populations.[11] Agriculture is essential to survival, and extensive land areas are necessary for farming. Still, how industrial agriculture is practised today is one of the most harmful industries on the planet. Farmland is typically considered green, lovely, and a picture of health. However, as farming is by and large practised now, this is far from the truth. The transformation of land—including forests, grasslands, and wetlands—to industrial agricultural landscapes represents one of the most destructive activities humankind engages in.

Geoff Lawton, an expert in soil and permaculture, highlights the paradoxical nature of modern agriculture. "The word agriculture comes from agrarian—meaning the soil—and culture—the enrichment of soil. Yet today, modern industrialised agriculture is a system that destroys soils, extracts soils and minerals, and degrades and erodes soils. We have lost touch with the natural systems of the culture of soil."[12] When soil is destroyed, its food-growing capacity and entire landscapes and ecosystems are destroyed.

In every part of the world, industrial agriculture presents considerable environmental threats. I recall a project I worked on in the Middle East, where a landscape strategy was being developed for a region equivalent in size to Belgium (22,000 sq. km). Among the challenges we encountered was the presence of commercial farms situated in the heart of the desert. These farms primarily produced fodder for thousands of camels owned by the wealthy elite, serving as status symbols. Unfortunately, the establishment of these farms caused devastation to fragile desert ecosystems, while the free-roaming camels, unsuited and disruptive to this environment, decimated thousands of hectares of delicate desert vegetation, consuming every green thing in sight.

These industrial farms, which brought little benefit to local communities, were primarily operated by large foreign companies heavily reliant on irrigation and fertilisers to sustain growth in such harsh conditions—where temperatures fluctuated between 25°C (77 °F) and 50°C (122 °F), and rainfall was scarce or absent. Consequently, the local groundwater aquifer, a vital natural underground reservoir, was on the verge of depletion, posing a severe threat to accessing fresh drinking water for the local population.

Approximately half of humanity depends on freshwater

extraction. It is difficult to summarise water withdrawals at the global scale as reliable data is limited to only a few countries.[13] However, we know that there is a rising demand for water extraction, together with increased water pollution.[14] (Worryingly, 80 percent of all wastewater is released into freshwater without treatment.)[15] Between 1900 and 2010, water withdrawals rose faster than population growth—the population increased by 340 percent, and concurrently water consumption increased by 630 percent.[16] Seventy-two percent of all freshwater withdrawals are for irrigation, not for drinking.[17] Groundwater extraction is unseen and under-researched and therefore, challenging to quantify. However, we know that between 2003 and 2013, thirty-seven of the world's largest aquifers exceeded their "sustainability tipping points."[18]

Too many ecosystems have been destroyed, aquifers depleted, rivers dried, soils flooded with excessive fertilisers and pesticides, groundwater contaminated, and fragile species made extinct for little gain in food security. Indeed, one of the greatest disasters of unsustainable farming is massive biodiversity decline and wilderness loss.

It's easy to believe that agricultural expansion is necessary to feed billions of people worldwide. However, industrial farms are often not growing food for people but for our livestock. (Like the desert example provided previously of fodder crops for camels.) Over a quarter of the earth's ice-free, habitable land is used for grazing livestock, and one-third of croplands are used for livestock feed production.[19] In Europe, the percentage of farmland area for livestock is even more remarkable—over 63 percent of arable land is used to produce animal feed instead of food for people.[20] Of all the cereal crops used, the majority was to feed animals, with only 24 percent to nourish people.[21]

Simultaneously, Europe finds itself in the predicament of overproducing meat and dairy, leading to the exportation of surpluses.[22] As a result, the EU has become the world's largest exporter of animal products, while heavily relying on imports of plant proteins, primarily sourced from Brazil and the United States.[23] Unfortunately, this excessive production of meat and dairy has come at a great cost to wilderness habitats and has replaced them with bereft monoculture croplands.

The production of meat is riddled with problems. Raising and culling animals for food consumption is far worse for the environment than growing and processing fruits and vegetables. In fact, meat production alone accounts for nearly 60 percent of all greenhouse gases from food production.[24] And let's not fool ourselves into thinking that this livestock is roaming on green pastures, far from it. In the United States, for example, only 3 percent of cattle are grass-fed, with 97 percent on feedlots (these are concentrated animal feeding operations congregating animals and production processes in a small land area). Feed is brought to the animals rather than the animals grazing in pastures or fields.[25] Apart from the evident issues regarding animal welfare, these feedlots are notorious for polluting the environment due to the mismanagement of waste. The copious amounts of manure and urine produced by livestock contaminate surface water, groundwater, and even drinking water sources. At the same time, the resulting emissions of enteric methane contribute a staggering 7 percent to total greenhouse gas emissions.

If you have not yet taken action, there is a significant difference you can make by shifting your dietary habits towards a more plant-centric approach, preferably sourced locally and from organic farms. By reducing meat consumption, along with limiting food waste, we can collectively generate a substantial impact. Through the fundamental law of supply and demand, adopting these practices will incentivise agriculture to embrace nature-friendly methods. Consequently, we will contribute to safeguarding remaining wilderness areas from devastating land-use changes and actively support the rewilding of farmlands, facilitating the restoration of vital habitats and ecosystems. By making these conscious choices, we all become agents of change, fostering a harmonious relationship between food production and nature.[26]

Forests

While global agriculture is expanding, the forest is declining. The two processes are fundamentally interwoven. Presently, forests cover approximately 30 percent of the world's land area.[27] However, the past 10,000 years have witnessed the loss of one-third of our forests—an area twice the size of the United States. Shockingly, half of this loss occurred within the last century alone.[28] In the span of just thirty years, a staggering 420 million hectares (more than one billion acres)[29] of forests have vanished, resulting in a significant decline in biodiversity and the release of massive amounts of CO_2 into the atmosphere.[30]

As a university student, I had a first-hand encounter with the devastating effects of deforestation. In British Columbia, it is commonplace for students to work as tree planters during the summer to finance their upcoming year's tuition. I, too, found myself in this role, tasked with replanting vast expanses of land that had been clear-cut by timber companies. Upon arriving in northern BC and settling into camp, I joined the other rookies for a drive to the designated block—a large area that had been logged, slashed, and burned. Dropped off at my assigned spot, I stood amidst a scene that resembled something out of an apocalyptic scene.

As far as my eyes could see, the landscape was devoid of life—barren, charred, and desecrated. The ground was littered with remnants of logging activities, burned-out oil cans, and other debris. A deep sense of loneliness engulfed me. I had not anticipated finding such desolation in the wilderness of British Columbia. There were no signs of life—no birds singing, no crickets chirping. The absence of shade from leaves and the tranquil rustling of trees in the wind added to the bleakness. Only the intense sun relentlessly scorched me with its searing heat. The deserted landscape felt overwhelmingly tragic, to the extent that there were moments when I had to pause my task of planting saplings into the scorched earth and weep, overcome with grief.

This personal experience served as a poignant reminder of the destructive impact of deforestation, not just in terms of the loss of trees but also the disruption of entire ecosystems and the utter loss of life.

Fortunately, trends show that forest areas in the Global North, including Canada, the United States, China, and Europe, have increased since that time. However, conversely, in the Global South, forests have considerably declined, still resulting in a steady global net decrease. A recent study in the journal *Nature* found much of the expansion in the Global South relates to "the production of beef, sugar cane and soybean in the Brazilian Amazon, oil palm in Southeast Asia and cocoa in Nigeria and Cameroon."[31]

Tropical forests are renowned for their spectacular variety of wildlife. Covering just 18 percent of earth's total land area,[32] they are home to 62 percent of its terrestrial vertebrate species—more than twice the number found elsewhere.[33] Specifically, 63 percent of mammals, 72 percent of birds, and 76 percent of amphibians live there.[34] Tragically, tropical forests continue to show significant losses every year.[35]

Tropical rainforests are even more threatened. They are one of the most endangered habitats on earth, occupying less than 7 percent of the planet's land surface.[36] Alarmingly, one-third of the original tropical rainforest has been lost, one-third is degraded, and only one-third is still intact.[37] Most deforestation occurs by logging companies for timber, and cleared areas are often turned into monoculture farmland devoid of life.[38] For example, vast areas of tropical rainforest have been replaced with oil palm trees cultivated for palm oil used in various products, from foods to cosmetics to cleaning solutions and fuels. Oil palm plantations now cover more than 27 million hectares (approx. 67 million acres) but contain virtually no biodiversity and push endangered species like orangutan, Borneo elephant and Sumatran tiger closer to extinction.[39]

Figure 8.3 *– Amazon Rainforest Clearing: Aerial photo highlighting the extensive deforestation in the Amazon rainforest caused by logging, mining, and other human activities.*

40

The loss of wilderness often initiates with the destructive practices of clearing existing habitats. Slash and burn, scarification and herbicide spraying are employed to decimate forests, woodlands, and grasslands, leaving no vegetation standing and obliterating both wilderness and wildlife in one fell swoop. Any surviving animals are displaced and severed from their sources of food and support for life.

The repercussions of above-ground vegetation loss extend to below-ground conditions with dire consequences. The layers of leaves and branches that once served to capture and retain rainwater are now absent, leaving the earth vulnerable to impact. Soils are left exposed and experience significant erosion during heavy rainfall, leading to subsequent landslides and water contamination. Without the organic matter replenished by fallen leaves, the soil lacks essential nutrients, and even the worms have nothing to feed on. A massive loss of life unfolds beneath the surface.

Root systems that once provided structure to the earth, serving as an essential binding force, decay within the ground. The intricate web of interlocking roots, along with the mycorrhiza and other vital fungi that symbiotically coexisted with them, wither away in the absence of a host to sustain them. Without trees, vegetation, and robust root systems, the soil is easily washed away during heavy rains and carried away by wind during droughts.

Grasslands

An illustrative example of the consequences of habitat destruction can be found in the history of the "Dust Bowl" in the United States during the 1930s. In an effort to replace wheat, corn, and other row crops typically imported from Europe, American farmers were encouraged to plough millions of hectares of grassland in the southern plains region during World War I. However, as the Great Depression unfolded, wheat prices plummeted, leading desperate farmers to further clear grasslands in the hopes of breaking even.

When a drought struck in 1931, the crops quickly failed in the barren and depleted soil that had been over-ploughed. Without the deep-rooted prairie grasses that once held the soil in place, the exposed dirt began to be carried away by relentless winds, vanishing into billowing dust clouds. The consequences were devastating, as massive dust storms ravaged the area, causing irreparable erosion and economic turmoil. The Dust Bowl impacted an expansive region, permanently damaging an area exceeding 40 million hectares (100 million acres) of cropland.[41] The Dust Bowl was the largest human-caused environmental disaster in history to date.

The detrimental practice of ploughing and tilling continues today, with persisting erosion. The more tilling, the weaker the soil, and the more chemical additives are required to mask the problem of degraded soils. Moreover, agriculture continues to push deeper into marginal land. In an article entitled "Cropland Expansion in the United States Produces Marginal Yields at High Costs to Wildlife," they note, "Our findings demonstrate a pervasive pattern of encroachment into areas that are increasingly marginal for production, but highly significant for wildlife, and suggest that such trade-offs may be further amplified by future cropland expansion."[42]

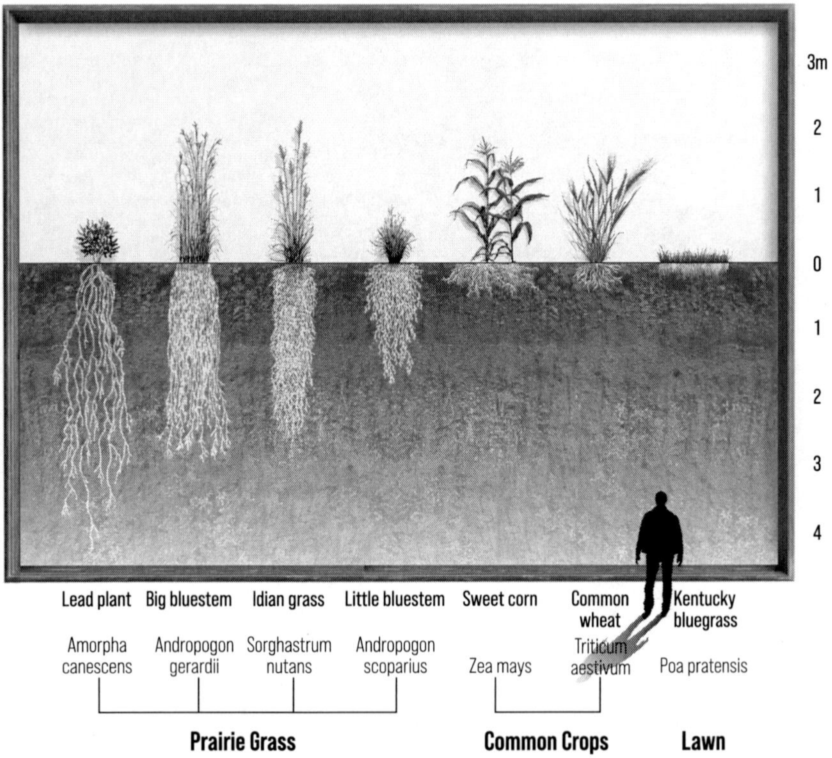

Figure 8.4 *– Root Systems of Prairie Plants: The root depth of prairie grass far exceeds its agricultural and lawn grass counterparts, helping to prevent the erosion of precious soils (© Alexandra Steed URBAN).*

43

The lessons learned from the devastating Dust Bowl of the 1930s seem to have been forgotten by subsequent generations. However, it is important for modern farms to rectify past mistakes by embracing regenerative methods and moving away from practices such as over-ploughing, monoculture planting, and excessive use of fertilisers and pesticides. As highlighted by Lawton, the current relationship between modern industrial farming and soil is flawed. Restoring a healthy connection to the earth is essential for the well-being of both natural and human communities.

The adoption of regenerative farming practices plays a pivotal role in facilitating this shift. The following points outline key strategies for improving soil health:

- Regularly monitor soil health on farms to assess its condition.
- Utilise cover crops and perennials to provide ground cover and protect bare soil.
- Introduce more trees or shrubs to farmlands, ensuring appropriate species selection and distribution.
- Design crop rotations that enhance diversity and promote soil health.
- Minimise tillage or transition to no-till methods to preserve soil structure and reduce erosion.
- Avoid the use of chemical fertilisers and pesticides, prioritising organic and natural alternatives.
- Implement integrated livestock and crop systems to harness their mutual benefits.
- Increase the incorporation of decomposed plant and animal matter back into the fields, enhancing nutrient cycling.
- Establish areas for stormwater attenuation to safeguard crops and serve as a water supply for the farm.
- Introduce uncultivated land with natural vegetation to mitigate erosion, reduce nutrient runoff, and support pollinators like bees.

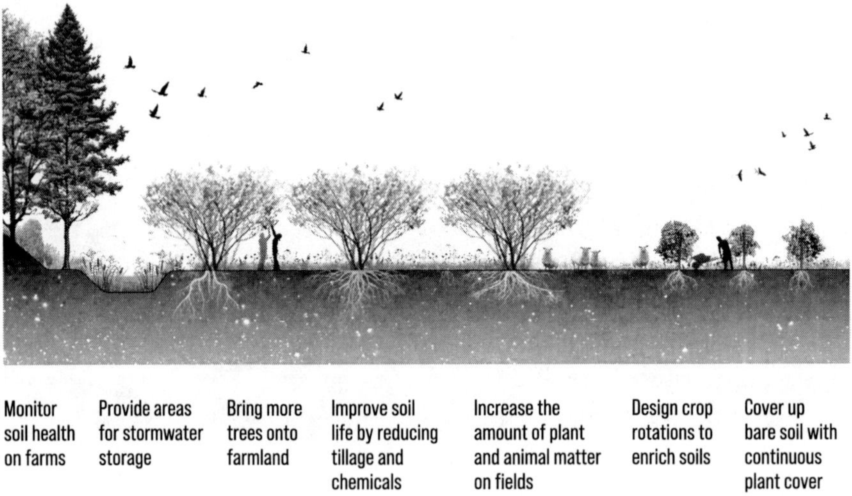

Figure 8.5 - *Agricultural Strategies for Improving Soil Health (© Alexandra Steed URBAN).*

44

You can make a significant impact by actively supporting farmers who embrace these healthy and regenerative measures. By choosing to purchase food from farmers who prioritise soil health, biodiversity, and sustainable farming practices, you can directly contribute to the success and expansion of these environmentally friendly approaches. Look for local farmers' markets, community-supported agriculture programs, or organic food cooperatives that follow regenerative farming practices. Additionally, educating yourself about sustainable agriculture and spreading awareness among your social circles can inspire others to make informed choices and support farmers who are dedicated to the well-being of the land. Together, we can collectively move towards a more sustainable and regenerative food system.

Wetlands

Forests, grasslands, wetlands, and coral reefs are all dynamic habitats that are facing significant threats from expanding farms and human activities. The decline of wetland areas is occurring at an alarming rate, disappearing three times faster than forests, according to the IPBES assessment.[45] Wetlands occur where water meets land, including peatlands, marshes, floodplains, mangroves, and even coral reefs. In the twentieth century, wetland conversion and loss were almost four times faster than before, with losses of up to 70 percent of wetlands in 1900.[46] Thousands of hectares were drained to provide agriculture, industry, and housing land.

Globally, humankind has treated wetlands as wastelands, dumping tons of sewage, industrial waste, fertilisers, pesticides, and other nasty things into these precious habitats (similar to the case of Essex). Activities such as shrimp farming for human consumption and other aquaculture businesses often destroy mangroves in their wake. With over 40 percent of the world's species reliant in some way on wetlands—including amphibians, crustaceans, and a variety of birds—the loss of these places is forcing many species to the brink of extinction.[47]

Coral reefs, another vulnerable habitat, have experienced substantial losses since 1950, with over half of the global coral reef cover disappearing.[48] Under business-as-usual scenarios, half of coral reef ecosystems worldwide will permanently face unsuitable environmental conditions, meaning coral reefs will die back, and other marine life will struggle to survive due to disruptions in the food chain.[49] Losses are due to ongoing disturbances to their habitat, induced by warming waters and runoff from agriculture and industry.[50] Tropical coral reef ecosystems, occupying less than 0.1 percent of the ocean floor, are home to at least 25 percent of known marine species.[51] The Great Barrier Reef is the largest coral reef ecosystem on earth and is considered the largest living structure, home to over 12,000 known species.[52] It's comparable to the Amazon rainforest of the seas.

Since 1995, the abundance of coral colonies has declined sharply,[53] following four mass bleaching events in 1998, 2002, 2016 and 2017.[54] Small colonies declined by nearly 80 percent along some areas of the reef.[55] These declines seriously inhibit the corals' reproduction processes, eroding their populations' recovery and resilience.[56] Humankind has long been replanting forests, but we are only now learning how to revive coral reefs. Together with other wetlands, they provide critical food resources, vast carbon sinks, and protection from storms and flooding for millions worldwide.

To address these environmental challenges, it is critical to support initiatives aimed at habitat restoration and conservation. Numerous charities and community groups are actively involved in coastal restoration efforts that you can contribute to through donations or volunteer work. By supporting these organisations, you can help protect and revive wetlands and coral reefs, which provide essential resources such as food, carbon sequestration, and natural protection against storms and flooding. Together, we can work towards the preservation of these invaluable ecosystems and the diverse species they support.

Freshwater

Each of us needs approximately two litres of water daily. This figure is modest. However, more concerning is the thousands of litres per day required to service water-intensive food production methods. Figures range from approximately 2,700 litres per capita per day in the UK to more than 3,800 litres per day in France.[57] To acquire these excessive amounts of water, countries worldwide have altered most of the longest rivers with dams to siphon off water for agriculture and industry. A study by researchers at the University of Cambridge found that meat production causes the biggest drain. "To produce 1 kg of protein from kidney beans required approximately eighteen times less land, ten times less water, nine times less fuel, twelve times less fertiliser and ten times less pesticide in comparison to producing 1 kg of protein from beef."[58]

Less direct human threats, such as land use and climate change, result in degraded soils and landscapes that have inhibited water infiltration and percolation. Reduced plant material results in less water capture and absorption capacity, and precipitation changes lead to more frequent and severe droughts and flooding. Humanity's wide-scale interference with freshwater has global effects, and the planetary boundary for freshwater indicates that it has been transgressed.[59] Heavy infrastructures and technological processes have profoundly changed the water cycle and compromised the stability of the earth's systems by doing so.

However, it is not only over-consumption of water that is at issue. Humans also continue to pollute available freshwater. Fertilisers are one of the leading threats—mainly in the form of phosphorus and nitrogen—unleashed into the soil in excessive concentrations and eventually washed into the water.[60] Rivers, lakes, aquifers, and oceans are all drowning in toxic chemicals, waste plastics, and other pollutants. These can become oxygen-starved aquatic environments—a process called eutrophication—which occurs when bacteria consume algae blooms that grow due to an increased nutrient load. The result has been nothing less than an environmental disaster, jeopardising the health of all life, including human well-being.

Oceans

Today, 40 percent of the ocean area is severely altered.[61] Again, much of the change is related to our food systems. The direct exploitation of organisms has had the most considerable negative impact—mainly caused by over-fishing.[62] The footprint of industrial fishing is four times larger than agriculture.[63] It overexploits one-third of global fish stocks.[64] Out of the most popular marine supplies, 75 percent are currently overexploited. These fish stocks are caught faster than they can reproduce. Thus, their populations decline.[65] The method of trawling, used by so many commercial fisheries, hauls in massive amounts of unwanted fish and other sea life and is then discarded—tragically wasteful. Like so many resources, fish stocks are not shared equally worldwide. Wealthy nations catch and consume most of the fish.[66]

The devastation of ecosystems and natural resources from commercial fishing is often hidden from view but is happening in massive quantities, with long-lasting consequences for the ocean's future. Once degraded, these natural resources are not easily replaced or renewed. Food security is threatened even after their exploitation stops, and health hazards and risks of natural disasters are increased.

A study by the Nature Conservancy has found that fishing not only depletes fish stocks and ruins ocean ecosystems but is responsible for "more than 100 million pounds of plastic from industrial fishing gear [that] pollute[s] the oceans each year—threatening marine life."[67] Discarded or lost fishing gear, often fishing nets, continues to entrap marine life. Entanglement can cause animals to become fatally or seriously wounded, drown, or be unable to escape from predators or catch food.[68] Plastic debris leaches chemical pollutants that disrupt the endocrine system if ingested.[69] If animals are exposed to these chemicals early on, they may become irreversibly infertile.[70]

As consumers, we must support companies that avoid the use and production of plastics, keep away from harmful products and seafood that endanger or threaten species (like certain cosmetics or jewellery made of coral), limit seafood purchases, and favour well-managed wild fisheries.

Oceans, like freshwater, are also gravely affected by nitrogen pollution. Nitrogen is the sixth most abundant element and is critical to the survival of all life on earth.[71] However, over the past 200 years, humans have significantly altered the global nitrogen cycle.[72] Now, 80 percent of the nitrogen found in our human tissues originates from chemically processed nitrogen used to make agricultural fertilisers.[73]

In aquatic ecosystems, inorganic nitrogen pollution causes acidification of the water, eutrophication, and impairing the ability of marine animals to survive, grow and reproduce.[74] The process of eutrophication, and the presence of algal blooms severely depletes oxygen and light levels. It causes cascades of detrimental effects for other organisms in the ecosystem, including death or impaired ability to catch prey. Low oxygen levels further promote the formation of harmful forms of inorganic nitrogen toxic to aquatic animals.[75]

These low oxygen levels in coastal ecosystems give rise to "dead zones," where most marine life flees or dies.[76] The number of dead zones has approximately doubled each decade since the 1960s—affecting an area of more than 245,000 square kilometres (over 152,000 square miles) worldwide.[77]

In conclusion, the degradation of wilderness areas due to human activities has had devastating consequences for the planet's biodiversity and the delicate balance of ecosystems. The changes to land use and relentless expansion of intensive agriculture and fishing practices have led to the loss of countless species, from birds and insects to mammals, reptiles, fish, and invertebrates. While these modern methods may yield short-term gains in food production, the long-term implications could be catastrophic, potentially resulting in a lifeless and desolate planet.

Continuing with the usual scenario will only bring suffering, darkness, and despair for humanity. However, the earth will persist, and nature will endure, even in the absence of humankind. To prevent further devastation and rather regenerate our planet, it is essential to protect the remaining wilderness areas and embark on substantial restoration efforts to revive degraded ecosystems. Central to this endeavour is a fundamental re-evaluation of the food industry, particularly in the realm of farmland cultivation. Our focus must shift towards caring for the land—soils, water and air—recognising its vital importance as the foundation of life.

David Attenborough's *A Life on Our Planet* serves as an urgent call to action, a global SOS to the world's people. But he does not stop there. His message is one of hope for the future. Attenborough emphasises that a rewilding of the world presents "our greatest opportunity."[78] Within their lifetimes, our children could witness a profound revolution from destruction to a restored and vibrant landscape. This transformation requires humanity to rekindle our love and reverence for the earth. The time to act is now. Fostering a deep connection with the land's essential elements of soil, water, and air is a vital first step.

9

Design for Life

COMMODITY TO COMMUNITY

"We abuse land because we regard it as a commodity belonging to us. When we see land as a community to which we belong, we may begin to use it with love and respect." [1]

—*Aldo Leopold*

IN PART 3, we investigated a wealth of distressing environmental data, presenting challenges that may seem insurmountable. From threatened cities grappling with floods and pollution, to staggering biodiversity losses, devastated forests, and lifeless ocean zones, the magnitude of these problems is daunting. These stories of tragedy stem from a deeply ingrained belief that the natural world exists solely for human convenience—to be controlled, commodified, and consumed.

Yet, there is value in examining these problems in detail. By painting a comprehensive picture of a broken system, we gain insight into the underlying issues and uncover potential solutions. Through the synthesis of information, a common thread emerges: all environmental ailments trace back to a dysfunctional relationship between humans and the earth, one that urgently needs mending.

In this chapter, I invite you to pause and reflect on a profound realisation: beneath our feet lies the promise of abundant life, and it is crucial that we restore our relationship with the land. The guiding principle that underpins all our endeavours is the restoration of this vital connection.

As we delve into the three fundamental elements of the land—soil, water, and air—we embark on a journey of understanding their significance. By structuring this book as a landscape strategy, we introduce the Guiding Principle—an overarching design tenet distilled from our comprehensive assessment. This principle serves as a guiding light, leading us towards a transformative vision of a reformed relationship between humanity and nature, ultimately giving rise to a new earth.

Within these pages, we explore how healing our connection with soil, water, and air becomes the bedrock of our revised framework. Recognising their essential role in the well-being of all life, we delve into case studies of regenerative landscape schemes. These practical examples serve as demonstrations of how we can actively support, reconnect with, and restore these three fundamental elements of the land.

Soil

Let's begin with soil. Our planet is called "earth" for good reason. All life on land depends on soil. No soil, no life. Throughout the ages, our ancestors possessed a deep understanding of the extraordinary and life-giving properties of soil. This wisdom is reflected in the etymology of our planet's name across languages, which often finds its roots in terms associated with "ground" or "soil."[2] The circle of life is most evident here, as represented in the adage "earth to earth, ashes to ashes, dust to dust."[3]

Wendell Berry, writer, agrarian, and environmental activist, posits, "The soil is the great connector of lives, the source and destination of all. It is the healer and restorer and resurrector, by which disease passes into health, age into youth, death into life. Without proper care for it we can have no community because without proper care for it we can have no life."[4] Berry cautions that if we neglect soil health, our health, and the health of our communities, will suffer. Without preservation and regeneration of the soil's health, culture cannot survive. All life comes from the soil, dies back into the ground, and springs to life again.

Fascinatingly, soil serves as the nexus where all components of the biosphere converge. When we examine the composition of typical soil, we find a rich blend: 45 percent minerals, encompassing sand, clay, and silt; 5 percent organic matter, consisting of living and once-living organisms such as plants, insects, and animals; and 25 percent each of air and water. Soil brings together all forms of life, a literal expression of the interconnectedness of all things.

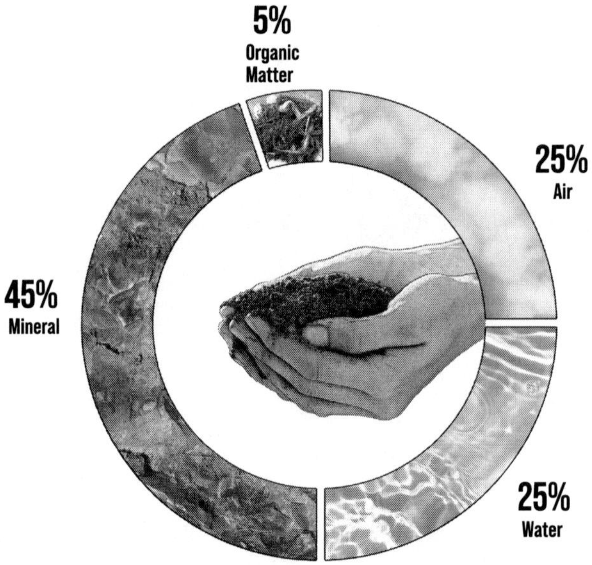

Figure 9.1 *– Soil Composition: The earth's make-up reflects the profound interconnectedness of all elements. Healthy soil is a perfect blend of life (© Alexandra Steed URBAN).*

5

It is easy to underestimate the significance of "dirt," particularly for those residing in cities with limited opportunities to get their hands into the stuff. Yet, there is nothing more essential. Soil's role in sustaining life cannot be overstated. It provides a plethora of functions that make life on earth possible. Many tomes have been written on the unseen beauty and potency of soil. Here, I touch on some critical reasons why society must revive our bond with soil. The below points provide a snapshot of some of the many precious services and functions that soil contributes to life on earth:

- Enables healthy plant growth by creating an optimal environment, facilitating nutrient, water, and air availability to plants and other organisms.
- Sustains various life forms, including humans, by providing essential food resources.
- Functions as a natural reservoir, effectively absorbing and retaining water while purifying it from pollutants and contaminants.
- Plays a crucial role in preventing natural hazards such as flooding, landslides, and dust storms.
- Operates as an efficient natural digestive system, decomposing and recycling waste materials.
- Harbours a diverse array of organisms, both visible and microscopic, that contribute to the overall health of the soil and its ecological processes. These organisms, ranging from earthworms to bacteria, are integral to soil functions.
- Serves as a significant carbon sink, storing a substantial portion of terrestrial carbon. In fact, approximately 80 percent of carbon stored in terrestrial environments can be found within the soil.

Undoubtedly, all life depends on the soil, especially the upper 20 cm (nearly 8 inches) of topsoil. Yet we are losing it at an alarming rate. Healthy soil takes hundreds of years to establish but can be lost instantly. Vulnerability to wind and water erosion, pollutants, run-off, or nutrient loss poses constant threats. It only takes a single flood or storm event to blow or wash it away for good.

In urban areas, the soil is often hidden beneath layers of asphalt or concrete, preventing essential interactions with water, air, plants, and animals. As a result, the earth loses meaningful connections and becomes devoid of purpose. In rural and wilderness regions, industrial and agricultural practices have similarly disrupted the soil's efficacy by isolating it from its natural community, including trees, plants, water, and other organisms. Activities like clear-cutting, ploughing, tilling, and the use of toxic chemicals have left the soil barren and unable to fulfil its potential. It is as if the processes of urbanisation, agriculture, and industrialisation have forcibly sterilised the ground and then blamed it for its lack of fertility.

Fortunately, numerous case studies have highlighted the benefits of enriching and rehabilitating the soil, although more examples are needed. The following pages showcase compelling initiatives that demonstrate the significant advantages of collaborating with soil as an essential member of the community rather than working against it. These examples serve as inspiration for the immense gains that can be achieved by cultivating a close association with the soil.

The Great Green Wall, Africa

The Great Green Wall initiative proposes a swath of vegetation 16 km (10 miles) wide and extending more than 7,000 km (4,350 miles) from Senegal in the west to Djibouti in the east. It is within the Sahel region: a vast semi-arid territory that links the Sahara Desert to the north and the tropical savanna to the south. This region of Africa suffers from widespread desertification due to years of extensive and severe drought, unsustainable agricultural land cultivation and overgrazing of livestock. (Desertification is land degradation in drylands whereby fertile areas become arid. The spread is often caused by human-induced change such as global warming and overexploitation of soils.) These practices have stripped the earth of sustaining vegetative cover.[6] The project's objective is to combat desert expansion and restore food security in the Sahel region. Initially, the approach involved planting a wall of trees, driven by good intentions. However, experience has revealed that in this semi-arid grassland, there are more effective solutions beyond solely relying on tree planting.

Much like the Great Plains Dust Bowl of the 1930s, described in Chapter 8, the problem in the Sahel is that the grasslands were devastated. Thus, unrooted and dry soil was blown away during dust storms. The ground was left barren, and life was hard for the people in the region who now struggled to grow food and access fresh water.

Since the Great Green Wall's initiation, the project partners learned that the answer to undoing desertification would not be found only in planting trees. In fact, most of the planted trees were dying. To tackle soil erosion and land degradation in this environment, a programme of indigenous land use techniques has proven incredibly successful, including increasing water harvesting and supporting natural greenery and tree protection. Mohamed Bakarr, the lead environmental specialist for the project, says, "It is not necessarily a physical wall, but rather a mosaic of land use practices that ultimately will meet the expectations of a wall. It has been transformed into a metaphorical thing."[7]

Figure 9.2 – *The Great Green Wall: Women taking action in agricultural fields to combat desertification, promote sustainable land management, and restore degraded lands in the region, contributing to the implementation of the Great Green Wall initiative.*

8

Those working in the area have witnessed a metamorphosis from a brown and lifeless desert to a green and vital landscape, transformed by the efforts of thousands of local farmers who have embraced regenerative agricultural practices to improve the ground conditions. They enhanced water infiltration with traditional techniques, including a grid of pits to capture and hold water, and placed stone barriers around crops to retain moisture during rainfalls. Moreover, they have learned to plant trees and crops together because the shade and cover of appropriate and carefully distributed trees benefit the soil immensely.

The local farmers have restored the earth with simple measures and radically increased food production. They have made great strides towards alleviating hunger and poverty in the region. This regenerative project will be the world's largest planned and designed living structure when complete.[9] It is only possible through the collaboration of many organisations and the hard work of the local communities.

Greening the Desert Project, Jordan

I was first introduced to the work of Geoff Lawton (introduced in Chapter 8) while working on a strategic landscape framework in the Middle East. Specifically, I was searching for exemplary sustainable farming initiatives in desert regions. The area I was focusing on faced challenges such as rapid depletion of the groundwater aquifer and the need for a less water-intensive approach to agriculture. In my research, I discovered Lawton's Greening the Desert Project in the Dead Sea Valley, Jordan, which serves as an exceptional and well-documented model for regenerative agriculture in desert environments.

Jordan, being the lowest place on land at 400 metres below sea level, experiences extreme temperatures, aridity, minimal rainfall, and shallow soils on rocky hillsides. Lawton and his team embarked on the 10-acre permaculture project in 2000, collaborating with local communities to transform the degraded site into a thriving oasis of rejuvenation. This project stands as an inspiring and remarkable example of how soil enrichment can lead to a rapid and complete transformation of a landscape.

To better comprehend the concept of permaculture, let us explore Lawton's definition as provided by the Permaculture Research Institute: "Permaculture (the word, coined by Bill Mollison, is a portmanteau of permanent agriculture and permanent culture) is the conscious design and maintenance of agriculturally productive ecosystems which have the diversity, stability, and resilience of natural ecosystems. It is the harmonious integration of landscape and people—providing their food, energy, shelter, and other material and non-material needs in a sustainable way. Without permanent agriculture there is no possibility of a stable social order."[10]

Lawton and his team applied this permaculture approach to revitalising the Dead Sea Valley landscape. The project employs solar power, biological wastewater treatment recycling, rainwater harvesting earthworks, and diverse interactive plant, animal, and tree systems. The team created an oasis in the desert with light-touch and organic methods, including selective tree planting and capturing all available water with shade, wind-buffering, and nitrogen-rich mulch. No chemical fertilisers are used. It proves that revitalisation is possible even in the most challenging sites on the planet when people engage with the natural systems in place.[11]

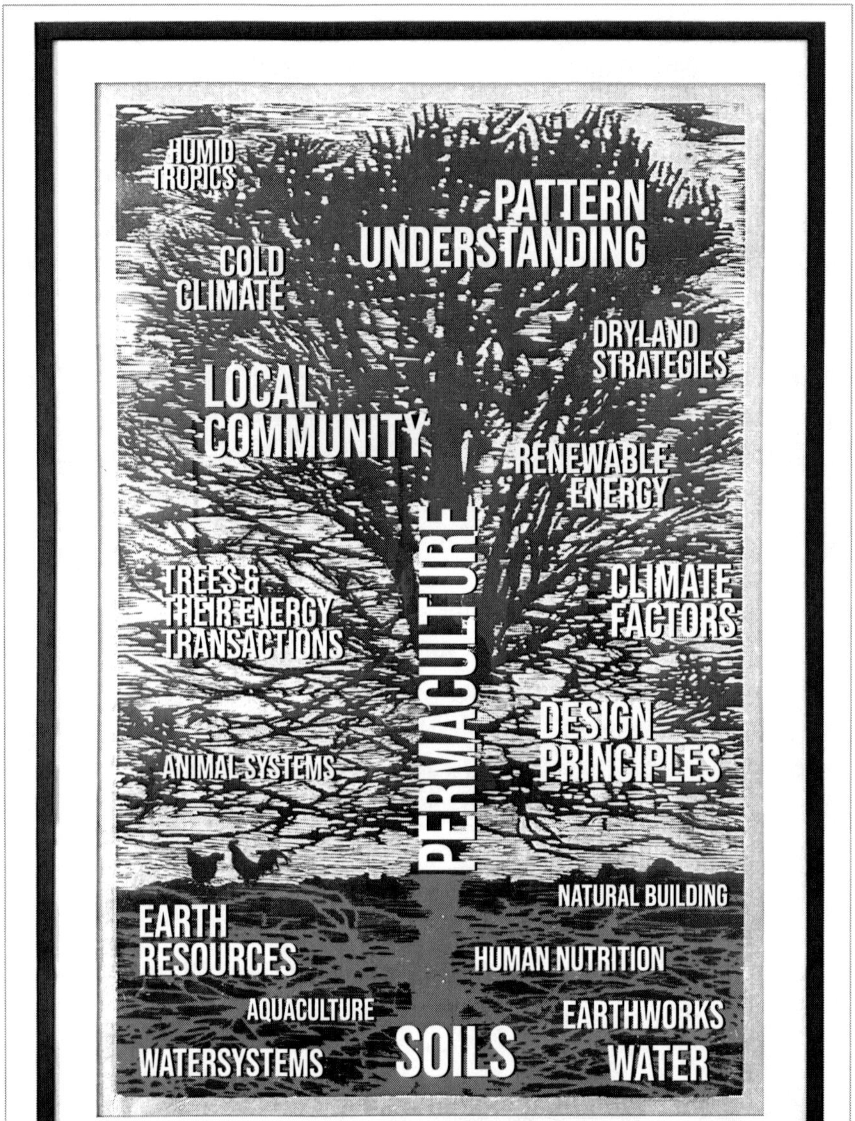

Figure 9.3 *– The Permaculture Tree: A visual representation of the permaculture system, showcasing its ability to meet humanity's food needs while simultaneously benefitting the environment (© Alexandra Steed URBAN).*

The local team in Jordan has taken proactive steps to assist local families in establishing their gardens, and they are also providing support to several nearby schools to do the same. This showcases the effective transfer of knowledge to local communities through a practical and interactive approach, where they actively engage in live projects. The success of the Greening the Desert Project has been so remarkable that it is now being replicated in various diverse locations throughout the region and country.

BEFORE **AFTER**

Figure 9.4 *– The Greening the Desert Project: These photos demonstrate the transformative power of permaculture, showcasing the remarkable conversion of a barren landscape into a thriving and productive garden within a short timeframe.*

13

Greenways, Canada

One of the most inspirational and memorable experiences of my career as a landscape architect took place in the City of Vancouver. From 2000, I had the privilege of being involved in the innovative Greenways program, which aimed to establish an interconnected network of green pedestrian and cycling routes throughout the city.[14] During this time, I had the opportunity to work on a project that involved redesigning a residential street using sustainable street design methods, and the impact of this initiative was extraordinary.

Collaborating with landscape architects, engineers, planners, and the local community, we set out to create a streetscape that was not only aesthetically pleasing but also functional and environmentally sustainable. Our approach encompassed several key elements. First, we narrowed the width of the street to encourage slower traffic and to increase permeable areas. Second, we introduced vegetated swales along the street to capture stormwater, filter out pollutants, and facilitate groundwater replenishment—an alternative to the common practice of channelling water directly into underground stormwater pipes. Furthermore, we adorned the street edges with native plants and trees, providing habitat support for local wildlife. To enhance sustainability further, we replaced paved car parking spaces with permeable gravel or grass, supported by a structural grid. Finally, we included an attenuation pond at the lower end of the street to mitigate the impact of high stormwater flows on a nearby stream, which had faced significant challenges due to the burial and piping of its course.

Upon completion of the redesigned street and the removal of the culvert, the project yielded exceptional results. Not only did the streetscape itself thrive, but the stream that had once been compromised saw a remarkable recovery, as evidenced by the return of spawning salmon the following year. What a victory! This triumph served as a testament to the integration of all elements in the landscape. It reinforced the understanding that nothing exists in isolation; rather, everything in the living world, including soils and water, is interconnected and interdependent.

Dubbed "Canada's First Sustainable Streetscape," the project has become a shining example of innovative street design and is continuously monitored to assess its long-term effectiveness. The exhilarating outcome of this early work served as a catalyst for my commitment to champion and advocate for regenerative practices in all my future projects.

Figure 9.5 *- Canada's First Sustainable Streetscape: This innovative design prioritises the well-being of people and the environment by integrating soil improvement, groundwater replenishment, stormwater storage, selective planting, and wildlife support into street infrastructure.*

15

Globally, there is a growing awareness and adoption of soil-enriching techniques. Across the world, numerous inspiring initiatives are underway, focusing on the restoration of wilderness areas, the regeneration of farms, the greening of streets, and even the rewilding of private gardens. These schemes demonstrate that improved soils hold the power to breathe life back into any landscape, regardless of its scale or location.

Water

Water is often referred to as the earth's lifeblood. It circulates through the earth's skin of soil and unites the land, ocean, and atmosphere into an integrated system. Everything on the ground, both plant and animal, depends on freshwater. (As you know, the human body quickly withers away after 3–4 days without water.) Just as our own bodies cannot survive for long without water, the entire natural world relies on freshwater to thrive. The significance of water extends far beyond its basic biological importance, as it plays a vital role in maintaining the health and balance of ecosystems. It regulates atmospheric conditions, temperature, and climate, while also serving as a fundamental resource that supports human civilisation in countless ways.

Water is constantly flowing between various parts of the biosphere in differing forms. NASA describes the hydrological cycle as "the pilgrimage of water as water molecules make their way from the Earth's surface to the atmosphere and back again, in some cases to below the surface. This gigantic system, powered by energy from the Sun, is a continuous exchange of moisture between the oceans, the atmosphere, and the land."[16] The water cycle is something that most of us were introduced to as school children. So familiar is it that it's easy to take it for granted and to forget just how miraculous the process is.

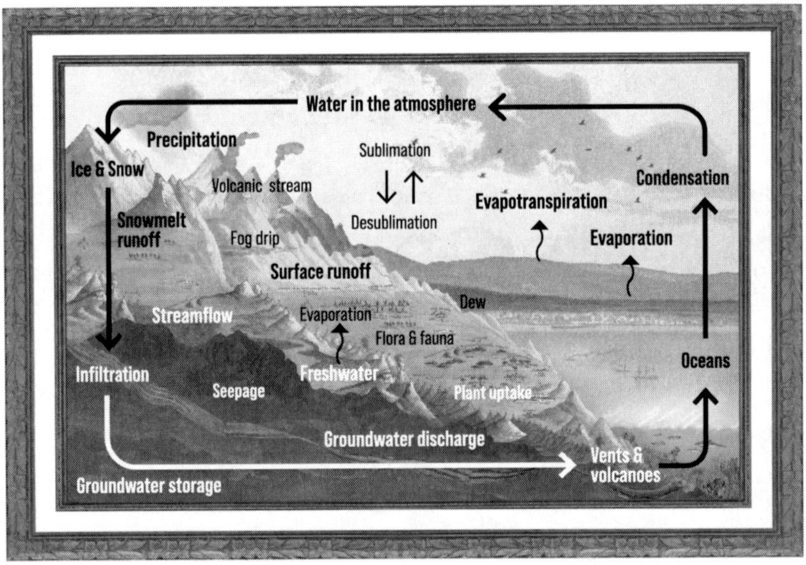

Figure 9.6 *– The Water Cycle: This image illustrates the perpetual journey of water, seamlessly cycling and exchanging between land, ocean, and air (© Alexandra Steed URBAN).*

17

When precipitation falls over the land, it can take several different paths. Some may evaporate and return directly to the atmosphere, some may percolate into the ground, and some may fall as surface water, shaping the land over which it passes. Other water may run off into local streams or rivers. Almost all water eventually reaches the ocean or other large waterbodies, only to set off on the eternal pilgrimage once again.

The water involved in this process is finite, not increasing or decreasing. Yet this constancy does not guarantee availability. Due to direct and indirect human forces, the earth's water is becoming more unpredictable, inaccessible, and unequally distributed. Society intercepts water for various functions worldwide, including domestic uses, agriculture, industry, and power generation processes.

Water does abound on the planet. 71 percent of the earth's surface is covered by water.[18] However, 97.5 percent of this amount is salt water, the remaining 2.5 percent is freshwater, and most are frozen in ice around the poles or locked underground in aquifers. Thus, only 0.26 percent of the total freshwater is readily available, concentrated in ponds, lakes, reservoirs, streams, rivers, wetlands and groundwater.[19]

To initiate effective restoration, we must focus on the watershed level, ensuring the uninterrupted flow of water throughout the earth's hydrological cycle and within specific terrestrial environments. A watershed refers to a defined area of land that channels water into a particular water body, encompassing the entire drainage system.[20] Unfortunately, the importance of watersheds is often overlooked in human development, leading to the degradation of local ecosystems and disregarding the vital role they play as the earth's life-giving bloodstream.

Across the globe, many nations have compromised the quality, accessibility, and availability of freshwater resources. However, there are opportunities to incorporate sustainable and resilient approaches to water management, even in the most severely affected environments. The following case studies serve as inspiring examples of ongoing restoration efforts being carried out internationally. These initiatives highlight the potential for positive change and offer valuable insights into how we can restore and preserve our precious water systems.

Sponge Cities, China

A decade ago, Kongjia Yu, landscape architect and founder of the design practice Turenscape, with a group of Chinese researchers, championed the concept of 'sponge cities' as a model for flood management, ecosystem restoration and urban heat stress reduction. The approach utilises the porous qualities of landscapes to catch, store and clean water. It welcomes nature back into cities, provides a nature-based solution to control and mitigate flooding, and addresses water scarcity and pollution in urban areas.[21] Yu's team achieved this by creating large landscapes dedicated to absorbing water naturally, filtering pollutants through the soil, and thus replenishing groundwater rather than forcing water immediately into a storm sewer network.

North China is facing the twin crises of water shortages and flooding. Engineering complex infrastructures to control water and expediently remove it from cities, primarily including storm sewer systems, has proven inadequate. Trying to arrange complete control over natural processes is never fail-proof. There is a better way. Yu explains, "Reverse-engineering a city to make it more spongey requires a mental rather than physical shift. It's a whole new philosophy of dealing with water. It is about how we plan and design our cities in an ecological way."[22]

In China, freshwater is running out, pollution is making much of the water unusable, and flooding is made worse by the climate crisis. Yu explains that though the hard, grey infrastructure of concrete, steel and pipes may help to address urgent problems, they do not address the more significant issues of environmental health and resilience. He says, "Sponge Cities are inspired by the ancient wisdom of farming and water management that use simple tools to transform the global surface at a vast scale in a sustainable way."[23] Yu urged his government to restore the essential relationship to water, soil and nature in threatened Chinese cities.

In 2015, the Chinese government agreed, announcing plans to roll out 30 pilot projects in cities including Beijing, Tianjin, Wuhan and Shenzhen. It set a target date of 2030 for completion.[24] Further ambitions include featuring sponge cities in 80 percent of China's municipal areas and recycling 70 percent of rainfall.[25]

***Figure 9.7** – Yanweizhou Park in Jinhua City: The park is a work of resilient and living infrastructure designed to adapt to dynamic water events and people flows. It is part of China's sponge city programme.*

[26]

Yanweizhou Park in Jinhua City, designed by Turenscape, is one of the completed sponge projects. This 64-acre wetland park has been designed to "make friends" with monsoon floods by creating a terraced river embankment with flood-adapted planting and paths. They are also designed to remediate and filtrate stormwater before entering the river system.[27] The inland area of the park is entirely permeable and allows large-scale flood attenuation. A resilient bridge and paths system is designed to adapt to stormwater flows while allowing people access to the park. Not only has this wetland park provided a nature-based solution to one of the city's biggest issues, but it has given Jinhua a distinctive and memorable landscape identity.

Worldwide, a multitude of similar projects are being implemented that align with the principles of "green and blue infrastructure," as discussed in Chapter 6. These initiatives recognise the invaluable services provided by nature and aim to create integrated networks of soft solutions for various challenges such as stormwater management, climate adaptation, biodiversity conservation, improved air quality, and clean water.

These projects prioritise collaboration with nature by leveraging its inherent capabilities. Instead of relying solely on heavily engineered solutions like dikes, dams, and storm sewer systems, they embrace nature-based alternatives. Strategies such as the establishment of swales, wetlands, mangrove forests, and reefs are employed as part of the landscape, harnessing their inherent ecological functions to address the identified challenges.

By embracing these nature-based approaches, these projects not only achieve their intended objectives but also foster the preservation and restoration of natural ecosystems. They demonstrate the potential of working hand-in-hand with nature to create sustainable and resilient solutions that benefit both human communities and the environment.

Oyster-tecture, USA

In New York, landscape architect Kate Orff, and her practice at SCAPE, are working to revitalise oyster reefs in New York Harbour in a project they call "Oyster-tecture."[28] The scheme holistically addresses the rising concerns of climate change, sea level rise, the impact of storm surges, and poor water quality while creating a waterside park and providing employment for local people. In an interview with *The New Yorker*, Orff explains, "We have to hit the reset button if we want nature to come back. There's no more natural nature. Now it's a matter of design."[29]

Orff explains that, in the past, "There were oysters, tide pools, grasses, lots of colourful marine life, and they were a big part of New York's coastal-protection system. They acted like breakwaters, absorbing wave energy and slowing the water before it hit the shore. We've spent the past one hundred years dredging out everything for shipping and hardening the edges. Now we have a different climate, and we need a different approach."[30]

Thus, the Oyster-tecture project harnesses the biotic filtration processes of oysters, mussels, and eelgrass to clean polluted harbour water, improve habitats, and restore biodiversity in tidal marshes.

SCAPE describes the project as "a living reef composed of a woven web of "fuzzy rope" that supports marine growth."[31] This innovative proposal demonstrates that exciting and beautiful solutions come to light by releasing the wondrous processes of the living world. There is no living without water, but now we must learn how to, once again, live with it.

Equally important to this project's design is the local community's involvement. This is essential in an era where public programs are being cut, and all development is profit-driven. Orff says, "If a community wants to make change in their environment, they're going to have to band together and do it themselves, and I feel that we as designers can and should play a role in facilitating that."[32]

With the Oyster-tecture project, the design team worked with the community to help them bring about positive change in their neighbourhood through a harbour pilot project. She explains, "Through our pilot project we were able to provide a channel and a means of organization for some of the incredible energy that already exists in those communities. I think that was our most important contribution."[33]

The implementation of this natural breakwater project provides a cost-effective solution for urban stormwater management while fostering community collaboration. Scientists, community leaders, governmental agencies, business owners, residents, volunteer groups, and designers join forces, working towards a shared goal to benefit the entire community. This collective effort demonstrates that sustainable solutions can be achieved through the cooperation and involvement of diverse stakeholders.

By engaging various entities, the project fosters a sense of ownership and responsibility among community members, as they actively contribute to improving their surroundings. Recognising stormwater management as a shared task, this holistic approach highlights the strength of collective action in creating positive change and benefiting the community as a whole.

Air

The enveloping presence of air is a constant in our lives. Just as fish navigate the depths of the ocean, we terrestrial creatures exist within an expansive sea of air. It surrounds us with an invisible, soft, pillowy blanket, just right for life—neither too hot nor too cold.

However, the pervasive nature of air often leads us to overlook its profound significance and purpose. The thin film of atmosphere encircling the globe performs remarkable functions. It safeguards all life on earth by creating a protective pressure that retains water on the planet's surface. Furthermore, it serves as a shield, absorbing harmful ultraviolet solar radiation and providing insulation that maintains the planet within the vital temperature range required for life to thrive. Though it may sound sci-fi, the atmosphere also protects us from meteorites by burning them up before they reach the ground.

The chemical makeup of the atmosphere is perfect to support life. Three elements comprise more than 99 percent of the air we breathe—nitrogen is 78 percent, oxygen is 21 percent, and argon is 1 percent.[34] The remaining percentage includes water vapour, carbon dioxide, and other trace gases, which, though relatively minor, significantly affect air quality.

Of course, humans are dependent on the oxygen found in the air. Many of us know how terrifying the experience of being trapped underwater without access to breathable air can be. Not having access to air is more terminal than not having access to fresh water. When starved of oxygen for just four minutes, permanent brain damage can occur, and as quickly as 4–6 minutes, the body can succumb to death.[35] Oxygen is not just a human requisite. All plants and animals need it to convert food into energy.

We are all too aware that humans are damaging the atmosphere's composition by increasing the release of carbon dioxide and other greenhouse gases into the air and creating global warming and climate change conditions. Aerosols also significantly influence the earth's systems, changing the hydrological cycle, causing global warming, and emitting atmospheric pollution. Moreover, due to increased dust and smoke from land-use changes, tiny particles released into the air alter the atmosphere's chemistry, make breathing difficult, and result in respiratory illness.[36] The ability to breathe clean air is no longer a given. WHO reports that 99 percent of the entire human population is now inhaling air that threatens health.[37] Air pollution kills seven million people per year.[38]

Human interference has had a profound impact on the delicate balance of the atmosphere, altering the very breath of life itself. However, there is hope in the form of inspiring case studies that demonstrate how humanity can actively contribute to the revitalisation of the atmosphere, allowing it to regain its health and fulfil its role in cradling life on earth.

Vancouver Parks, Canada

I was born in the naturally spectacular city of Vancouver, surrounded by impressive mountains, rivers, and sea. Vancouver is consistently ranked among the world's most liveable and green cities, due to its healthy environment.[39] Air quality is an essential dimension of this ranking. Undoubtedly, Vancouver's natural landscape setting is a critical reason for its high liveability score. However, significant efforts have always been made to keep the city's environment healthy.

Shortly after the City of Vancouver's inception in 1886, one of the newly formed local government's first moves was to formally open Stanley Park as a green lung in the city centre. They had a vision for the park to be "the most beautiful park in the world."[40] Even in those early days, with a city population of only about 1,000 people, city officials had the foresight to protect nature in the city's centre for future citizens. The park is 1000 acres in area, predominantly forest, and makes up the northwestern half of Vancouver's Downtown Peninsula. The parkland is equal in size to the built-up part of the city centre, providing just as much space for nature as for civilisation.

Stanley Park, a true gem of nature, sustains a dynamic array of ecosystems, wildlife, and plants, while serving as a vital habitat and playing an important role in stormwater management and climate cooling. Unlike many city parks that were meticulously designed by a single landscape architect, Stanley Park has evolved naturally as a protected and managed forest. Having had the privilege of spending numerous joyful days there during my childhood, I cherish the memories and the countless opportunities for recreation, leisure, and cultural enrichment that this beautiful park offers.

Figure 9.8 *– Stanley Park: A green lung for the city, sitting next to Vancouver's downtown core. It is a critical component of Vancouver's vitality and liveability.*

[41]

The vision and commitment to keep Vancouver green and fresh

are still as strong today as when Vancouver was initially established. Take, for example, the innovative streets programme I referred to previously. One of my former university professors pitched the concept of greenways to the City of Vancouver to knit the city together with a network of eighteen routes for pedestrians and cyclists. Fortunately, the local government accepted and launched the programme.

Greenways encourage people to leave their cars and walk or cycle instead, take up recreation opportunities, and enhance nature corridors in the city.[42] The myriad benefits include decreased air pollution, improved health and fitness, enhanced filtration of stormwater run-off and pollutants, increased biodiversity, beautification of streets with trees and planting, and greater opportunities for socialising and fun. The city-wide greenways have been very successful, and the programme was extended to include neighbourhood greenways that rely on community involvement to care for the green streets. Plans are underway to expand the network so that all city residents live within a five-minute walk of a greenway.

Vancouver, like London, recently undertook a "Natural Capital Valuation" of its parks, which attempts to articulate the somewhat invisible and difficult-to-quantify economic value of parks and green spaces to justify their protection and maintenance.[43] (Unfortunately, economic rationale is still required, but such is our world.) The report measures tourism, recreation and physical health, property premiums, stormwater management, air quality, and temperature regulation. It indicates, "Preliminary calculations show that the tourism value of Vancouver's parks ranges between $198 million to $1.3 billion per year, their recreation value is worth at least $31 million per year, and their physical health value is worth at least $47 billion." It adds that this Canadian dollar value only represents annual revenue, not asset value. As in the case of Central Park, asset value would far outweigh the market value and opportunity cost if it were to be converted to residential or commercial land use.[44] The people of Vancouver have always appreciated the intrinsic value of the healthy environment and stunning landscape—it is what has attracted most residents to call Vancouver home. Now they have the figures to back it up.

Gardens by the Bay, Singapore

Other cities, such as Singapore, are making remarkable progress in enhancing urban air quality, even though they may not rank as well on the air pollution index. Despite its small size, occupying only 700 square kilometres (270 square miles), Singapore accommodates a population of 5.7 million Homo sapiens, making it Asia's most densely populated country.[45]

Tragically, Singapore has experienced the loss of over 95 percent of its original flora and fauna since British colonisation in 1819. The extractive mindset of the British colonisers led to the rapid degradation of the island's landscape. However, recognising the need to address the environmental challenges, including the lack of green spaces and high levels of air pollution, the Singaporean government implemented the Singapore Green Plan. This comprehensive plan focuses on key areas such as air quality, climate change, water and land conservation, and the promotion of nature and public health.[46] Despite its limited space, Singapore has embraced the vision of becoming a "garden city" by adopting innovative and creative approaches to reintroduce nature into the urban landscape.

Singapore now has the motto, "Singapore—City in a Garden."[47] It has made impressive progress at bringing nature back to the city, so much so that it feels like the buildings originally grew up through the garden. A lush environment permeates all of Singapore. Take, for example, the iconic Gardens by the Bay project. Not only is the garden significant for Singapore, but it has become emblematic worldwide of a city committed to living harmoniously with nature. Indeed, the government has invested heavily in the re-creation of the landscape. Green roofs, green walls, hanging gardens, nature trails, and parks carpet the city in green. With the blossoming of green, the air quality has improved to be better than in many cities in Asia.[48]

Figure 9.9 *– Gardens by the Bay: A symbol of Singapore's metamorphosis. This expansive nature park covers over 100 hectares (250 acres) and is globally acclaimed for its iconic Supertrees, designed by landscape architects Grant Associates.*

49

The case studies presented above illustrate the potency of rotating our perspective from Portrait to Landscape, recognising the interconnectedness of the community of life and unlocking nature's intelligence to restore and rejuvenate landscapes at all scales and in every location.

Soil, water, air. Life's source, blood, and breath. All life is contingent on these three things. If we can get our relationship to these things right, everything else will fall into place, including the healing capacity of plants, animals, and entire ecosystems.

The Community of Life

Unfortunately, our current approach to human development is often self-centred and exploitative, overlooking the wondrous context of life. Economic growth takes precedence, while the needs of other life forms and the health of our environment are neglected. We must reframe our perspective and consider the built environment, urban life, agriculture, and wilderness areas through the lens of depleted soils, polluted waters, declining plants, and suffering animals. How often are other life forms considered in plans for growth and development? How often is the built environment seen through the eyes of the land? How often do we listen to the wisdom of nature?

Nature's voice must be heard. Rather than asking what society can extract from nature, let's ask what society can contribute to nature. Instead of viewing nature as a commodity to be exploited, we need to adopt a mindset where nature is seen as our extended community to be loved and cared for. A mutually beneficial relationship with nature allows both humanity and the natural world to thrive. This requires a paradigm shift and ecological reparations. Imagine the possibilities if we embrace a caring and inclusive community mindset that values the well-being of all life.

The book's final section outlines a transformative journey, redefining our relationship with the earth and its promise of abundant life. It bridges the awakening of an eco-consciousness to the deliberate cultivation of landscapes worldwide. This vision calls upon individuals from diverse sectors and backgrounds—government officials, landowners, planners and designers, educators, students, and everyday individuals—to collaborate in bringing this vision to life. Topics such as investment, legislation, landscape-led development, education reform, and raising a skilled workforce of stewards are explored, providing practical guidance for implementing a Portrait to Landscape approach in our daily lives.

This transition from a self-centred worldview to a community-focused perspective signifies a profound awakening and unwavering commitment to the planet's recovery. The framework presented in this book provides a clear and actionable pathway towards a more integrated and authentic coexistence, guiding us to heal our landscapes and forge a better future for all. By addressing the symptoms and root causes of our world's ailments, including our broken relationship with the land and nature, we lay a solid foundation for the bountiful rejuvenation of our earth.

PART IV

Key Moves

10

True Investment
EXTRACTION TO REPARATION

"Land is power, land is wealth, and, more importantly, land is about race and class. The relationship to land—who owns it, who works it and who cares for it—reflects obscene levels of inequality and legacies of colonialism and white supremacy." [1]

—*Nick Estes*

THE GLOBAL EXCHANGE and investment in land involve vast sums of money. However, for those in positions of power and privilege, such as global corporations, billionaires, and colonialists, land is often viewed merely as real estate, property, and a commodity. Their focus is evidently on maximising financial gains through land ownership and control of natural resources, while giving little back to the land. This narrow and self-centred approach is inherently unsustainable.

To strive towards a more beautiful future, humanity needs to ask different questions and seek better answers. The world's powerful must radically rethink their mindset and replace the question of extracting from nature for short-term profits with one that focuses on supporting nature and repairing planetary health and stability in the long-term. Citizens have a role to play in encouraging leaders and elites to adopt this reorientation, especially within the established domain of economics.

Innovative models, like Kate Raworth's *Doughnut Economics*, offer a holistic approach that situates economic growth within a sphere of environmental and social responsibilities.

This chapter explores top-down measures necessary to bring economic activity within safe planetary limits. It argues that those who have disproportionately benefitted from land ownership and the exploitation of natural resources should bear the responsibility of investing heavily in nature's recovery.

Without enforcing reparations, world leaders will struggle to fulfil their promises to address climate change, halt ecological decline, and achieve the United Nations' sustainability targets. It is the collective responsibility of citizens to raise their voices, elect leaders who prioritise the earth's wellness, support governments in making necessary changes, and utilise their consumer buying power to drive positive change.

A critical first step in this process is understanding who owns the land. By shedding light on land ownership patterns and disparities, we can uncover the imbalances and inequities that perpetuate unsustainable practices.

Who Owns the Land?

"Meet Farmer Bill: America's Leading Farmland Owner," reads the headline on *The Land Report*'s winter 2020 issue.[2] Billionaire, technocrat, software developer, business magnate, but farmer? No way. Bill Gates knows nothing of farming and cultivating the land, yet he is hoovering up farms in a massive land grab, now making him the most prominent private farmland owner in the United States. In total, Gates has accumulated over 108,000 hectares (267,000 acres) of land, including almost 100,000 hectares (247,100 acres) of farmland, diversified in over nineteen states, in less than a decade.

Nick Estes, a citizen of the Lower Brule Sioux Tribe and

Professor of American Studies, has written an article called, "Bill Gates is the biggest private owner of farmland in the United States. Why?" In it, Estes notes that Gates' landholdings are "twice the acreage of the Lower Brule Sioux Tribe, where I'm an enrolled member. A white man owns more farmland than my entire nation!"[3] Gates isn't the only billionaire with vast landholdings. Other individuals, including Amazon CEO Jeff Bezos, CNN founder Ted Turner, and Liberty Media chair John Malone are all in the game, fast becoming the world's largest landowners.[4] For these men with billions to invest, it's a no-brainer.

Surprisingly, it is not unusual for one man to own as much land as an entire nation. For circa 10,000 years, land ownership has been concentrated with the top 1 percent of society. Land ownership has always defined the wealthy. It is not distributed fairly but is held in the hands of a few. Land, not cash, is the most common characteristic of wealth worldwide.[5]

Guy Shrubsole, researcher and campaigner, introduces his book *Who Owns England* by noting, "Who owns land matters. How landowners use their land has implications for almost everything: where we build our homes, how we grow our food, how much space we leave for nature."[6] Let's not fool ourselves into believing that most landowners hold dear the type of land ethic that Aldo Leopold promoted. These powerful landowners typically have little closeness to or care for their land. Far too many abuse their landholdings with greed and short-term profits in mind, despoiling habitats and wiping out wildlife in exchange for profitable extractive and exploitative processes, including industrial agriculture, deforestation, mining, and other damaging processes and infrastructures.

The ethical management of land, and its fair use and enjoyment, is far from the current state of things, but it's a concept fundamental to securing an improved quality of life for all. Shrubsole reminds us, "Talking about land ownership has been taboo for far too long. Raise it in public debate, and sooner or later you're accused of the "politics of envy," for asking questions about how we might best use and share out our most scarce common resource. But it's not a sign of envy. It should just be common sense."[7] So let's talk about it here.

While researching this book, I was shocked to discover that most countries have never recovered from feudalism and mediaeval forms of land ownership. This structure reigns in countries including the UK, Canada, and Australia. India has been notably disturbed by the ravages of this system. Yet, unbelievably, more than 85 percent of the world's population is still subject to feudal control.[8]

The most significant legal landowner is the Family of King Charles III, who owns a staggering 1/6 of the planet's land. Anyone who thinks they "own" land in the Crown's territories is actually a tenant of the British monarch. Two-thirds of Antarctica and over 90 percent of Canada remain in their portfolio. Throughout most of human history, 3 percent of the population—kings, queens, aristocrats, and religions—has owned land, while the remaining 97 percent own nothing.[9] And let's not forget that most of these espouse an archaic patriarchal system, passing land from male heir to male heir. Women have little ownership of the world's habitable land.

Just how much land is available globally? Let's look at the numbers. The world's ocean covers approximately 71 percent of the earth's surface, leaving 29 percent land cover. In absolute numbers, this equates to circa 50 billion hectares (124 billion acres) of total surface area, with 15 billion hectares (37 billion acres) of that being land.[10] To indicate size, in the UK, a typical football pitch takes up about one acre, which is slightly smaller than an average American football field of 1.2 acres.[11] That's circa 1.6 hectares (4 acres) for every person on the planet when calculated using 2050 population estimates. If only it were as equitable as that.

The eight wealthiest individuals globally, all men, own as much as the poorest half of humanity. Since 2020, the world's richest 1 percent have accumulated almost twice as much new money as the rest of the global population combined,[12] and are responsible for twice as many emissions as the poorest 50 percent.[13]

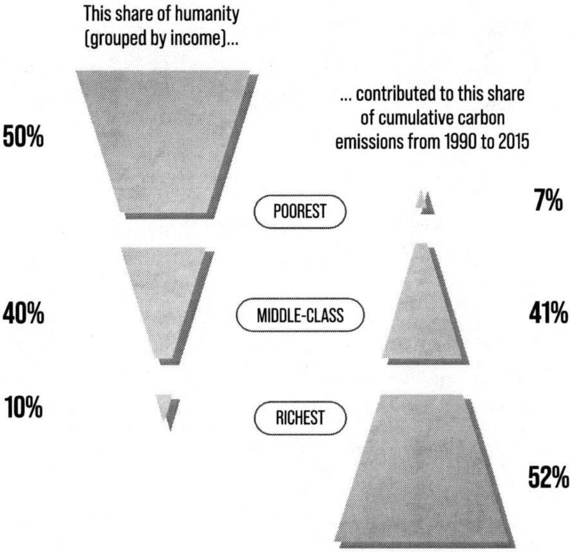

Figure 10.1 *– The Wealth Pyramid: A striking portrayal of global wealth distribution, highlighting the profound extent of financial inequality worldwide. The majority of this wealth is concentrated in land assets (© Alexandra Steed URBAN).*

14

A recent Oxfam study found globally, the top 1 percent of fortunes soared USD 26 trillion (63 percent) of all new wealth since 2019, while USD 16 trillion (37 percent) went to the rest of humanity.[15] Daily, this amount equates to billionaire wealth increasing by USD 2.7 billion, while the wealth of the bottom half of humanity drops by USD 500 million.[16] Women and children suffer the most. Much of this expansion in wealth is due to soaring land values, with approximately two-thirds of the world's global wealth now locked up in land.[17] The land grab of the rich is on the back of the poor's dispossession.

The intrinsic value of land is undeniable, and it remains the most valuable and life-sustaining resource. However, this precious and fragile resource has been subjected to years of exploitation by greedy landowners, including corporate giants, billionaires, and powerful individuals who have profited greatly without taking responsibility for its long-term care. Their actions have caused planetary devastation, yet they continue to engage in degrading practices without facing the consequences. It is clear that relying on their voluntary change is insufficient, and they must be held accountable.

To address this issue, citizens worldwide must become advocates for the preservation of nature and actively elect politicians who share this commitment. Governments have a significant role to play by enacting legislation and implementing policies that swiftly shift away from harmful colonial extraction and exploitation of land towards regenerative practices. Additionally, those who possess large landholdings must take the initiative to invest in and give back to the land, recognising that proper investment should never involve the destruction of the very resource that sustains life. Failing to take these actions promptly risks pushing the earth beyond its tipping point, making it increasingly difficult to restore a state of equilibrium.

In tackling the monumental challenges facing our planet, it is essential to consider and engage in discussions surrounding three key measures that require significant government efforts. These measures serve as catalysts for addressing pressing environmental concerns and should encourage debate on the most effective strategies to safeguard the future of our planet.

1. Enforce Taxation of Large Landowners

Hefty upfront investments are imperative to transform the world's landscapes sustainably. Despite the availability of funds, the wealthiest individuals, multinational corporations, and colonial powers retain vast fortunes derived from land values and resource exploitation, evading their fair share of taxes and dodging responsibility for the ecological devastation caused by their actions. Governments must take action by collecting rightful taxes from the top one percent, compensating those most affected by loss and damages, and redirecting budgets towards sustainable land investments instead of subsidising destructive practices.

World leaders avoid the topic of taxing the wealthy even more than the topic of land ownership. This evasion can no longer persist. Overcoming the world's crises is unlikely unless governments commit to equitable taxation. The pervasive use of tax havens by international billionaires to dodge taxes and safeguard their immense wealth must be directly confronted. Yet few governments are willing to address the issue.

Money stored offshore in tax havens equates to approximately 10 percent of global GDP. Multinational corporations stash a further USD 500 billion annually in tax-free jurisdictions, with the most serious losses presented to low and lower-middle-income countries.[18] The world's ultra-wealthy are well aware that investing in land enables them to avoid capital gains and inheritance taxes while also presenting an opportunity to achieve carbon-neutral goals and offset their substantial corporate emissions.[19] Buying up land has proven to be another way for the billionaire class to avoid paying taxes and accumulate even more wealth.

Why is no one talking about this? Even at the World Economic Forum in Davos, Switzerland, a meeting convened for government, big business, and civil society to discuss world crises and priorities for the year ahead, the subject of taxes is conveniently overlooked. Oxfam Director Gabriela Bucher does not back away from the challenge. She explains, "Taxing the super-rich and big corporations is the door out of today's overlapping crises. It's time we demolish the convenient myth that tax cuts for the richest result in their wealth somehow 'trickling down' to everyone else. Forty years of tax cuts for the super-rich have shown that a rising tide doesn't lift all ships—just the superyachts."[20]

Decades of tax evasion by the most prosperous, enabled by world governments, have led to grave inequalities. The poorest individuals regularly pay a higher percentage in taxes than billionaires. For example, the Oxfam report "Survival of the Richest" notes that Elon Musk paid about a 3 percent actual tax rate between 2014 and 2018, while Jeff Bezos paid less than 1 percent.[21] The report compares their tax rate to that of a Ugandan market trader, Aber Christine, who spends 40 percent of her profits on tax. It goes on to note that in the last forty years, tax rates for the wealthy have been slashed in countries from Africa to Asia and the Americas. The goods and services tax increase fell disproportionately on the poorest individuals in the same period.[22]

Instead of pouring billions into rocket launches to Mars, we should first sort out the damage we've caused on our earth. If only more billionaires would follow the footsteps of those like Patagonia's founder Yvon Chouinard who, rather than engaging in land exploitation or contributing to space pollution, is giving away all company profits to fight climate change and invest in natural recovery. He says, "Instead of extracting value from nature and transforming it into wealth for investors, we'll use the wealth Patagonia creates to protect the source of all wealth."[23] Investing wealth gained from nature back into the land sounds precisely like the common sense needed today.

Along with collecting taxes due, international governments could impose a wealth tax. The analysis provided by the Fight Inequality Alliance, Institute for Policy Studies, Oxfam and the Patriotic Millionaires has found "an annual wealth tax of up to 5 percent on the world's multi-millionaires and billionaires could raise $1.7 trillion a year, enough to lift two billion people out of poverty, fully fund the shortfalls on existing humanitarian appeals, deliver a ten-year plan to end hunger, support poorer countries being ravaged by climate impacts, and deliver universal healthcare and social protection for everyone living in low- and lower middle-income countries."[24] A tax of 5 percent is a modest fee considering the highly detrimental consequences of the super-rich's actions on the environment and biodiversity.

Isn't it time for our world's governments to prioritise their constituents over hobnobbing with billionaires and focus on establishing fair and enforceable tax systems? Too many ultra-powerful individuals and corporations escape accountability and responsibility for their actions, profiting from rising land values and natural resources without shouldering any cost. Just imagine the possibilities if even a fraction of their accumulated wealth was reinvested in the land to combat climate change, ecological decline, and pave the way for a sustainable future.

2. Unlock Funds to Pay for Loss and Damages

As outlined in Chapter 2, the world's wealthiest have contributed most to the global crisis, and thus they should be held accountable for compensating developing nations that endure the harshest effects. These impacts manifest as rising sea levels, prolonged heatwaves, desertification, species extinction, and crop failures, escalating in severity and frequency.[25] For example, the African continent is least responsible for climate change yet is most vulnerable to its impacts. Why should countries and continents like Africa, which have contributed little to climate change and ecological collapse, be responsible for cleaning up the mess of the worst perpetrators?

Establishing a Damage and Loss Fund was a key topic of COP27, but questions remain about quickly getting it off the ground. Total damages caused by climate change could cost developing countries $290-580 billion by 2030 and exceed $1 trillion by 2050.[26] An idea to unlock the resources of global financial institutions (such as the World Bank, International Monetary Fund and African Development Bank) was raised at the climate conference to transform the world's ability to finance climate action and nature restoration.[27] At the meeting, there was a collective call from countries worldwide for these banks to scale up funding to tackle the climate crisis. The Bridgetown Initiative, created by Barbados Prime Minister Mia Mottley, calls for special drawing rights for developing nations. The proposal is to unlock these funds for climate mitigation and reconstruction after a climate disaster.[28] Harnessing the trillions tied up in these banks is a significant way to meet rising needs quickly.

The UN Secretary-General António Guterres insists that corporate polluters must pay. He urges the enforcement of windfall taxes on fossil fuel companies that continue to rake in profits while wrecking the planet.[29] One report found that Europe's five biggest oil majors are responsible for a whopping $13tn (£11.5tn) of damage in the past thirty years, with considerable costs to society, including pollution, carbon emissions, and deteriorating public health, while simultaneously benefitting from massive profits.[30] If these gigantic fossil fuel companies were held accountable for their emissions, they could be legally obligated to pay an annual sum into a polluters-pay climate fund for affected developing countries.[31]

Without imposing financial accountability on giant corporate polluters for the consequences of their damaging actions, it is improbable that they will cease polluting. Consequently, the planet will remain under constant pressure, lacking the ability to initiate a meaningful recovery.

3. Channel Government Budgets into Reversing Climate Change and Restoring Nature

It is disheartening that even now, in the throes of a planetary catastrophe, a significant portion of global GDP continues to subsidise destructive land use, with minimal investment directed towards reversing climate change and ecological decline. Governments must take immediate action to cease funding the fossil fuel industry and redirect budgets towards clean, restorative practices, technologies, and infrastructures.

Let's consider how much this would take. Yuval Harari, Itzik Yahav, and their team at Sapienship have already done the work. Their research on "The Actual Cost of Preventing Climate Breakdown" found that we are talking about increasing investment by a mere 2 percent or approximately USD 1.7 trillion—interesting to note that this is the exact figure quoted by Oxfam, that a meagre 5 percent wealth tax could achieve.[32] Many green jobs and other economic opportunities would be created, not to mention the huge savings made in health care by reducing air pollution, among other benefits. Governments could finance wide-scale change for a relatively low price tag by redirecting current investment from degenerative into regenerative land uses, especially agriculture and forestry.

Sapienship reminds us that politicians are skilful at reallocating resources swiftly. It is not difficult for governments to move budgets around. "They do it all the time."[33] For example, in 1945, the US government moved 36 percent of its GDP into winning the war. During the economic crisis 2008, the US government shifted 3.5 percent to save large financial institutions from collapse.[34] In 2020, 14 percent of global GDP was levied to deal with the COVID-19 epidemic.[35] Harari and his team have also determined that a one-off payment of approximately USD 800 billion, or 1 percent of GDP, would be enough to protect the Amazon Rainforest.[36] But rather than investing wisely, governments still spend an equivalent amount annually on direct subsidies for fossil fuels.[37]

You can exercise your voice as a responsible citizen to vote into office politicians who understand the gravity of environmental challenges. You can hold them accountable to shift these small percentages of GDP to prevent climate change and to save biodiversity. Participating in protests, rallies, and petitions can also make a difference in demanding that governments prioritise the right areas of investment.[38] Additionally, as a consumer, you can speak with your purse and choose to support companies that espouse sustainable techniques and processes.

However, further public debate is needed to catalyse definitive actions from the highest levels of society. This chapter underscores the importance of policymakers and governments redirecting investment and elevating the pursuit of landscape reparations. This includes enforcing taxation on large landowners, allocating funds to compensate nations facing the most severe damages, discontinuing subsidies for polluting corporate giants, and reallocating government budgets towards regenerative and sustainable infrastructures. It is time to evolve from a mentality of exploiting the land to one of giving back to our most precious resource, the earth.

As a generation of people, will we invest in things that matter? The land—soils, water and air—is fragile and finite. The earth sustains us, and it is our responsibility to alleviate the extraordinary pressures we have placed upon it. By genuinely investing in long-term landscape cultivation and adopting humble governance and management of human behaviours within it, we have the potential to create a tremendously beneficial impact.

11

Humble Governance

DOMINATION TO COLLABORATION

"You are not Atlas carrying the world on your shoulder. It is good to remember that the planet is carrying you." [1]

—*Vandana Shiva*

THE EARTH IS generous to us, sharing with us abundant gifts—nourishing food, pure water, fresh air, and incomparable beauty. Unfortunately, we often take these life-sustaining blessings for granted. The prevailing economic systems, driven by globalisation and corporate capitalism, rooted in a history of colonialism and Western ideologies, have trapped many within a paradigm of division and domination. Trapped in this worldview, it becomes impossible to be responsible stewards of the planet or good caretakers of the earth community. Let us not forget the wisdom of Einstein, who urged us to liberate ourselves from a delusion of separateness by embracing all living creatures and the whole of nature.[2]

Caring for the living world and managing our actions within it is our highest calling as humanity—not as masters of creation, but as attentive custodians and benefactors. If we ground ourselves in humility and integrity, we can transcend the confines of a narrow worldview and expand human consciousness to embrace the interconnected web of life.

We need not reinvent the wheel to forge a new path forward. Aldo Leopold's land ethic and Vandana Shiva's Earth Democracy, as discussed in Chapter 3, along with other ecocentric philosophies, offer comprehensive and collaborative models for responsible governance. By embedding nature-centred values into national legislation, we can refocus our governance structures toward wisdom, cooperation, and compassion for all life.

This chapter highlights two overarching and significant measures that will set us on a revolutionary trajectory. The first is protecting, recovering, and enhancing vast wilderness areas worldwide. The second is regenerating extensive agricultural landscapes, bolstered by robust incentives, guidelines, and management plans to ensure their sustainable upkeep. As citizens of the earth, we are all connected and, therefore, all responsible for implementing just and compassionate governance, creating a world where peace, justice, and sustainability prevail. It becomes evident that while governments play a central role, the active involvement of communities and individuals like yourself is indispensable for the successful implementation of integrated governance.

Protect Wilderness

Most of nature has no voice or rights concerning its governance or protection. Therefore, humanity, who can speak, has a duty to act on the living world's behalf. Several individuals, communities, and organisations are doing just that. Shiva and other members of the Global Alliance for the Rights of Nature (GARN)—a global network of organisations and individuals committed to the universal adoption and implementation of legal systems that recognise, respect, and enforce the "Rights of Nature"—have enshrined the concept of Earth Democracy within the Universal Declaration of the Rights of Mother Earth.[3] They explain that, "natural communities have the right to exist, maintain, and regenerate their vital cycles."[4]

***Figure 11.1** – Assembly of the Earth: This captivating illustration depicts the profound concept of nature's rights as protected by constitutional law. Drawing inspiration from* Parliament of Plants, *by Studio Céline Baumann (© Alexandra Steed URBAN).*

[5]

GARN understand a top-down and ground-up approach is required. They have united a wide array of individuals and groups who all bring something valuable to the table. "Our members are a diverse network of scientists, attorneys, economists, indigenous leaders, authors, spiritual leaders, business leaders, politicians, actors, homemakers, students, activists: people from all walks of life who are looking to transform our human relationship with our planet."[6]

The declaration is a first step towards establishing nature's sovereignty. More work is required to bring it into the international rule of law. They say, "An essential step in achieving this is to create a system of jurisprudence that sees and treats nature as a fundamental, rights-bearing entity and not as mere property to be exploited at will."[7] The full declaration is included in this book's Appendix.

Establishing universal rights for nature will take considerable effort and, as GARN understands, require the involvement of everyone. While this endeavour may take time, governments can take immediate action with the support of citizens by making significant investments in nature conservation and stewardship. This involves designating vast areas of wilderness for protection and restoration, accompanied by the enactment of robust legislation and policies that ensure sustainable management practices and effectively curb destructive land use.

Given the current state of affairs, it is evident that stewardship cannot be expected to naturally emerge among most landowners. However, valuable lessons can be learned from Indigenous Peoples who, when not disrupted by colonial forces, have safeguarded their lands for millennia. Notably, reputable conservation organisations committed to long-term nature conservation provide commendable frameworks for managing and protecting wilderness areas. By integrating the wisdom of these traditional practices and establishing effective governance structures, great strides towards restorative landscape management can be made at a meaningful scale.

Even if you are not directly involved, it is essential to stay informed about the necessary actions and lend support to those actively engaged in this vital cause. The following pages outline the essential measures required to advance these goals and ensure a sustainable future for our planet.

1. Conserve 50 Percent of the Earth's Land and Seas

The world's leading conservation organisations have reached a consensus that designating 50 percent of land and seas as protected areas, free from human disturbances, is necessary. This ambitious goal, as discussed in Chapter 1, reflects the pioneering work of Aldo Leopold, who successfully advocated for the legal protection of the Gila Wilderness in New Mexico, making it the world's first designated wilderness.[8] Leopold's visionary understanding of the importance of wilderness protection has proven to be incredibly prescient. Today, approximately 13 percent of the United States is designated as protected land.[9]

According to the International Union for Conservation of Nature (IUCN), the leading global authority on nature conservation, nearly 17 percent of land areas, 15 percent of freshwater, and 7 percent of oceans are currently protected.[10] The international community has made significant progress on protected area coverage. Still, one-third of key biodiversity areas lack any form of protection.[11] Moreover, the quality of protection and restoration provided falls short. More needs to be done.

In pursuit of the ambitious goal of protecting 50 percent of all land and seas, the "Joint Statement on Post-2020 Global Biodiversity Framework" has set out a "New Deal for Nature and People" that was subsequently agreed upon at COP15. This agreement sets a target to safeguard 30 percent of the planet's areas for nature by 2030. The statement asserts:

> "The Deal must integrate seamlessly with the Sustainable Development Goals and the Paris Agreement. Using 2018 as a baseline year, it must prevent extinctions, reverse the decline of species populations; stabilise or increase natural ecosystems and habitats and their services—while restoring degraded lands. Protected and conserved areas must focus on those areas important for biodiversity, including species richness, Key Biodiversity Areas, Ecologically or Biologically Significant Areas, intact ecosystems and ecosystem services including climate mitigation through carbon sequestration. To meet this vision, the entire planet must be managed sustainably, supported by truly sustainable production and consumption, a circular economy, and the sustainable and equitable sharing of benefits from nature."[12]

The IUCN offers invaluable guidance on the identification, protection, restoration, and management of natural landscapes. Through collaborations with communities, organisations, and governments, they play a vital role in developing effective strategies. Central to their approach is a clear understanding of what constitutes a protected area. According to the IUCN, a protected area is "A clearly defined geographical space, recognised, dedicated and managed, through legal or other effective means, to achieve the long-term conservation of nature with associated ecosystem services and cultural values."[13]

The IUCN has classified protected areas into six distinct categories based on their management objectives. It is important to recognise that while each nature site is unique, they all warrant protection measures, stringent development controls, and restoration programs. The table below outlines the six types of protected areas as defined by the IUCN.

IUCN Category	Definition	Primary Objective
Ia: Strict nature reserve	Strictly protected areas set aside to protect biodiversity and also possibly geological/geomorphological features, where human visitation, use and impacts are strictly controlled and limited to ensure protection of the conservation values. Such protected areas can serve as indispensable reference areas for scientific research and monitoring.	To conserve regionally, nationally or globally outstanding ecosystems, species (occurrences or aggregations) and/ or geodiversity features: these attributes will have been formed mostly or entirely by non-human forces and will be degraded or destroyed when subjected to all but very light human impact.
Ib: Wilderness area	Usually large unmodified or slightly modified areas, retaining their natural character and influence, without permanent or significant human habitation, which are protected and managed so as to preserve their natural condition.	To protect the long-term ecological integrity of natural areas that are undisturbed by significant human activity, free of modern infrastructure and where natural forces and processes predominate, so that current and future generations have the opportunity to experience such areas.
II: National park	Large natural or near natural areas set aside to protect large-scale ecological processes, along with the complement of species and ecosystems characteristic of the area, which also provide a foundation for environmentally and culturally compatible spiritual, scientific, educational, recreational and visitor opportunities.	To protect natural biodiversity along with its underlying ecological structure and supporting environmental processes, and to promote education and recreation.
III: Natural monument or feature	Areas set aside to protect a specific natural monument, which can be a landform, sea mount, submarine cavern, geological feature such as a cave or even a living feature such as an ancient grove. They are generally quite small protected areas and often have high visitor value.	To protect specific outstanding natural features and their associated biodiversity and habitats.
IV: Habitat/ species management area	Areas that aim to protect particular species or habitats and management reflects this priority. Many category IV protected areas will need regular, active interventions to address the requirements of particular species or to maintain habitats, but this is not a requirement of the category.	To maintain, conserve and restore species and habitats.
V: Protected landscape/ seascape	Where the interaction of people and nature over time has produced an area of distinct character with significant ecological, biological, cultural and scenic value: and where safeguarding the integrity of this interaction is vital to protecting and sustaining the area and its associated nature conservation and other values.	To protect and sustain important landscapes/ seascapes and the associated nature conservation and other values created by interactions with humans through traditional management practices.
VI: Protected area with sustainable use of natural resources	These areas conserve ecosystems and habitats, together with associated cultural values and traditional natural resource management systems. They are generally large, with most of the area in a natural condition, where a proportion is under sustainable natural resource management and where low-level non-industrial use of natural resources compatible with nature conservation is seen as one of the main aims.	To protect natural ecosystems and use natural resources sustainably, when conservation and sustainable use can be mutually beneficial.

Table 11.1 *– International Union for Conservation of Nature (IUCN) Protected Area Categories.*

14

While there are now significant pockets of protected nature areas, they often face fragmentation due to urbanisation and industrialisation, hindering species migration. However, extensive research on wildlife and ecosystem health has underscored the critical importance of connectivity. It is essential to facilitate the movement of species between highly biodiverse sites that often span political boundaries. Nature disregards arbitrary borders, making it crucial to incorporate cross-border approaches and foster collaboration among neighbouring communities and governments as integral parts of conservation strategies. This recognition of the fluidity of natural systems and processes should be encouraged and supported by raising awareness among elected officials and advocating for their inclusion in strategic plans. Furthermore, individuals may be inspired to join community-led movements or support environmental charities spearheading such initiatives.

It is noteworthy that many nature sites have been protected not only by governmental entities but also by communities, indigenous peoples, private organisations, and individual landowners. Their contributions to protected area systems can be exceptional. Different governance types are often defined by the entities holding authority and responsibility for the protected areas. The IUCN has provided a helpful breakdown of four governance types, as outlined below: [15]

Governance by government

- Federal or national ministry/agency in charge (e.g., a ministry or park agency)
- Sub-national ministry or municipal government in charge
- Government-delegated management (e.g., an NGO or private operator)

Shared governance

- Collaborative management (various degrees of influence)
- Joint management (pluralist management board)

- Transboundary management (involves two or more governments)

Private governance

- By individual owners; by non-profit organisations (NGOs, universities, cooperatives)
- By for-profit organisations (individuals or corporate)—incentive schemes such as revenues from ecotourism or reduction of levies and taxes often support this type

Governance by indigenous peoples and local communities

- Indigenous peoples' conserved areas and territories
- Community conserved areas—declared and run by local communities

It is now the collective responsibility of governments and individuals to ensure the implementation of these nature protection guidelines set forth by the IUCN. The IUCN has developed a comprehensive range of documents that provide detailed guidance on how to effectively carry out this task. It goes beyond merely identifying areas to be preserved; it entails establishing robust management regimes led by attentive individuals who possess the knowledge and dedication to care for the earth.

Even in urban areas, there are plenty of opportunities to get involved in nature conservation. For example, I worked with a community group called Grove Park Neighbourhood Forum in South London, campaigning to create a nature reserve as part of their Neighbourhood Plan. This area boasts unique ecosystems, including wet woodlands, chalk grasslands, and ancient woods, which require protection and restoration. The community was resolute in saving these landscapes from detrimental development proposals and preserving the land for the enjoyment of present and future generations, as well as for wildlife. Through collaborative efforts, significant progress has already been made towards the preservation of this land. Similar community initiatives are prevalent and always in need of support. You can contribute by donating, volunteering your time and energy, advocating to the government, and informing your neighbours. Importantly, visit nature reserves and bring your children along. Instilling a love for nature from an early age is crucial for raising individuals who care about and nurture the natural world.

Undoubtedly, there is a great deal of work to be done by governments, conservation organisations, landowners, and communities worldwide to protect 50 percent of the earth's land and sea. Even achieving the 30 percent target by 2030, as agreed upon at COP15, would be an extraordinary accomplishment.

2. Empower Indigenous Peoples as Landscape Guardians

The conservation community acknowledges that empowering the leadership of Indigenous Peoples and local communities is paramount if we are to have any hope of achieving the protection targets. Without them, there is little hope of recovering the earth's ecosystems on which life depends.[16] Fortunately, things are moving in the right direction, and the efforts of indigenous peoples, local communities, and private entities are finally receiving recognition for their enduring stewardship of the planet. It is intrinsic to their way of life. Though commonly undervalued and under-reported, these communities contribute tremendously to the future security of people and nature. Indigenous people still manage territories which protect and sustain an extraordinary 80 percent of the planet's biodiversity and a third of global forests. Humanity cannot save our world without them. So much can be learned about living in balance with nature by imitating their respectful relationship with the land.[17]

Geographies worldwide are beginning to embrace indigenous knowledge and leadership in wilderness management. One of these is Canada. An investment of up to CAD 340 million has been announced to support Indigenous leadership in nature conservation. The Canadian Government news release states, "The

Indigenous Guardians and Indigenous Protected and Conserved Areas initiatives recognise the many lessons that can be learned from Indigenous partners when it comes to protecting nature and rely on Indigenous experience and Traditional Knowledge to ensure lands and waters are safeguarded for generations to come."[18] Funding will be used towards Indigenous Protected and Conserved Areas (IPCAs). It is a vital step to safeguarding Canada's lands and waters and plays a central role in conserving 30 percent by 2030.

In the US, some areas are being returned to Native American tribes committed to managing the land with great respect and a familial relationship with the living community.[19] Likewise, the Daintree tropical rainforest in Queensland, northern Australia, has now been handed back to its original custodians. These Eastern Kuku Yalanji people will manage it together with the Queensland government.[20]

Indigenous peoples are now being granted the long-awaited opportunity to have their voices heard. In a historic environmental triumph at the 2021 IUCN Members Assembly, indigenous representatives from over 500 nationalities presented a compelling case for safeguarding 80 percent of the Amazon rainforest by 2025. The overwhelming support received for this proposal marks a significant milestone, setting a ground-breaking example for ecosystem protection and restoration efforts globally. It serves as an inspiration and model for other regions, accentuating the importance of inclusive collaboration and the integration of indigenous wisdom in preserving our natural heritage.[21]

3. Bring Environmental Protection into Legislation

Aside from designating protected nature sites, it is imperative to have clear and enforceable legislation and policies that embed stronger environmental protection into law across all landscapes. This includes the establishment of binding targets for air and water quality, biodiversity conservation, and waste reduction. It is crucial to limit harmful activities while providing financial incentives to promote sustainable practices and processes among landowners and managers.

Although progress in this area remains insufficient, there are encouraging examples of global commitments to environmental preservation. Denmark's green tax reform, implemented in the 1990s, has successfully reduced greenhouse gas emissions by half, with further ambitious targets outlined in its Climate Act.[22] Some countries, such as Belize, Greenland, and Spain, have introduced legislation to ban new gas and oil exploration licenses.[23] Others, including Bhutan, The Gambia, Nepal, and Rwanda, have developed inspiring and innovative forest policies to halt deforestation and ensure sustainable forest management.[24] The UK Environment Act includes legally binding targets on species abundance by 2030.[25]

Most noteworthy is Ireland. The Citizens' Assembly on Biodiversity Loss has called for a referendum to protect biodiversity, potentially enshrining nature rights comparable to human rights within the Irish constitution.[26] Similarly, the country of Aruba is adding the Rights of Nature, as declared by GARN, into its constitution. These pioneering steps could be game-changing, hastening the movement from arrogant and dominant to humble and inclusive governance.

Increasingly, countries around the world are legislating environmental laws and creating new policies to protect nature, some even at a constitutional level. However, every nation still has a long way to go in providing legislation and policy to achieve a sustainable future. Strengthening the environmental rule of law is vital to effectively address the pressing challenges of pollution, biodiversity decline, and climate change.[27]

Regenerate Agricultural Landscapes

Given that nearly half of the world's habitable land is dedicated to agriculture, it is imperative that we pay special attention to its management.[28] Yet, the absence of policies and protection mechanisms, similar to those in place for protected wilderness areas, leaves agricultural lands highly vulnerable. Ironically, food production methods persist as the land's greatest threat, even though farming depends on the healthy functioning of ecosystems to produce food; healthy soils, fresh water, plentiful pollinators and a dependable climate are critical for food security. Indeed, agriculture is shaping the face of the land, the earth's fate, and our species' survival. Similar to the need for wilderness protection, we urgently require legislation and policies to support sustainable agriculture. Harmful industrial farming practices must be abolished, and we must empower small-scale farmers, particularly women, who possess intimate knowledge and love for the land they cultivate. These concepts are further elaborated upon below, organised into three key categories.

1. Halt Subsidies for Harmful Agricultural Practices

It may not come as a surprise that the world's largest private landholdings are primarily dedicated to agriculture. However, what is truly astonishing is that a mere 1 percent of farms own and operate 70 percent of the world's farmland.[29] As a result, a small number of owners and multinational corporations exert control over the majority of habitable land.

Unfortunately, these large agricultural companies, such as Monsanto or Bayer, have little connection to or concern for the well-being of the land they own. The trend has been towards expanding industrial farms, characterised by monocultures and heavy reliance on chemical fertilisers, with fewer sustainably managed small farms. These practices have proven detrimental to biodiversity, pollute and deplete freshwater sources, and contribute to soil erosion. The harmful actions of large private landowners profoundly impact our food systems and land health. Farming is moving in the wrong direction.

While the super-rich hold sway over most farmland, they also receive significant rural subsidies, further exacerbating the concentration of wealth while depleting valuable natural resources. Governments around the world provide substantial subsidies to farmers. The Organisation for Economic Cooperation and Development's (OECD) "Agricultural Policy Monitoring and Evaluation 2020" report found that the fifty-four countries studied allocate over $540 billion annually in total support to the agricultural sector.[30] Alarmingly, almost 90 percent of these global farm subsidies, according to the Food and Agriculture Organization (FAO) of the UN, harm people's health, contribute to the climate crisis, and degrade nature.[31] Moreover, these subsidies disproportionately disadvantage women and smallholder farmers in the sector. The issue of small farms and women farmers deserves special attention and will be addressed in the final point of this chapter.

The report also notes that unhealthy products (like sugar) and intensive greenhouse emission commodities (like beef and dairy farmers) receive the most support worldwide, creating little incentive to promote the growth of healthier and more nutritious foods, such as fruits and vegetables.[32] In essence, the polluters not only evade accountability but are also rewarded for their actions. Without immediate reform, these harmful subsidies will exacerbate the planetary crisis. It is imperative that investments in unsustainable agricultural practices be redirected towards more sustainable alternatives without delay.

As mentioned earlier, you can make a difference through your consumer choices. Opting for unprocessed and non-genetically modified foods helps avoid supporting industries that have ravaged precious ecosystems. Instead, choose locally sourced and sustainably grown food, particularly fruits and vegetables, which are nutritious and cost-effective. By investing a little time in researching and understanding sustainable agriculture, these choices become clearer and more impactful.

2. Develop Legislation and Policies to Support Sustainable Agriculture

The need for a transition to sustainable agriculture has become increasingly urgent in response to a convergence of pressing challenges anticipated in the coming decades. Poverty, hunger, wasteful food production systems, land and freshwater scarcity, soil depletion, pollinator decline, pollution, biodiversity loss, and climate change are all critical issues that require attention—just one of these issues would be overwhelming in itself. Undoubtedly, the world must move towards sustainable agriculture.

Industrial agriculture methods are intensifying the threatened environmental conditions on which food production relies, such as healthy soils, access to fresh water, a variety of pollinators, and stable climates.

Figure 11.2 – *Contrasting Industrial vs Sustainable Agricultural Practices: Widescale industrial agriculture methods wreak havoc on land health. Planting monoculture crops, implementing genetic modification, using chemical fertilisers and pesticides, practicing intensive irrigation, excessive tilling, leaving bare soil, and destroying existing vegetation have devastating effects on ecosystems (© Alexandra Steed URBAN).*

Sustainable agricultural practices and biodiversity conservation are mutually dependent. Adopting practices like crop rotation, embracing biodiversity, planting cover crops and perennials, reducing or eliminating tillage, integrating livestock and crops, and managing entire systems are essential for restoring land health. Governments must develop legislation and policies that facilitate access to sustainable methods for farmers and ensure their effective implementation.

Figure 11.3 – *Sustainable farming restores land health and showcases the compatibility and complementarity of food security and nature conservation (© Alexandra Steed URBAN).*

33

In previous chapters, we explored the concept of sustainable agriculture, which encompasses various names and forms like agroecology, permaculture, regenerative, conservation, organic, natural, or inclusive agriculture. The FAO describes its vision for sustainable food and agriculture as, "a world in which food is nutritious and accessible for everyone and natural resources are managed in a way that maintain ecosystem functions to support current as well as future human needs."[34] Regardless of the terminology used, sustainable agriculture entails non-negotiable characteristics. It can take diverse forms and involves practices such as crop diversification, reduced use of synthetic pesticides and fertilisers, no-tillage, managed grazing, and the preservation of essential and appropriate habitats like wetlands, hedgerows, and meadows.

The FAO has established five fundamental principles of sustainable farming that serve as a basis for developing policies, regulations, strategies, programs, and incentives: [35]

1. Improving resource efficiency
2. Conserving, protecting, and enhancing natural ecosystems
3. Protecting and improving rural livelihoods and social well-being
4. Enhancing the resilience of people, communities, and ecosystems
5. Promoting good governance of natural and human systems

The IUCN also supports sustainable agriculture through its "Sustainable Agriculture and Land Health Initiative" which aims to foster dialogue between the agriculture and nature conservation sectors.[36] The initiative's primary objective is to accelerate the transition to sustainable agriculture that ensures land health and avoids land degradation, water pollution, pollinator decline, and compromised ecosystem services like water supply and climate regulation.

When sustainably managed, agricultural lands can contribute significantly to food security and the target of protecting 30 percent of the planet's land area for nature by 2030. However, despite the evident benefits of sustainable agriculture, the FAO confirms that few countries have implemented substantial reforms to make their agriculture systems healthier, more sustainable, and equitable. Deep and wide change is required.[37]

There are positive transformational examples taking place worldwide that can serve as models for other initiatives. In the European Union, the Common Agricultural Policy (CAP) reform incentivises crop diversification. Farmers receive direct payments for implementing improvements such as growing multiple crops simultaneously for diversification, maintaining grasslands, and establishing forested areas. Reforms also require that 4 percent of farmland be non-productive, including fallow land, with direct payments allocated to eco-schemes such as organic farming.[38] Similarly, in England, the Environmental Land Management scheme (ELMs) is an integral part of the 25-Year Environment Act. ELMs provide economic compensation to farmers in exchange for delivering public environmental goods such as clean air and water, protection from environmental hazards, nature conservation, and climate change adaptation.[39]

The Republic of Korea has introduced subsidies and direct payments to farmers to encourage environmentally friendly farming practices and reduce the use of chemical fertilisers. In China, the Conversion of Cropland to Forest Program (CCFP) was implemented to address soil erosion, desertification, and floods while alleviating poverty. The program has successfully reforested over 28 million hectares of land.[40] The Indian state of Andhra Pradesh has initiated a programme based on traditional farming methods.[41] Small landholders, including poor farmers and women, are critical stakeholders in the process. The scheme preserves ecosystem services and biodiversity on farms, strengthens crop resilience to climate change, improves soil fertility, and enhances incomes.[42]

Indeed, numerous inspiring examples of sustainable land management and agricultural practices exist. Governments worldwide must urgently introduce more environmental legislation and policies concerning farming to drive a profound transformation that ensures food security and nature conservation. Understanding the necessity of sustainable agriculture is essential, even if you are not a farmer, an elected politician, or a public servant. As a consumer, you have agency within the food industry. Choose to support sustainable practices by avoiding processed and modified foods and opting for locally and sustainably grown produce, especially fruits and vegetables. If you have access to a garden, consider cultivating sustainable techniques by growing your own food. If you don't garden, even tending a pot of herbs in the kitchen can be restorative. Such hands-on experience, though small, will help to reconnect you with the system of food production, where food comes from, and to appreciate how nature sustains us.

Industrialised agriculture is changing the shape of the world's landscapes and seriously jeopardising ecosystems and biodiversity. It is imperative to rehabilitate our approach to food production, farmland management, financial incentives, resource distribution, and investment. These changes are vital for healing the earth and securing our future. Also essential to sustained transformation is empowering the knowledge and skills of women.

3. Invest in Small Farms and Women Farmers

Investing in small farms, principally women farmers is vital to eradicating extreme poverty, hunger, and nutrition. Despite the dominance of large industrial farms, around 80 percent of the world's food is still produced by small farms.[43] Women, who account for an average of 43 percent of farmers in developing nations, play a central role in food production, even though they face significant discrimination.[44] They produce generous amounts of food for their families and surrounding communities. Food is life, and investing in and supporting small farmers, especially women, could radically alter the state of things. Therefore, it is essential to channel investments through various sources, including government programs, NGOs, and individual contributions.

Unfortunately, the plight of women worldwide does not receive sufficient support. However, it is widely acknowledged that supporting and enabling women is one of the most important ways to end world hunger and achieve a healthy planet. Women are disproportionately affected by hunger and malnutrition—many cannot own land, access water, have a bank account, take a loan, or contribute to community decision-making. Furthermore, corporate investments in farmland further dispossess women of their land rights, jeopardising their expert knowledge, stewardship of nature, and overall well-being.[45]

FAO Director-General José Graziano da Silva explains, "It's all about opportunity. Evidence shows that when women have opportunities, the yields on their farms increase—also their incomes. Natural resources are better managed. Nutrition is improved. And livelihoods are more secure."[46] Neven Mimica, European Union Commissioner for International Cooperation and Development, echoes this sentiment, highlighting that, "We know that agricultural yields would rise by almost a third if women had the same access to resources as men. As a result, there would be up to 150 million fewer hungry people worldwide. And we know that children have significantly better prospects for the future when their mothers are healthy, wealthy, and educated. Especially during the first 1,000 days of a child's life." He goes on to say, "If we are serious about putting an end to poverty and hunger once and for all, then we all need to step up our support for rural women. As an investment in families, in our communities, in our wider societies, and in our planet's future."[47]

The world is failing to support women. The need for gender equality is prominently featured in the UN's Sustainable Development Goals (SDGs), which are directly related to hunger, malnutrition, and land-related goals.

Of the seventeen SDGs, seven are particularly relevant: No Poverty, Zero Hunger, Gender Equality, Sustainable Cities and Communities, Climate Action, Life Below Water, and Life on Land. However, the SDG Land Tracker analysis reveals that sustainable land management is still not a priority in many countries. This indicates a shortfall in efforts to empower women and achieve gender equality.[48]

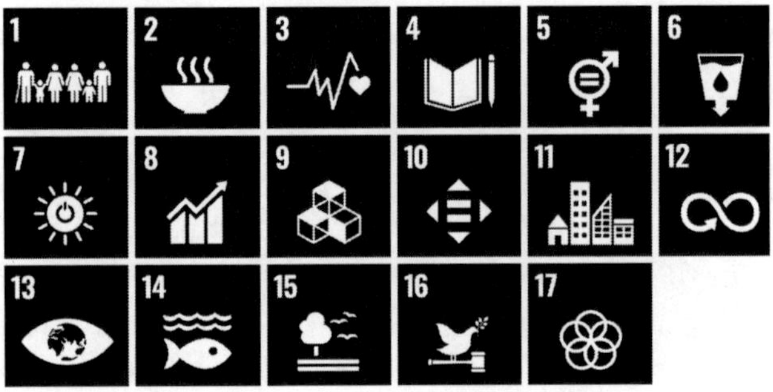

1 NO POVERTY
2 ZERO HUNGER
3 GOOD HEALTH AND WELLBEING
4 QUALITY EDUCATION
5 GENDER EQUALITY
6 CLEAN WATER AND SANITATION
7 AFFORDABLE AND CLEAN ENERGY
8 DECENT WORK AND ECONOMIC GROWTH
9 INDUSTRY, INNOVATION AND INFRASTRUCTURE
10 REDUCED INEQUALITIES
11 SUSTAINABLE CITIES AND COMMUNITIES
12 RESPONSIBLE CONSUMPTION AND PRODUCTION
13 CLIMATE ACTION
14 LIFE BELOW WATER
15 LIFE ON LAND
16 PEACE, JUSTICE AND STRONG INSTITUTIONS
17 PARTNERSHIPS FOR THE GOALS

Figure 11.4 *– The UN's 17 Sustainable Development Goals.*

[49]

The global campaign "Stand for Her Land" aims to consolidate grassroots and national-level efforts to strengthen women's access to land and overcome persistent barriers.[50] It emphasises that land rights are fundamental human rights and highlights the ongoing struggle for equality. Positive advancements have been seen in some regions, such as newly adopted legislation in China that strengthens women's land rights by registering their names on land certificates, ensuring equal rights for male and female household members, and repealing provisions that previously disadvantaged farmers who moved to urban areas.[51] These achievements mark significant victories for women's rights and access to rural land.

Let's look deeper into Vandana Shiva's transformative work in India. She has translated her philosophical concepts of Earth Democracy and the Rights of Nature into a practical farming approach. Motivated by the disastrous effects of industrialisation on Indian agriculture, Shiva sought to find a regenerative alternative.

In the 1980s, the plight of Indian farmers and the alarming rate of suicides caught her attention, compelling her to extensively study the agricultural sector to uncover the underlying causes. Her research revealed that the Green Revolution, which introduced modern farming practices in the 1960s, had undermined India's long-standing agricultural and economic foundations. These practices replaced traditional protective farming policies with toxic chemical fertilisers, pesticides, and genetically modified seeds. As a result, Indian farms and farmers have been experiencing widespread failure, leading to desperation and, tragically, suicide.

In response to this crisis, Shiva established the Navdanya Farm in Dehradun, India, as a women-centred movement dedicated to preserving biodiversity, native seeds, food sovereignty, and the well-being of small farmers.[52] The farm has grown into a forty-seven-acre organic farm, seed bank, and biodiversity research centre. Through practical demonstrations, Shiva and her colleagues embody the vision of Earth Democracy—a place deeply rooted in the earth where ecological responsibility and economic justice are practised in daily life. Women play a vital role in cultivating a liveable future through sustainable and regenerative farming practices.[53] Shiva believes that empowering women is essential to achieve a healthy planet. She says, "We are either going to have a future where women lead the way to make peace with the earth or we are not going to have a human future at all."[54]

Like many other sustainable farming institutions worldwide, Navdanya welcomes the participation of individuals and offers training programs, volunteering opportunities, and relies on donations. They are eager to engage others in their mission. Through her work, Shiva urges a shift in focus from economic systems of food production and commodification to a holistic approach that measures the health and well-being of ecosystems and communities. She critiques the reductionist measure of "yield per acre" and advocates for a comprehensive "health per acre" measurement that prioritises nutrition output while minimising input costs. This paradigm shift recognises that food production should not be solely about total calories produced and consumed.[55]

To address the monumental challenges at hand requires equally significant solutions. The regeneration of regional ecosystems cannot be achieved through quick fixes. Protecting nature is not a luxury and caring for the earth's community with compassion is essential for our future. Sustaining a healthy biosphere involves integrated land, water, and air management, conservation of nature, restoration of biodiversity, soil erosion control, food security, access to clean water, ocean protection, and empowerment of local communities and women. Governance should be guided by principles of diversity and inclusion, drawing on earth-centred and community-focused knowledge systems, as exemplified by Navdanya's Earth Democracy model.

In conclusion, effective governance for the protection, restoration, and long-term stewardship of the biosphere transcends the sole responsibility of the government. It necessitates the active involvement of every individual. By recognising and appreciating that the earth carries us, and not the other way around, we can approach the task of stewardship with humility and a profound sense of responsibility.

The notion of stewardship goes beyond preservation or conservation; it encompasses a holistic perspective that integrates ecological integrity, social equity, and economic viability. By embracing this broader view, we can co-create resilient and sustainable landscapes that support the well-being of both nature and humanity, forging a path towards a future where the earth and its inhabitants thrive in harmony. To achieve this, it is crucial to involve diverse stakeholders, including community organisations, non-governmental organisations, businesses, and academic institutions.

This inclusive approach to stewardship extends beyond rural landscapes and reaches urban and peri-urban environments as well. These densely populated areas, with their distinct challenges and opportunities, necessitate immediate adoption of innovative practices in planning, design, development and management that effectively reconcile human needs with the well-being of the planet.

12

Landscape-Led Development

DEVELOPMENT-DRIVEN TO CONTEXT-INSPIRED

"The world is abundant, we require only a deference born of understanding to fulfil man's promise…He must become the steward of the biosphere. To do this he must design with nature." [1]

—*Ian McHarg*

AMIDST THE EVER-INCREASING demands of burgeoning city populations, there arises an urgent need for a fresh perspective on urban landscapes—one that encompasses the preservation, restoration, and enrichment of nature. It is no longer sufficient for protected landscapes and management practices to be confined solely to rural or wilderness areas; they must seamlessly extend into urban spaces. An innovative landscape-led approach must be enshrined in legislation and integrated into the blueprints of our towns and cities, guiding development, curbing detrimental consequences, and nurturing vibrant, natural communities.

Examination reveals a fundamental flaw in the prevailing development paradigm: a backward process where development takes precedence and landscapes are an afterthought. This pervasive system often goes unquestioned and unnoticed. The following pages propose a radical reset, where development becomes sensitively integrated within the broader landscape, inspired by the context rather than solely driven by human impositions.

The creation of strategic landscape frameworks becomes paramount, where landscapes are considered as integrated wholes rather than fragmented parcels. Recognising that natural systems and processes span vast expanses and rely on connectivity, our plans must evolve to embrace the functioning of landscapes across regional boundaries, linking wilderness and rural areas into suburban and urban domains. The planning approach should foster the integrity and unity of these regional landscapes.

Ultimately, landscape-driven strategic thinking, comprehensive environmental analysis, audacious vision, and steadfast stewardship, will yield not only thriving communities but also the restoration of our planet. By repositioning nature at the forefront and adjusting our focus to the land, an integrated, holistic, and inclusive outcome organically grows.

While this chapter primarily caters to individuals involved in environmental legislation, planning policy, urban design, and development, its relevance extends to all those responsible for land or invested in their community's plans. Strategic planning and the state of the built environment impact everyone's lives, sometimes in profound ways. Hence, each person should be empowered with the knowledge of a landscape-led approach, for it holds the potential to both conceptually and tangibly re-shape our world.

Landscape-Led

Landscape architect and writer Ian McHarg popularised a planning and design method that starts with the land in his 1967 classic book, *Design with Nature*. (His book is mentioned in Chapter 7, regarding the South Essex case study.) In it, he argues that landscape health is imperative and must be understood before any development modifications are made. As a doctor's practice is based on their patient's anatomy, biology, and physiology, McHarg explained how planning and design must be based on a landscape's physical attributes and ecology. Both institutions must have the aim of limiting harm and improving health.

McHarg's landscape-led imperatives are set within a grander vision, "Let us green the earth, restore the earth, heal the earth."[2] He believed understanding and respecting natural processes and systems is fundamental to this vision. He also saw the benefit of conserving the most vital parts of the landscape and providing appropriate development constraints to the less sensitive areas. By following these principles, the damaging impacts of developments are limited. Moreover, when sensitively sited and constructed, buildings and infrastructures are themselves protected from natural hazards.

McHarg's ideas played a critical role in the rising environmental consciousness of the 1960s. *Design With Nature* was published shortly after Rachel Carson's *Silent Spring*. His book was one of few written about the human relationship with the environment. Lewis Mumford, the American historian and literary critic, wrote: "*Design With Nature* is a notable addition to the handful of important texts that begin, at least in Western tradition, with Hippocrates' famous medical work on Airs, Waters and Places: the first public recognition that man's life, in sickness and in health, is bound up with the forces of nature, and that nature, so far from being opposed and conquered, must rather be treated as an ally and friend, whose ways must be understood, and whose counsel must be respected."[3]

McHarg possessed a deep understanding of the interconnectedness of all life and the importance of safeguarding and enhancing the health of landscapes, particularly the vital elements of soil, water, and air, in order to maintain the well-being of our species. Furthermore, he demonstrated remarkable foresight by acknowledging that, "The most important issue of the twenty-first century will be the condition of the global environment."[4] In response to this impending challenge, he advocated for a landscape-led approach to human growth and development.

So much can be learned through McHarg's commitment to starting with the land, designing with nature, and acting as stewards of the biosphere. He was committed because he foresaw the great need for an ecological approach in an era of unprecedented environmental threats.

In the realm of property development, the term "landscape-led" has gained popularity. It is often bandied about to suggest that a particular project has organically grown from its surrounding landscape. However, in reality, this is rarely the case. Developers frequently employ this phrase to cater to environmental concerns without truly embracing its underlying promise.

The dominant focus of land-use planning, development, and management practices remains primarily socioeconomic. Assessments of land revolve around factors such as proximity, connectivity, and cost. Growth predominantly disregards natural processes and values. In the realm of most development endeavours, the living landscape is resisted, overlooked, and isolated. Property boundaries, development parcels, and political divisions often fail to recognise the natural systems on which they are built. Conversely, the living world does not acknowledge human-imposed divisions and boundaries. Traditional property development rarely collaborates with or designs sensitively alongside nature. However, this must change.

It is high time for our planning systems to embrace a nature-based, living infrastructure, landscape-led approach. To achieve sustainable development, the entire community—both human and non-human—must be taken into consideration. This approach holds tremendous possibilities in addressing the challenges posed by climate change, ecological decline, and population growth. Such a transformative shift will enable us to integrate natural systems, the built environment, and social equity. Undoubtedly, adopting a landscape-led approach to growth and development will restore health and balance to our communities and our precious planetary abode.

Design with Nature

Designing with nature is a straightforward and logical concept, although it is often overlooked. It aligns with the overarching design principle outlined in Chapter 9: Design for Life. As you may recall, the proposal suggests that global well-being can be restored by rehabilitating our relationship with the three fundamental elements of the land: soil, water, and air. It's not a complex scientific theory or a lofty philosophical idea; it's mostly just common sense. The key to sustainable planning and development lies within nature itself. We need to seek guidance from the land, plants, and animals on how best to collaborate. Understanding the natural processes and systems within a landscape is necessary. Indigenous cultures have long comprehended their environments and respected their dependence on them for sustenance. Western societies must now learn to pay attention, listen, and engage with the intelligence and life inherent in the land.

Let me be clear—I am not suggesting that nature is simple, uncomplicated, or unsophisticated. Quite the opposite; nature is awe-inspiring, enigmatic, and ultimately beyond complete comprehension. However, humanity possesses sufficient insight and tools to gather a foundational level of understanding about the natural processes within a landscape to guide development. Professionals in disciplines such as ecology, geography, landscape architecture, planning, and engineering, among others, can combine comprehensive site environmental data with the community's local knowledge and historical context to unveil a framework for sustainable development.

Environmental studies are an imperfect science and an evolving field of investigation. Undoubtedly, future research will challenge some of our current assumptions. However, scholars and professionals already possess ample evidence to recognise that partnering with nature fosters the creation of healthy places. We have a firm foundation on which to build. As McHarg posits, "If one accepts the simple proposition that nature is the arena of life and that a modicum of knowledge of her processes is indispensable for survival and rather more for existence, health and delight, it is amazing how many apparently difficult problems present ready resolution."[5] When we take the time to observe natural processes and systems, we not only discover that nature offers pre-existing solutions to guide and support human projects, but that its services are freely provided.

Regrettably, conventional plans often disregard the bountiful offerings of nature. Instead, they rely on heavy-handed, overly engineered, or technological solutions in an attempt to dominate and control natural forces. Yet, this approach is not only inefficient but also futile, a mere joke in the face of nature's power. This point was exemplified in Chapter 9 through the case study of Kongjia Yu's concept of sponge cities. The inadequacy and over-reliance on storm sewer systems were starkly highlighted in that example. As the saying goes, what we resist, persists.

The case of South Essex's polluted wetlands, discussed in Chapter 7, further illustrates this issue. By imposing waste upon wetlands, these absorbent landscapes become filled with toxic substances that seep into the soil, water, and air, contaminating these life-sustaining elements. This devastation not only affects local ecosystems but also diminishes coastal food sources, depletes freshwater supplies, and even harms air quality. Contamination leads to human diseases, including widespread respiratory illnesses. Furthermore, wetlands that once provided protection against coastal storms and flooding have been stripped of their absorptive capacity.

Another prevalent but hazardous practice worldwide that disregards natural systems and jeopardises human well-being is constructing homes on floodplains. Regardless of how well these houses are built, they are inevitably susceptible to flooding and destruction, putting individuals at risk of injury and homelessness. How many times must we witness the tragedies experienced by cities like New Orleans, where engineered flood barriers succumbed to the force of Hurricane Katrina? Similarly, Jakarta, constructed on swampy terrain, has depleted its aquifers and is now sinking. Yet, in numerous locations around the world, developers persist in building on high-risk sites with the blessing of local governments. With a fundamental understanding and integration of landscape conditions, many of these issues could easily be avoided.

When we design with nature, we are also designing for ourselves. By safeguarding natural communities, we are protecting human communities. This fundamental principle holds true now more than ever in a world where the destinies of all species and humanity are inextricably intertwined. When society acknowledges how landscapes function and respects nature's life-sustaining services, we automatically limit harm to human development. Undoubtedly, communities need a deeper understanding of earth's systems to fortify themselves, especially in the face of destabilising climate changes.

Those involved in planning and design must perceive a landscape from the perspective of the land itself. What better way to achieve this than to explore urban life not only through the lens of humans but also through the vantage point of the land, natural systems, and processes? We can view it through the struggles of a tree disconnected from its community, through depleted and chemical-laden soils, through culverted and contaminated rivers, through fragmented plant communities, or even through the eyes of a bird soaring above.

Figure 12.1 *– Urban Design from a Multispecies Perspective: How often do we examine the planning and design of urban environments through the eyes of nature – trees, rivers, soils, plants, animals. For example, by considering the vantage point of a bird soaring through the sky, we gain a fresh outlook on urban development (© Alexandra Steed URBAN).*

6

By adjusting our perspective to consider the life of air, water, soil, plants, and animals, a new model of designing that encompasses the community of life will emerge. Such a landscape-led approach will reveal insights and depths in the fields of planning and development that are often overlooked by conventional methods.

Armed with knowledge of natural processes and systems, we gain clarity on the optimal and most valuable use of specific landscapes. The initial step involves identifying the landscapes that are most vulnerable and in need of protection. Some landscapes are simply too precious to be tampered with, and thus, their preservation must take precedence over all other land uses. Examples include pristine wilderness areas, wetlands, marshes, floodplains, aquifer recharge zones, woodlands, and forests, which must be safeguarded to continue providing their invaluable services. McHarg's book provides a preliminary list of these sensitive landscapes, conveniently summarised in Table 12.1.

Landscape Features		
Name	**Description**	**Compatible Uses**
Surface water and riparian lands	Only land uses that are inseparable from waterfront locations should occupy them; and even these should be limited to those which do not diminish the present or prospective value of surface water for supply, recreation or amenity.	Ports, harbours, marinas, water-treatment plants, water-related industry, open space for institutional and housing use, agriculture, forestry and recreation.
Marshes	In principle, land-use policy for marshes should reflect the roles of flood and water storage, wildlife habitat and fish spawning grounds.	Recreation, certain types of agriculture, isolated urban development.
Floodplains	All development should be excluded save for functions which are unharmed by flooding or for uses that are inseparable from floodplains.	Ports, harbours, marinas, water-treatment plants, water-related and water-using industry, agriculture, forestry, recreation, institutional open space, open space for housing.
Aquifers	All prospective land uses should simply be examined against the degree to which they imperil the aquifer, those which do should be prohibited, for example, development that includes the disposal of toxic wastes, biological discharges or sewage. The use of injection wells, by which pollutants are disposed into aquifers, should be discontinued. Aquifers may be managed effectively by the impoundment of rivers and streams that transect them.	Agriculture, forestry, recreation, industries that do not produce toxic or offensive effluents. All land uses within limits set by percolation.
Aquifer recharge areas	The point of water interchange could potentially be a location where the normally polluted rivers may contaminate the relatively clean - and in many cases pure - water resources in aquifers. These points of interchange are then critical for the management and protection of groundwater resources.	As aquifers
Prime agricultural lands	Prime agricultural soils are uniquely suitable for intense cultivation with no conservation hazards and provide the country's scenic beauty. The protection of all farmland is difficult but the protection of the best soils in a metropolitan area would be desirable.	Agriculture, forestry, recreation, open space for institutions, housing at 1 house per 25 acres.
Steep lands	Steep lands are central to the problems of flood control and erosion. For reasons of erosion, steep slopes should be in forest and not cultivated or developed.	Forestry, recreation, housing at maximum density of 1 house per 3 acres, where wooded.
Forests and woodlands	Forest improves micro climate and it exercises a major balancing effect upon water regimen —diminishing erosion, flood and drought. The scenic role of woodlands is apparent, as is their provision of a habitat for game; their recreational potential is among the highest	Forestry, recreation, water management, wildlife habitats, housing at densities not higher than 1 house per acre.

***Table 12.1** – Table of Land Features and Suitability for Urban Use: Summarised from text within McHarg's* Design With Nature.

7

These invaluable landscapes, which face global threats, possess far greater long-term value when preserved rather than developed. By assessing the suitability of land for different purposes, we can pinpoint locations that are most appropriate for human development, such as urban and industrial areas, agriculture, and recreational spaces. Simultaneously, we can protect sensitive landscapes that harbour unique natural resources, thriving best with minimal human interference.

In addition, it is crucial to safeguard culturally significant landscapes, including heritage areas, archaeological sites, monuments, and more, from detrimental activities. By clearly delineating areas of ecological and cultural significance, governments, planners, and communities can establish a comprehensive guide that identifies landscapes unsuitable for development. However, effective plans should go beyond limiting harm; they should also incorporate strategies for the recovery and enhancement of landscapes, fostering genuinely sustainable environments and restorative communities.

It is pivotal to grasp that sound planning for growth can coexist with the protection and design of dynamic landscapes—these two goals are not mutually exclusive. Nature and culture are not at odds but rather compatible and complementary. What is needed is a well-defined environmental framework for future plans, offering guidance to local authorities and communities, and providing essential guidelines for development.

In the following sections, I present a landscape-led approach to planning, design, and development that can be entrenched in national legislation, regional spatial strategies, local plans, and design guidelines. This approach is designed to achieve the objectives of sustainable and regenerative development, ensuring that landscapes are at the forefront of decision-making processes.

Strategic Landscape Frameworks

Drawing from years of experience and bolstered by robust research, it becomes evident that the implementation of strategic landscape frameworks is imperative for facilitating ecologically sound planning. To this end, the following steps are integral to the process:

1. Comprehensive geographical surveys
2. Baseline analysis and assessment
3. Community collaboration and stakeholder engagement
4. Visioning and setting objectives
5. Strategic framework
6. Planning policy and design guidelines
7. Management strategy

1. Comprehensive Geographical Surveys

A thorough understanding of the land is paramount, conducted through watershed-level or regional-scale surveys to commence the process. This comprehensive assessment maps the interplay of natural processes and systems within the area, encompassing geology, hydrology, and soils. In recognising the intricate interconnectedness of ecosystems, it becomes apparent that random development parcels cannot adequately address their complexity. Hence, taking a holistic and integrated approach often entails traversing political boundaries and development plots to gain a comprehensive view of the land. As the assessment progresses, coordination between landscape plans and local plans, as well as property divisions, becomes essential.

Fortunately, the collection of survey information is no longer arduous. In today's era, the accumulation of environmental data has reached such magnitude that, as Johan Rockstrom asserts, "we have a new consciousness embedded inside the planet."[8] It is imperative for those involved in planning and design to tap into this rich resource. One significant source of information is the wealth of data contained within Geographical Information Systems (GIS), which serves as a comprehensive index of the world, offering valuable location intelligence. By creating, managing, analysing, and mapping diverse data types, GIS seamlessly integrates location data with descriptive information, revealing patterns, relationships, and geographic context.[9] Notably, it was a student of McHarg's who developed GIS, motivated by his proposition to base planning and design on ecological data.[10]

The digital nature of this information offers the advantage of efficient sharing and distribution. Many local authorities now maintain accessible websites housing up-to-date data, facilitating the streamlined capture of baseline information.

2. Baseline Analysis and Assessment

After conducting the surveys, the collected baseline data must undergo assembly, review, and assessment. This analysis includes crucial factors such as heritage and cultural zones, population and community data, existing planning policies and regulations, and proposed development sites. Understanding the overlaps, conflicts, and synergies among this information is a pivotal step.

Decades ago, Professor Mary Jacqueline Tyrwhitt, an expert in City Planning and Landscape Architecture, introduced the "overlay technique" to accomplish precisely this task[11] (with McHarg being one of her students, unsurprisingly).[12] In the 1950 English publication *Town and Country Planning Textbook* the overlay technique is described as a method of layering mapped data on transparent paper at the same scale.[13] By "sieving" the information through this overlay process, essential relationships between distinct features can be discerned. This approach enables the identification of suitable locations for different land uses and specific building types.[14] While the overlaying is now predominantly performed using computer-based GIS programs, the effectiveness of this method remains unchanged.

Despite the wealth of sophisticated information available to us today, it is often not effectively utilised, analysed, or synthesised to inform decisions regarding future land use planning. Society may be information-rich but knowledge-poor in this regard. However, information in the realm of development becomes truly valuable when it is effectively assessed and synthesised.

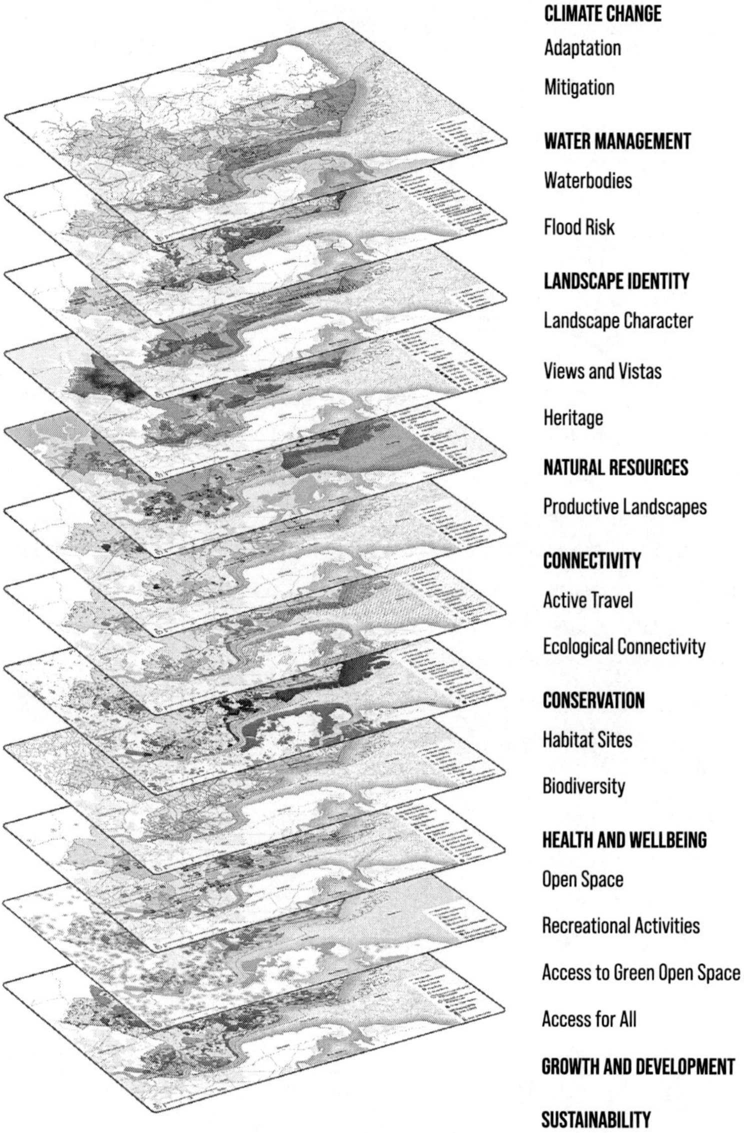

Figure 12.2 *– The Overlay Technique: An example of a digital application of the overlay process for the South Essex Green and Blue Infrastructure Study (© Alexandra Steed URBAN).*

The graphical representation of layered information should not be underestimated. It is almost miraculous how much becomes revealed through visual illustrations that may not be fully understood when confined to words alone. Unfortunately, the baseline drawing process is often not successfully coordinated in the planning process. This detachment from comprehensively viewing the landscape is a significant contributing factor to the inappropriate developments that have wrought devastation upon our landscapes.

3. Community Collaboration and Stakeholder Engagement

Mapping landscapes comes alive through interactive workshops conducted with local community members. By engaging with the people who intimately know and have a deep connection to the land, valuable insights into the beauty and functionality of the landscape are revealed. These workshops involve actively listening, learning, and understanding the community's relationship with the place, capturing their stories and blending their collective experiences with environmental data on physical maps. In doing so, the true essence and character of a place, often referred to as the "genius loci" as beautifully described by Alexander Pope (see Chapter 5), are uncovered.

The symbiotic relationship between community and place is undeniable—they shape one another. To harness the most meaningful ideas from the local community, it is important to ensure engagement with diverse members representing various ages, ethnicities, backgrounds, income levels, and gender identities. Adopting an inclusive approach is essential to prevent bias and promote the well-being of the community. Going beyond traditional consultation methods, actively reaching out to the community through visits to local community centres, schools, and gathering places, as well as leveraging social media platforms, facilitates engagement with a broad cross-section of the community. Throughout this process, it is paramount to listen not only to human voices but also to the voices of the soil, water, air, plants, and animals. By keeping ecological and baseline data readily accessible, and by listening to people who know the land well, nature's perspective is given a voice in the decision-making process.

An exciting pathway forward is empowering the local community to take charge of shaping their own local plans, with the guidance and expertise of skilled professionals (as exemplified by the Grove Park Neighbourhood Plan in Chapter 11). Increasingly, communities are embracing this approach, recognising the untapped potential within their community and striving for outcomes that surpass the limitations of conventional approaches.

4. Visioning and Setting Objectives

The most powerful vision for a place arises from the fusion of people and nature, community and landscape. Without a strong vision, communities lack something meaningful to rally behind, and transformative change becomes unlikely. Conveying plans through tedious technical documents filled with jargon fails to inspire action, ignite the imagination, or instil hope. Strategic plans rely on meaningful visions, co-created with the community and presented in beautiful illustrations. This inspired approach sparks enthusiasm, instils hope for the future, and provides a shared aspiration to strive for.

An authentic vision for a place must grow organically from its specific landscape; it cannot be imposed. Again, Alexander Pope's wisdom resonates: "all must be adapted to the genius and use of the place, and the beauties not forced into it, but resulting from it."[16] By combining a profound understanding of a landscape's distinct physical qualities, natural processes, and cultural history, creative possibilities for its transformation come to light.

Vitruvius Pollio, the ancient Roman architect of the first century BC, aptly identified the three pillars of harmonious design: *firmitas, utilitas, and venustas.*[17] These elements represent the land's suitability, functionality for the community, and beauty in design. As recognised by Alexander Pope and the English Landscape Movement, great beauty, purpose, and productivity are interwoven. Authentic and harmonious places for the entire community emerge when a landscape's unique attributes are acknowledged, respected, and further enhanced in the planning and design process.

Figure 12.3 *– A Place-Specific Vision: Inspired visions grow out of the community. They harmoniously bring together strength, utility and beauty. This visualisation was prepared as part of the visioning exercise for the South Essex Green and Blue Infrastructure Study, described in Chapter 7 (© Alexandra Steed URBAN).*

18

A true vision emerges when a landscape embraces the diverse community members and enables each to synergistically contribute in their unique way, much like a symphony composed of different instruments and parts. It is in this orchestration that a masterpiece unfolds, reflecting the beauty and power of collaboration. This is the essence of a genuine vision.

A set of objectives should be established to ensure the realisation of the vision and to guide future planning and design. These objectives should be derived from the baseline assessment and combined with the insights gathered from the community. This integration ensures that the design principles and objectives are firmly rooted in the unique characteristics of the landscape.

To illustrate this concept, let's consider an example of how themes and objectives could be established for a specific community. The chosen themes are derived from the existing landscape, while the objectives outline how the design will enhance and enrich each theme. Together, they significantly contribute to the overall sustainability of the scheme. These are not intended to be prescriptive and may not be applicable in all situations. However, they serve to demonstrate how well-defined objectives can support a vision. As the planning and design process unfolds, the team can refer to mutually agreed-upon objectives to maintain focus and alignment with the vision.

Theme	Objective
Climate change	Establish a resilient infrastructure
Water management	Work with hydrological systems
Landscape identity	Celebrate a sense of place
Natural resources	Support natural resource productivity
Connectivity	Improve connectivity
Conservation	Protect and enhance biodiversity
Health and wellbeing	Promote livable and healthy places
Growth and development	Define a resilient growth structure
Sustainability	Ensure sustainable management

***Table 12.2** – Landscape Themes and Objectives (© Alexandra Steed URBAN).*

Description
An innovative and adaptable landscape will be created, capable of meeting significant 21st century challenges, including climate change and biodiversity loss. A living infrastructure that addresses social systems and nature will co-evolve in a mutual and complex interaction in this constantly transforming estuarine environment.
Design for a changing estuary will welcome, and accommodate, sea level rise and increasing tidal and stormwater flooding events. The balance of green and blue infrastructure will shift in response to these effects brought on by climate change, and South Essex, like a sponge, will be able to absorb the change dynamically.
South Essex is a blend of many things: land/sea, urban/rural, old/new, industrial/natural. It is also a place of constant change, like the true nature of a transitioning estuary. But it is precisely this change and contrast that make South Essex dynamic, diverse, attractive and unique. These qualities will be celebrated.
Our landscape infrastructure will cultivate natural resources for productive purposes, including sustainable food, energy and other ecosystem services. Each site will be considered as part of a larger network, having multi-functional purposes, and a long-term strategy for creative after-use and re-purposing.
The green and blue infrastructure will connect the people of South Essex, and connect them to their environment in a complete network of corridors. The wildlife and ecological networks will be improved between sites of high quality habitat stepping stones, allowing species to move and to adapt.
South Essex will face the challenge of biodiversity loss head-on, and will protect, conserve and enhance areas of habitat to support biodiversity in a connected network. Moreover, biodiversity net gain will be a requirement for all new development, ensuring that habitats and wildlife are left in a measurably better state.
Create South Essex green and blue infrastructure will protect and improve people's health and wellbeing by promoting favourable environmental conditions through green urban initiatives and by creating opportunities for outdoor recreation and daily experience of wildlife nearby their homes.
Great demands for growth, including new jobs and homes, have been set for South Essex. But a delicate balance must be struck between urban growth and natural systems. Our green and blue infrastructure will address and define this balance and in turn create high-quality, appealing, healthy and distinctive places.
In order to ensure high-quality and effective green and blue infrastructure in the long-term, a strategy must be put in place to provide research, investment, and government legislation to support these efforts. An education and communication strategy should be developed to garner interest, support and continued momentum.

***Table 12.3** – Landscape Themes and Objectives with descriptions (© Alexandra Steed URBAN).*

19

5. Strategic Framework

With a thorough baseline analysis, a well-defined vision, and clear objectives in place, a strategic framework can be crafted to translate the concept into a spatial plan that unifies all ideas into a cohesive and elegant picture. This framework outlines the landscapes to be protected, restored, and improved, encompassing diverse types such as ancient woodlands, rolling grasslands, and coastal marshes. It categorises various landscape uses, including nature reserves, formal parks, recreational areas, green spaces, water bodies, and watercourses. Moreover, it identifies suitable areas for development in less sensitive landscapes.

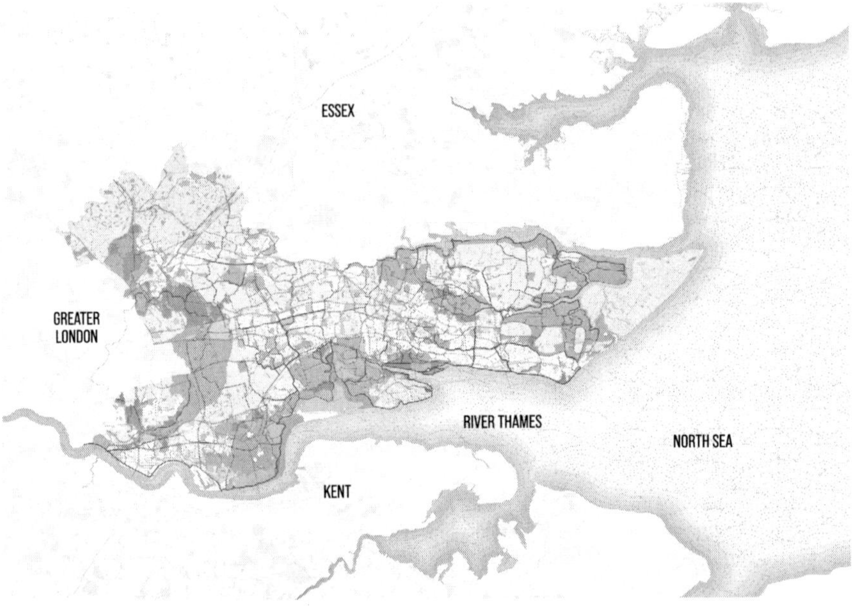

Figure 12.4 *– Strategic Framework Plan: Example taken from the South Essex Green and Blue Infrastructure Strategy Plan. This plan highlights areas of protected landscapes, nature reserves, agriculture areas, parks, greenways, watercourses and coastal paths (© Alexandra Steed URBAN).*

20

Designing the landscape to benefit both wildlife and humans is a significant undertaking that requires a thorough and thoughtful process. The same overlay technique employed during the assessment stage can be applied to illustrate the proposed layout and showcase the essential relationships between elements, ranging from protected landscape areas to agricultural lands, recreational areas, and planned development sites. This integrated approach is vital. The Strategic Framework Plan figure exemplifies the type of plan that might be produced.

Recognising the importance of seamlessly integrating developments within the landscape, rather than imposing upon it, is paramount. This perspective dispels the misconception that human civilisation, progress, and development are inherently incompatible with nature. On the contrary, when we collaborate with nature, we mitigate risks associated with development and position ourselves within a life-sustaining environment that promotes health and well-being. The landscape supports development when it is understood, respected, and nurtured, but achieving this requires planning for the landscape ahead of development. Attempting to force the landscape to accommodate poorly situated buildings can lead to disastrous outcomes.

6. Planning Policy and Design Codes

A landscape framework's effectiveness relies on its translation into written policies that guide the planning process. Without integration into local and strategic plans, the framework becomes redundant. Its success hinges on adoption by authoritative local planners responsible for approving land uses and future growth.

To support these plans and policies, design codes are essential. Design codes provide detailed visual guidance, clarifying the approach and principles of the landscape framework. They facilitate alignment with the framework's vision and landscape objectives for planners, landscape consultants, architects, engineers, and developers involved in the design and development process.

Design codes are comprehensive sets of guidelines and

standards that specify requirements for the design and development of an area or project. They address various aspects, including building aesthetics, materials, landscaping, street layouts, parking, signage, and more, contributing to the visual and functional quality of the built environment. Developed based on a broader planning framework or policy document, design codes ensure consistency, coherence, and adherence to the desired vision for the area. They can be tailored to specific contexts, considering unique characteristics of neighbourhoods, districts, or development sites.

Design codes foster a shared understanding among stakeholders, enabling informed decision-making. Through specific guidelines and physical parameters, design codes facilitate the realisation of the strategic vision within new or regenerated projects.

7. Management Strategy

Ultimately, it is vital to establish a governance structure and management strategy to guarantee the enduring safeguarding, restoration, and nurturing of the landscape. In a world confronted by persistent risks of misuse, pollution, and destructive activities, the landscape necessitates ongoing care and cultivation, as it cannot autonomously sustain its well-being in the face of overwhelming human threats. However, one of the most significant challenges I have encountered is the reluctance to allocate funds for management and maintenance. Unfortunately, budgets for landscape upkeep and public spaces have suffered deep cuts over the years. For instance, England's parks have experienced a real-terms funding reduction of £330 million per year since 2010.[21] Consequently, public open spaces are often sold to private entities that are not accountable to the general population.[22]

Stewardship and governance play pivotal roles in the success of any strategy, particularly when dealing with living, evolving landscapes. Long-term management is a major challenge, as land-based approaches are frequently underfunded. While urban areas may have Park Boards or similar bodies overseeing green and blue spaces, peri-urban or rural landscapes often lack well-funded governing entities for landscapes, if any.

A landscape-led approach is particularly imperative for peri-urban areas, which sit between wild, rural, and urban landscapes and often suffer the most from the expansion of metropolitan areas. Despite their significance, these areas do not neatly fit into the protection and management strategies offered to national parks or urban green spaces. However, they offer exciting opportunities to shape, restore, and connect extensive ecological networks on the outskirts of cities while fostering social and economic activities.[23]

The outlined steps demonstrate the process of a landscape-led planning, design, and development approach. By conducting comprehensive environmental surveys and engaging the community in baseline assessments, a solid foundation is laid for further work. This leads to the development of a bold vision and strategic framework supported by planning policies, design guidelines, and management plans. By reframing our focus to include all of nature and adopting an integrated and inclusive mindset, holistic outcomes naturally emerge.

Over the past few years, I've had the honour of collaborating with my team on two significant landscape frameworks: the South Essex GBI, as described in Chapter 7, and a regional landscape framework for AlUla, Saudi Arabia. Remarkably, these projects were undertaken concurrently, despite their contrasting geographical and cultural contexts. Nevertheless, the land-led approach we employed demonstrated its equal effectiveness in both settings.

In the following pages, I provide a detailed account of the AlUla project and conclude with a discussion of other exemplary regional-scale landscape-led projects. These examples illustrate the outcomes achievable when we lead with the land in the planning, design and development process.

The AlUla Framework Plan: A Vision for Sustainable Development

Imagine a land of extraordinary natural beauty and historical significance, nestled in the heart of North-West Saudi Arabia. AlUla, a sprawling region spanning over 22,300 square kilometres (76,000 square miles), is a true marvel that intersects ancient civilisations, rich biodiversity, and threatened heritage. To preserve, restore, and cultivate this unique landscape, a meticulous and sensitive approach was essential.

Figure 12.5 *– View Over the AlUla Oasis: A palm-filled desert oasis nestled beneath the Hijaz Mountains and forged by ancient lava flows, wind erosion and watercourses.*

24

The ambitious vision for AlUla is to transform it into a premier global destination, renowned for its nature, culture, and heritage. To bridge the gap between this vision and reality, the Landscape Framework Plan was carefully crafted, serving as a holistic and integrated blueprint for sustainable development. This comprehensive document encompasses a range of elements, including a GIS Database, Analysis, Baseline and Thematic Reports, Strategic Environmental Assessment, Vision and Charter, Framework Plan and Proposal Maps, and Design Guidelines.

With the Framework Plan and Guidelines serving as guiding beacons, AlUla's trajectory towards 2035 is firmly established. They provide the necessary impetus for implementation, ensuring measurable gains in biodiversity and the protection of extensive natural and cultural heritage areas. AlUla's transformation into a global destination hinges on this inspirational framework.

At the heart of this endeavour lies a commitment to internationally recognised design and sustainability standards. Referencing esteemed organisations such as the UN Agenda for Sustainable Development, UNESCO World Heritage, the International Council on Monuments and Sites, and the International Union for Conservation of Nature (IUCN), the AlUla project ensures the highest levels of excellence in its design and preservation efforts.

***Figure 12.6** – The Ancient Site of Hegra in AlUla: This photo is of the author on site in ancient Hegra, built more than 2,000 years ago by the Nabataeans. It is Saudi Arabia's first UNESCO World Heritage Site (© Alexandra Steed URBAN).*

25

The IUCN, in particular, played a pivotal role in identifying and categorising protected areas within the landscape. Its guidance facilitated the integration of nature conservation within agricultural and other developed zones, fostering a symbiotic model of human activity and ecological integrity.

As landscape architects, we understood the need for bold action to preserve the wonders of AlUla's remarkable environment. Together with the client and the broader design team, we recognised the importance of allocating vast areas for nature conservation. Our strategy included enhancing, restoring, and connecting habitats, as well as reintroducing endangered wildlife species critical to the region's ecosystem.

Throughout history, AlUla's diverse environment has thrived through the coexistence of varied habitats and human activity. However, in recent times, agricultural practices, overgrazing of camels, urban expansion, and other human-induced factors have posed significant threats to this delicate balance. Habitat loss and fragmentation have disrupted species interactions and depleted biodiversity, leaving only fragmented patches of native habitats.

To counteract these challenges, the Framework Plan incorporates policies and strategies focused on restoring and safeguarding precious ecosystems and wildlife. By implementing this plan, AlUla's landscapes can be preserved, wildlife can flourish, and species can be rejuvenated for the mutual benefit of habitats, communities, and visitors.

Figure 12.7 *– Reintroducing Species: Wildlife management strategies for the protection and re-introduction of species, including the Arabian Leopard, Sand Gazelle, Arabian Oryx, and Ostrich, amongst others, are integrated into the AlUla Framework Plan (© Alexandra Steed URBAN).*

[26]

The associated policies and strategies encompass various essential aspects:

- Preserving ecological connectivity across AlUla, including a migratory bird strategy.
- Designating and restoring IUCN protected nature conservation areas, covering 80 percent of the county area.
- Promoting native and adaptive planting to reverse land degradation and promote biodiversity.
- Implementing wildlife management strategies, including the protection and reintroduction of species such as the Arabian Leopard, Sand Gazelle, Arabian Oryx, and Ostrich.
- Maximising long-term biodiversity opportunities in all developments and optimising environmental rehabilitation for net gains in biodiversity.
- Developing flood risk management strategies and a Wadi Restoration Strategy to manage floods effectively while regenerating the wadi corridor.
- Creating management plans for a network of protected areas, including AlUla National Park, Sharaan Nature Reserve, Cultural Oasis, Environmentally Sensitive Rangelands, and Special Areas that contribute to the region's unique landscape character.

The AlUla Framework Plan and Guidelines serve as an exemplary model for sustainable development. It outlines a grand-scale vision for enhancing and connecting biodiversity, with far-reaching benefits extending beyond AlUla to Saudi Arabia and the world. The international recognition and endorsement of the AlUla Framework at the 2020 G20 Riyadh Summit further validate its significance.[27]

Above all, the AlUla Landscape Framework Plan adheres to McHarg's fundamental principle of designing with nature. By prioritising the protection of precious landscapes, controlling harmful activities, and carefully planning construction in the least sensitive areas, the framework sets a shining example of sustainable development. It demonstrates how humans can coexist lightly with landscapes while preserving their integrity.

As we explore landscape-led strategies, it's inspiring to see remarkable examples from around the world. One such exemplary project is the Emscher Landscape Park in Germany. This ambitious strategy has revitalised a once-industrial and heavily polluted region into a flourishing green landscape.[28] Located in the Ruhr region, Emscher Park was historically dominated by coal mining and steel industries, leaving behind a legacy of environmental degradation. However, through visionary planning and dedicated efforts, the park has undergone a complete metamorphosis. Today, it stands as a testament to the power of landscape-led initiatives in restoring and reimagining a post-industrial territory.

The thirty-year project began in the 1990s and focused on rehabilitating the Emscher River, its many tributaries, and the river valley. The project has fundamentally altered the perception of the area, its environmental quality, but also its economic strength. It is now a highly attractive place for residents, businesses, and visitors alike. The park is known for its retention of iconic industrial features that landscape architect Peter Latz has repurposed within the Landschaftespark in Duisburg-Nord—definitely worth a look.[29] The project includes approximately twenty municipalities, 450 completed projects, and 450 square kilometres of rejuvenated landscape.[30]

The transformation of Emscher Park showcases how thoughtful design and skilful restoration can breathe new life into a landscape scarred by human activity. By embracing nature-based practices and integrating ecological principles, the park has emerged as a vibrant and thriving testament to the resilience of nature.

***Figure 12.8** – The Iconic Landschaftespark Duisburg-Nord: Once a contaminated industrial river valley, Emscher is now a flourishing landscape. Industrial artefacts have been repurposed into recreational and cultural facilities for the public's enjoyment.*

31

Another such stunning endeavour took place in the region of Valencia, Spain. Here, landscape architect Arancha Munoz spearheaded the development of a ground-breaking landscape strategy for the territory. With an overarching objective to preserve and enhance the landscape for generations to come, this strategy was given the utmost priority in the region's planning policy.[32] It recognised the landscape as a vital resource, fundamental to the quality of life for its inhabitants. Munoz proudly states, "Valencia is the first region to enshrine landscape protection in its legal framework and embrace the principles of the European Landscape Convention."

A brilliant example of the successful implementation of this landscape strategy is Cabecera Park, a collaborative effort by Eduardo de Miguel and Arancha Munoz. This visionary project not only connects the city of Valencia with its surrounding communities but also reclaims and restores over a kilometre (0.6 miles) of the River Turia's banks. The park's design serves multiple essential functions: safeguarding the city from flash floods, purifying the river water, fostering biodiversity and thriving habitats, and improving the overall health and stability of the soil. As a result, Cabecera Park has transformed into a vibrant and flourishing landscape, enriching the lives of the people of Valencia.

Figure 12.9 *– Cabecera Park: Situated in Valencia, this park utilises innovative landforms and varying elevations along the banks of the River Turia to establish a rejuvenating and sustainable landscape.*

33

This remarkable achievement in Valencia showcases the profound impact that a landscape-led approach can have on a region. By recognising the significance of the landscape as its greatest resource, Valencia has set a precedent for other municipalities to follow. This commitment to a place-inspired approach not only secures a prosperous future for Valencia but also serves as an inspiration for other regions to integrate similar strategies into their planning policies.

Another notable example is the Room for the River project in the Netherlands.[34] As a response to increasing flooding and decreasing floodplain and river capacity, this government program encompasses thirty-four projects involving four major rivers—the Rhine, Meuse, Waal, and IJssel. The objective is twofold: managing floods effectively and creating a comprehensive river landscape masterplan on a vast scale. By providing rivers with safe space to flood and improving the surrounding landscapes' quality, the project embraces a landscape-led approach to flood management and river restoration.

Figure 12.10 *– Room for the River: Aerial view of Deventer and the IJssel river, part of the room for the river high water protection program.*

35

While these examples highlight the potential of landscape-led strategies, it is right to acknowledge that such initiatives are still relatively few and far between. Without robust landscape frameworks that are grounded in the integration of natural systems and provide a solid foundation for development, we risk repeating past mistakes.

It is crucial to recognise the flaws of conventional approaches that still disregard or diminish the natural world in planning and development. Adopting a landscape-led perspective cherishes a collaborative relationship with the land, valuing its inherent worth, and leveraging its life-sustaining functions to foster global sustainable growth and development.

To bring about meaningful change, multiple stakeholders must play their part. Governments can legislate landscape-led approaches, making it mandatory for landscape professionals to contribute to regional growth plans. Those in the development industry must educate themselves about this approach and incorporate it into their work. Moreover, communities can embrace this approach to shape contextually inspired neighbourhood plans that reflect their unique attributes.

Indeed, genuinely landscape-led development presents a transformative approach to planning, design, and development. By prioritising the preservation, restoration, and integration of natural systems, we can create resilient, adaptable, and regenerative environments that benefit both humanity and the earth. When we embrace the wisdom of the land and learn from its intricate workings, we possess the power to shape a brighter and more prosperous future for our planet and all its inhabitants.

While it may present a formidable challenge for our generation to break free from deeply ingrained structures driving growth and development, we must recognise that the children of today hold the key to our future. By nurturing their innate love for nature from an early age, we can lay the foundation for a more sustainable and harmonious world and empower them to become stewards of the land. In doing so, we not only ensure a brighter future for our children but also cultivate a generation that cherishes and protects the precious resources of our planet.

13

Green Education and Skills

IGNORANCE TO INTELLIGENCE

"When we set up schools, colleges, and universities as places of learning, and gather together the most precious segments of the population—children and youth—education, and what we do in our seeds of learning, ought to have a bigger purpose, a larger purpose than is the case today. That's why we begin with the most basic and the most fundamental claim on teaching and learning, and that is the claim of planet Earth herself. We call it 'natural greenery' or 'environmental greenery.' We belong to this Earth. We owe to this Earth for our survival, for our nourishment, for our fulfilment."[1]

—Darius Radkevicius

THE WORLD IS in dire need of a generation that has an inherent love for nature embedded in their very DNA. A deep and instinctive connection must become the norm, cultivated from an early age. This starts within the home, where admiration, awe, and respect for the living world are passed down from one generation to the next. Children must be given the freedom and encouragement to explore the wonders of the natural world, to understand its intricate processes and systems, to acquaint themselves with its diverse inhabitants. Simultaneously, schools can play a pivotal role by placing learning within the context of life and guiding students to integrate their way of living with a cultivated sense of care for the earth. Learning how to relate to nature in unity is fundamental to raising responsible global citizens, as it inevitably influences every action we take as humans. This connection is not isolated or separate from other considerations but instead seamlessly interwoven into the fabric of our existence.

Of course, I am not suggesting that we pass on our burdens to the younger generation and wait for them to sort out our relationship with the earth. On the contrary, people of every age and every generation must actively participate in the process of relearning and embracing the art and science of caring for our planet. Relying solely on the hope of a future generation of well-rounded individuals will not adequately address the imminent challenges we face. And we certainly cannot afford to wait for the next cohort of grown-ups to bring about the necessary change. Urgent action is required, yet we are confronted with a significant shortage of individuals in the global workforce who possess the knowledge and skills needed to drive this dramatic transformation. Therefore, there is an immediate and pressing need to provide training opportunities for individuals in various specialised green skills. Fields such as green finance, environmental law, protected area management, strategic ecological planning, landscape architecture, soil science, permaculture, sustainable forestry, landscape construction, and other professions related to landscape protection, recovery, and management are currently lacking the resources and expertise they require.

In this chapter, I argue that the world needs to recruit you—though you may not be directly involved, you are indirectly—and you can help. Everyone is a student, everyone a teacher, and we hold the power to teach and influence those around us. As members of communities, we possess the capacity to exert influence and bring about positive change. This includes enrolling ourselves in the global green workforce, whether formally or informally. Regardless of our individual roles or professions, every action we undertake can be executed with a landscape mindset, understanding the broader implications and striving towards a Portrait to Landscape shift in our physical reality.

By embracing our collective responsibility and actively engaging with a landscape-led approach, we have the power to foster a sustainable future. In the chapter ahead, we will delve into the ways each of us can contribute, shedding light on the significance of our actions. We will explore the immense potential of an education system aligned with ecocentric values and a global workforce united by a shared commitment to preserving and restoring our natural environment. Together, we can shape a world where a deep respect for the land is embedded in our core, where landscapes are prioritised, ensuring the well-being of both humanity and the earth we call home.

The Seeds of Knowledge

The country of Bhutan is way ahead of the curve. They prioritise a respectful relationship between people and planet in everything they do. They are the first and only carbon-negative country in the world. Seventy-five percent of the country is under forest and scrub cover, with more than half of the total area protected for all time with some form of conservation status. [2] The forests provide massive carbon sinks and, as part of the Eastern Himalayan Range, are one of the few remaining biodiversity hotspots in the world.[3]

In the early 1970s, Bhutan's then-king, His Majesty the Fourth King of Bhutan, famously pronounced that "Gross National Happiness is more important than gross national product."[4] Since then, the proclamation has been translated into a vision for the kingdom, underscored by the philosophy that holistic, inclusive, and sustainable development cannot be pursued only with socioeconomic development but in tandem with the pillars of environmental sustainability, cultural integrity, and good governance. The Bhutan National Report for the United Nations Conference on Sustainable Development 2012 calls for "a new global economic paradigm founded on environmental sustainability and social equity to promote happiness and well-being of all forms of life on earth."[5]

Bhutan's leaders recognise that education is the only way to enshrine the concept and national vision of Gross National Happiness (GNH). Education has a central place in advancing the progress of sustainable development, and it is critical to raising responsible citizens of the planet. Bhutan has initiated the "Green Schools for Green Bhutan" program to carry out this vision. They explain that green is a colour and a metaphor for anything that supports and sustains life—"human life, animal life, plant life, birds and every manner of life in its infinite variety."[6] They start with the premise that honouring and appreciating the gifts of planet earth is the most important lesson and that after this, everything else falls naturally into place. They nurture a sense of harmony, belonging, and solidarity in their schools, which the students take into the world.

One such school is the Jigme Losel primary school in the Bhutanese capital, Thimphu, awash with green. Plants precariously perch on every surface and play a central role in the curriculum revolving around natural stewardship and care for plants, gardens, and community. "Let nature be your teacher" is the school's unofficial logo. In an interview with *The Guardian* newspaper, the headteacher, Choki Dukpa, explains, "Environmental sustainability and nature is central to the way we teach here." She says the green approach is not just about the environment but a philosophy. "It's a values-led approach to education that stems from the belief that education should be more than academic attainment. It should be about expanding children's minds and teaching what it is to be human—and at the forefront of this is the conservation of the natural environment."[7] It's about maintaining the integrity of the human/nature relationship and teaching children that we belong to nature, that the earth sustains us, and that we must reciprocally sustain the earth.

Bhutan's Green Schools programme provides a perfect example of green education. Meeting the vision of a green future and having the background and skills necessary to bring this vision about requires respect for nature and environmental sustainability. Green skills must be the seeds of the education system and the world's future leaders and citizens. This can be brought about by instilling a land ethic in our children and in educational curriculums from an early age.

If you are an early years educator, you can follow the example of Jigme Losel school, and bring plants into the classroom, plant seeds together, take the children on visits to local nature reserves, and grow a school vegetable garden that contributes to their snack time, and reuses their lunch waste as compost. Of course, governments can bring about educational reforms, but we can't rely on that. Many of you are parents or caregivers and have the capacity to introduce or get involved with these activities. Schools are often under-resourced and grateful for volunteers, so consider how to get involved. Indeed, nurturing a healthy attitude and relationship with nature from day one, at home, nursery and primary school, and through to graduation will open young minds to a broader understanding of community and a more integrated way of living in the world.

A Green Curriculum

Regrettably, education systems worldwide tend to prioritise a purely academic approach, focusing on subjects such as mathematics, science, language, history, and geography. However, there is a significant deficit when it comes to teaching environmental stewardship, our relationship with the land and community, our ability to care for ourselves and the planet, and our understanding of the elements that bring joy, peace, beauty, and meaning to our lives.

In our increasingly urbanised and technologically-driven world, where we have become progressively disconnected from nature, introducing children to the land requires deliberate effort. Many children have limited access to natural environments, lacking gardens or any form of outdoor space. Some may even struggle to find any green spaces, let alone wild places. For some, their only interaction with nature comes through screens. Reflecting upon this dislocation and disconnection from life, it becomes evident that such a state is synonymous with dystopia.

Nurturing a sense of care and love for nature should begin from an early age, as we now recognise its critical importance for the future survival and well-being of humanity. When cultivating this love and knowledge proves challenging within the home and garden, it becomes even more imperative for the education system to shoulder this responsibility. To raise responsible global citizens, we must replace a reductionist education approach with an inclusive and integrated curriculum, taking inspiration from programs like the Green Bhutan initiative. Holistic learning approaches will equip children for the ultimate task that lies ahead for all humans—caring for the planet that sustains us.

One such example is the Green School in Bali. After watching *An Inconvenient Truth*, the 2006 documentary film about the actual and imminent dangers of global warming, parents John and Cynthia Hardy vowed to do whatever they could to improve their own children's future possibilities and others.[8] They opened the Green School—a beautiful, open bamboo construction flooded with natural light and situated within 8 hectares (20 acres) of flowing gardens, complete with their own buffalo.

Here they teach and practice holism with the hope that, in John Hardy's words, if a student graduates "as a whole person, chances are she'll demand a whole world—a whole world—to live on."[9] He says, "We have to teach our kids that the world is not indestructible." Children here learn sustainable construction methods, how to recycle materials, build composting toilets, lay footpaths made of local stone, manage stormwater, and grow and cook their food. The Hardy's have created a model for a new holistic system of education that has now spread to Tulum, South Africa and New Zealand, educating the world's future green leaders.[10]

Though ideal, we can't all open our own schools, or live and send our children to school in forested places like Bhutan and Bali. Most kids' lives are worlds away, city-dwelling, and in polluted, concrete jungles. Stephen Ritz is a teacher and parent in just such a place—the South Bronx, New York. With tremendous enthusiasm, he started the Green Bronx Machine campaign. He believes that integrating plant-based teaching will bring about healthier, happier kids.[11] Most of these youth live below the poverty line, many with disabilities. He considers, "kids should not have to leave their communities to live, learn, and earn in a better one." [12]

With a vision to connect his students with the natural world, he decided to bring the landscape directly into their classroom by introducing seeds. Together, they attentively nurtured these seeds, transforming their classroom into an indoor edible wall. What started as a simple initiative flourished into something truly remarkable. The students, now empowered and inspired, took on the role of contractors, actively installing 100 green walls in various schools and institutions within their community. Not only were these young people able to raise money for their school, but they've been able to give back to others in their community—seniors, people without homes, and those in need. Ritz says, "So we started giving back. And that's when I realised that the greening of America starts first with the pockets, then with the heart, and then with the mind."[13] That is an excellent point. The investment must come up front, along with a paradigm shift, education, and training that brings that shift into being.

Around the world, there are progressive models of education springing up, from the Green Schools in Bhutan and Bali to the Green Bronx Machine to the global Eco-Schools movement, which operates in sixty-eight countries across the globe, to help and empower young people to take positive actions for a sustainable future for all.[14] This movement is heartening to see. They provide excellent models that can be scaled up and applied across many schools. They demonstrate how we can prepare our future leaders with the skills necessary to care for the world in which they live.

Working with Local Communities

It is not all up to the kids. Adults too, must recognise that we cannot simply rely on the next generation to drive transformation. The need for land protection, restoration, and stewardship is urgent, and it requires the active participation of individuals, communities, and agencies across the globe. You have the power to make a difference by taking a hands-on approach and getting involved with your local community or supporting another community in need.

There is a wealth of community-led initiatives and training programs available worldwide, offering opportunities to learn and contribute to sustainable practices. These programs cover a wide range of topics, from working with the land and sustainable food production to waste recycling, greening urban streets, and establishing community gardens. The possibilities are endless.

In this book, I have highlighted several inspirational projects and movements that have been initiated and led by communities. These include the Green Streets program in Vancouver, the Friends of the High Line in New York, the Grove Park Neighbourhood Plan in South London, the London National Park City. Many of the projects mentioned also include learning and training opportunities, such as the Navdanya Biodiversity Conservation Farm in India, and the Greening the Desert Project in Jordan. Some of these projects have grown to have global reach.

While based in Australia, Lawton's Permaculture Research Institute, introduced in Chapter 9, contributes to communities globally by training people to live in balance with the land. The Institute is a not-for-profit organisation with a mission, "to work with individuals and communities worldwide, to expand the knowledge and practice of integrated, sustainable agriculture and culture using the whole-systems approach of permaculture design. This will provide solutions for permanent abundance by training local people to become leaders of sustainable development in their communities and countries." [15]

Lawton has taught more than 15,000 students worldwide, in more than fifty countries, with the aim, "to drive the establishment of self-replicating educational demonstration sites across the globe."[16] He and his colleagues are passionate about sharing their knowledge with anyone and everyone who will take an interest and get involved, as they know through their experience with numerous projects around the world that the application of permaculture provides a solution to the multiple crises that the planet is facing—climate crisis, soil erosion crisis, food security crisis, pollution crisis, and so on. They believe humans can become the most beneficial element on earth, rather than the most damaging.

John D. Liu is another pioneer in communicating and educating others about organised landscape restoration programmes' efficacy in healing the earth. In 1995, Liu was involved in producing a film about the revitalisation of the Loess Plateau in China, a region about the size of France. Centuries of overuse and overgrazing in this region led to the devastation of the land, excessive erosion and widescale poverty. With his own eyes, Liu witnessed how local people working together, supported by international and government funding, transformed this degraded and barren landscape into a thriving, verdant ecosystem.

Figure 13.1 – *The Loess Plateau: Once a degraded and barren landscape, this region was transformed into a thriving, verdant ecosystem by targeted investment into restorative landscape strategies implemented by the hands of local communities.*

17

This renewal was not achieved in a heavy-handed manner but through a combination of restorative landscape strategies, including terracing, sediment traps, check dams, tree-planting, and regenerative agricultural methods. The spectacular results completely blew him away, and from that moment on, Liu decided to commit his life to educating others about how to rehabilitate our exhausted landscapes at a grand scale.[18]

In 2017, Liu founded Ecosystem Restoration Camps, a non-profit worldwide movement that trains people with the skills required to restore damaged ecosystems at a regional scale. Their mission is, "To work together to restore ecological functionality, to build Research, Training and Innovation Centers for Ecological Restoration, to engage people in the inquiry of ecological restoration, and train people in how to restore degraded lands in perpetuity."[19] They have dozens of camps around the world, called "local living labs." Campers work together with the local community, knowledge-sharing and learning restoration techniques that can be applied in many environments internationally.[20]

Programmes such as Lawton and Liu's have wide-scale impact. These are reinforced by literally thousands of other programmes, projects, and initiatives around the world encouraging re-greening and the transformation of barren landscapes to thriving places for nature, from street greening projects to community gardening, to green roofs, stream keepers, watershed restoration, or re-wilding schemes. The transfer of knowledge from one person to the next in these community schemes is invaluable, shows the generosity of spirit so often demonstrated in greening projects, and brings about benefits for the whole community and the planet.

Some of the projects featured in this book may already exist in your own community, or perhaps you can easily identify similar initiatives nearby. The abundance of such projects reflects the widespread recognition of the importance of landscape-led transformation. There are numerous ways for you to get involved and contribute to these endeavours. The world needs many educated in the art and science of aligning our actions with natural processes and systems for the sake of sustainable and resilient landscapes. Many individuals need the training to drive the necessary transformation at a faster pace. Does that include you?

Formal education plays a significant role in preparing a skilled workforce to address the environmental, landscape, and sustainability challenges we face. From design and planning professionals to conservation managers, forestry workers, farmers, and fishermen, including those in engineering and construction, a diverse range of skills is needed. With a competent and knowledgeable workforce, we can effectively meet the escalating demands of nature restoration.

Skilling Up

Indeed, to facilitate the broad-scale change necessary to achieve global targets, such as protecting 30 percent of land and seas by 2030 and limiting global warming to 1.5°C (35°F), many hands are required, including individuals, communities, and agencies with the necessary skills for landscape regeneration. Currently, there is a global shortage of skilled professionals in the environment, landscape, and sustainability sectors, and this gap will only widen as the demand for planning, design, protection, restoration, and management intensifies. If you are seeking a career or considering a career change, your expertise and contribution could greatly benefit the world.

A comprehensive study conducted by the Landscape Institute, the chartered body for the landscape profession in the UK, has shed light on the current state of the landscape sector and its readiness to address future demands. The study has revealed an impending crisis in design, implementation, management, and maintenance skills, highlighting the urgency to meet the growing need for landscape-led approaches. In their study, they note that the core landscape activities, as listed in the following table, are planning, design, building, management, and conservation of spaces, supported by investment and research, education and policy.[21]

Investment
Public or private investment into spaces, capturing activity from developers

Core landscape sector

Planning	Design	Build	Management	Conservation
Technical and policy response to deliver investment, including assessment	Design landscape features, based on plans including architects	Construct the design, including planting	Management and maintenance of landscapes	Conservation or protection of landscapes
• Town planning officers • Chartered architectural technologists • Architectural and town planning technicians	• Landscape Architects • Architects • Draughtspersons • Civil engineers • Construction project managers and professionals • Building and civil engineering	• Managers and proprietors in agriculture and horticulture • Managers and proprietors in forestry, fishing and related services • Gardeners and landscape gardeners • Agriculture and fishing trades	• Groundsmen and greenkeepers Adjacent occupations: • Horticultural traders • Forestry workers • Fishing and other elementary agriculture occupations	• Conservation professionals • Environment professionals • Conservation and environmental associate professionals

Research, education, and policy support
- Natural and social science professionals

Adjacent occupations:
- Biological scientists
- Social and humanities scientists

Table 13.1 - *The Core Landscape Sector: This table displays some of the primary skills required to be capable landscape stewards (© Alexandra Steed URBAN).*

22

THE CRITICAL NEED for these skills is not specific to the UK. Globally, there is a demand for landscape skills, knowledge, and experience greater than ever before.[23] For example, the IUCN has identified the urgent need for more managers, staff, and stewards in nature conservation areas worldwide, along with an elevation of the profession of protected area management. As they explain, "The future of the planet's biodiversity and life support systems is a complex, multi-skilled profession, worthy of respect, recognition and support."[24]

They understand that managing protected areas is becoming more demanding and diverse, with expectations to:

- Protect species, habitats and ecosystems
- Maintain ecosystem services, vital for local and national economies
- Support local sustainable development and use of natural resources
- Provide opportunities for tourism and recreation
- Promote equitable forms of governance
- Adopt entrepreneurial approaches for generating vitally needed funding
- Argue the case for protected areas in government legislative and decision-making processes
- Manage large, complex organisations and work in partnership with other sectors

You can see from the above points, that a wide array of skills is required, including green finance, legal, and complex management. As the IUCN report suggests, culturally, working with nature is not perceived as a pursuit with high value. Salaries reflect this undervaluing of landscape planning, design, and management occupations. With salaries relatively low compared to other comparably skilled professions and disciplines, it's difficult to attract and sustain talent. Those involved in the more physically intensive sub-sectors, build and management, tend to have earnings below national averages.[25]

Furthermore, the landscape sector frequently faces the perception that its expertise is less valuable compared to other sectors involved in land development. "Soft" expertise involving natural materials and processes is sometimes considered less sophisticated, less serious, non-essential, and subordinate to other skills involved in the built environment. In the development sector, "hard" infrastructure, engineering and building components are typically treated as more critical and prioritised over landscape and ecological considerations.

Moreover, landscape professionals' strategies often lack a prominent role in development decision-making, and their involvement, if any, is often delayed until after crucial decisions have already been made. Additionally, their contributions may go unrecognised and uncredited, further marginalising their work and diminishing the perceived importance of landscape design and its shaping impact.

To ensure a landscape-led approach in the development process, the importance of individuals with landscape expertise, including ecologists, soil scientists, landscape architects, local communities, and stakeholders, must be acknowledged, and provided with equitable recognition, adequate fees, and sufficient resources to carry out their valuable work alongside other disciplines in the built environment.

Active participation in community planning processes allows everyone to contribute their concerns and advocate for a landscape-led approach that encompasses the needs of the entire community. Engaging with your community to develop a neighbourhood plan can be a meaningful way to promote inclusive and sustainable development.

In addition, rural areas require special attention, particularly regarding agricultural transformation and the preservation of rural lands for the sake of planetary health. The knowledge and commitment of agrarians who have a deep connection to the land are indispensable. However, small-scale farmers face significant challenges, including economic constraints, with their assets tied up in the land while struggling with limited cash flow. As a result, many farmers are compelled to sell their farms to larger landowners and lease the land back from them to continue farming.[26]

Much more investment is required to encourage these small-scale farmers to persevere and to support them with sustainable farming methods. Financial incentives that promote sustainable farming practices can empower farmers to produce food while contributing to important land regeneration initiatives that bring significant environmental benefits. Additionally, as consumers, our choices play a crucial role in supporting and promoting healthy farming practices.

The majority of landscape transformations aimed at nature recovery will take place in rural areas, as farmland is the primary location of land use change worldwide. These agricultural landscapes represent a significant opportunity for implementing large-scale biodiversity conservation, carbon sinks and flood attenuation measures. Incorporating sustainable nature-based solutions in agricultural areas, as discussed in Chapter 8, not only benefits the environment but also contributes to the long-term success of farms.

Introducing nature conservation practices in farmland also facilitates the connectivity between isolated nature-protected areas, such as nature reserves or national parks. Often, private farmlands or ranches act as barriers between these protected areas. By integrating landscape vegetation such as wetlands, woodlands, hedgerows, native grasslands, and wildflower meadows within appropriate farming areas, habitat connectivity between protected areas can be restored.

Furthermore, leveraging farmland can effectively address the impacts of climate change and the increasing occurrence of extreme flooding. Managing rural areas as critical components of regional flood strategies offers a nature-based solution to mitigate the effects of more frequent and intense storms. Additionally, implementing robust water storage strategies on farms helps address drought conditions. It is essential to disseminate knowledge about these strategies to those responsible for managing farmlands.

The inclusion of natural flood management techniques on farms enables the capture, slowing down, and storage of floodwater. This approach provides a range of benefits, including replenishing groundwater and aquifers, preventing soil erosion, enriching soils, irrigating crops, filtering pollutants, and supporting wetland species, including important sites for migratory birds. The Natural Flood Management diagram illustrates various ways in which flood management can be appropriately integrated into farmland.

Figure 13.2 – *Natural Flood Management on Farms (© Alexandra Steed URBAN).*

27

It is imperative that we create more opportunities for farmers in coastal zones to adapt their farmland to the challenges of sea level rise. They should be educated about the potential benefits of utilising their land as blue carbon sinks, biodiversity net gain sites, and for innovative marine farming methods. For instance, subsidies can be provided for farmland that restores coastal marshes as flood buffer zones and wetland carbon sinks, benefiting migratory birds.

Additionally, specialised marine farming, such as cultivating seaweed and shellfish, can offer lucrative prospects while promoting environmental sustainability. Skilled individuals are needed to support these endeavours, including the cultivation of crops like marsh samphire and environmentally robust species such as mussels, oysters, and clams.

Figure 13.3 *– Coastal Farming: Many farms along coastlines will need to adapt to sea level rise and increasing storms. This diagram illustrates some methods which simultaneously address the climate, nature, food and health crises (© Alexandra Steed URBAN).*

28

Large-scale investment is necessary to train a competent workforce capable of integrating new sustainable crops and nature conservation practices into rural areas, particularly in the face of changing climate conditions.

Time is of the essence. We must prioritise education, training, and investment to equip a workforce capable of embracing landscape stewardship, planning, designing, developing, and managing our way into a new paradigm that aligns with nature. The survival of our species depends on individuals who possess a deep understanding of the land, its processes, and the responsibilities of stewardship. This responsibility falls on each and every one of us. The environmental challenges we confront are daunting and reversing conditions like climate change and ecological decline requires widespread involvement, resilience, and unwavering commitment over the long term.

Undoubtedly, the world needs individuals trained in specific landscape management skills and expertise, ranging from wildlife management to ecological planning and landscape construction. We must invest in universities, colleges, apprenticeships, and other programs to train a generation of skilled professionals. Furthermore, we must incorporate a green philosophy into the education system to instil a love for nature from an early age, foster respect for nature's intelligence, and encourage individuals to act from a place of wisdom. The world needs a generation of people who cultivate an ecocentric worldview in their chosen work and in all aspects of their daily lives.

14

Tend Your Plot

IMPOTENCE TO AGENCY

"We must cultivate our garden." [1]
—*Voltaire*

VOLTAIRE'S FAMOUS PHRASE, "One must cultivate one's own garden," remains profoundly relevant in the present, just as it did when written in the eighteenth century. In his novel *Candide*, the protagonist and his companions embark on a journey filled with numerous atrocities, experiencing war, shipwrecks, earthquakes, disease, hunger, and torture. Towards the conclusion of the story, they reach Turkey, where they encounter an elderly Turk residing in a suburb of Istanbul. Despite the despair they feel for humanity, the old man imparts quiet wisdom and hope by sharing the solace his family finds in the bountiful and delightful surroundings of their productive farm. He encourages Candide and his companions to follow suit, directing their attention away from the wrongdoings of others and towards cultivating their own plots.[2]

In today's world, while not everyone may have the opportunity to manage their own farms or gardens, each of us holds the power to cultivate our own lives and make conscious choices about how we inhabit the earth. We mustn't solely rely on governments or organisations to bring about the changes we desire, nor should we solely focus on large-scale national or international endeavours. Instead, we can direct our attention to our metaphorical plots and take personal responsibility for the impact we have on the environment. Remember, you are an integral part of nature—a capable and productive citizen of the earth. Daily, you can live in this truth by taking immediate, consistent, and persistent actions; actively living out your role as an earth steward.

Our individual relationships with nature will manifest in unique ways. For some, it may begin with small-scale projects in their local areas, such as tending a small garden, supporting local family-owned farms, collaborating with the community to develop sustainable neighbourhood plans, or participating in elections to support politicians who share their land ethics. Others may find fulfilment in guiding their children to develop a love for nature, writing books, pursuing training in sustainable design, or fundraising for women farmers in India. There are countless ways to contribute as an earth steward and engage in a profound awakening to the living world that surrounds us. Each of us must take responsibility for cultivating our own gardens, knowing that the rewards we reap from our efforts will far surpass our contributions.

In this chapter, I provide a summary of the most impactful and immediate actions you can take on a daily basis to contribute to the regeneration of the earth. The transformation from Portrait to Landscape will occur one person at a time, and your individual actions matter greatly.

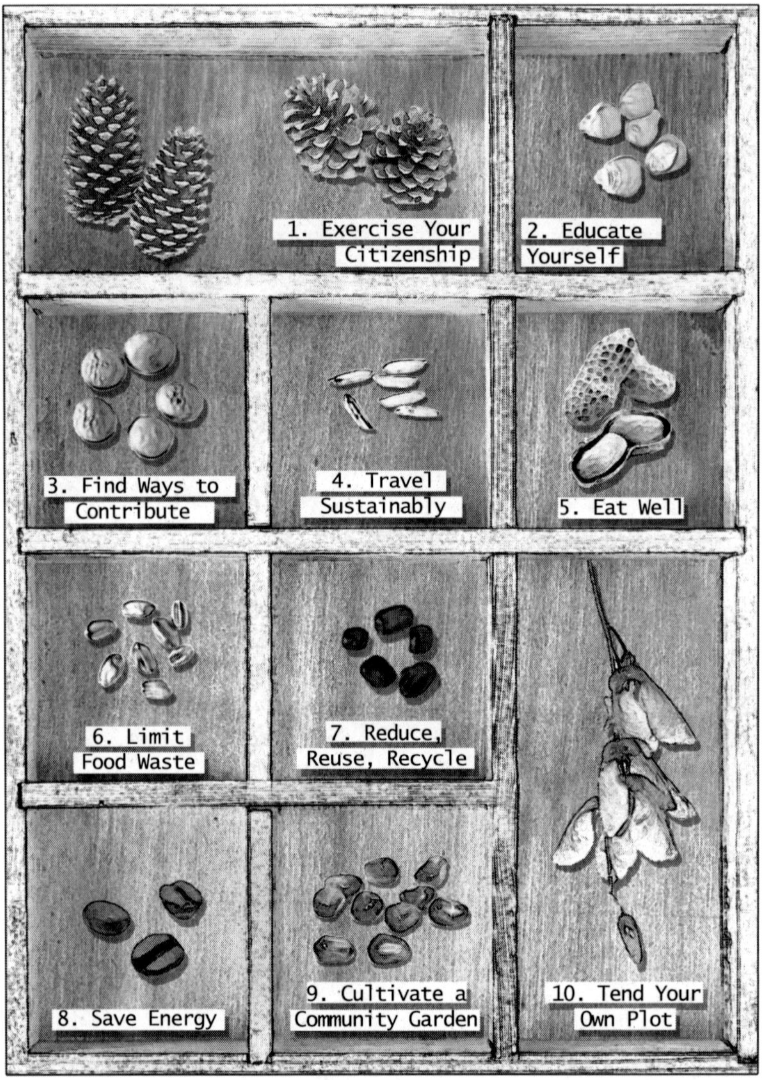

Figure 14.1 *– The Seeds of Change: 10 actionable steps individuals can take to contribute to the earth's regeneration (© Alexandra Steed URBAN).*

3

1. Exercise Your Citizenship

Each of us has been given a voice, and there is plenty of reason to use it now. Exercising your civic responsibilities—not only enjoying its privileges and protections—and actively participating in political decisions is crucial to bringing about change. This calls for a collective effort involving not only governments but also the private sector, academic institutions, civil society, and most significantly, the influential voices of women, youth, and each one of us.

Our world leaders have made many promises, stretching from the Montreal Protocol in the 1980s, the "UN Framework Convention on Climate Change" in the 1990s, the Kyoto Protocol in the 2000s and the Paris Agreement in the 2010s. Unfortunately, the commitments made thus far fall short of what is required. Regrettably, our governments, despite these inadequate pledges, are failing to fulfil their obligations and are not making sufficient progress towards meeting their targets.[4] Moreover, the global response to the COVID-19 pandemic has tragically reversed advancements in various areas related to the attainment of the 2030 Sustainable Development Goals (SDGs).[5]

Taking action to hold world leaders accountable is in our hands. We have numerous avenues to do so. By exercising our right to vote, signing petitions, participating in protests and rallies, engaging with local politicians through letters, and sharing vital information on various platforms, including blogs and social media, we can make a difference. Let's not forget the power of face-to-face conversations with colleagues, friends, and family, discussing important matters that contribute to saving the world. I trust this book has provided you with a comprehensive understanding of the facts and ignited your curiosity to embark on further research, enabling you to step forward confidently.

2. Educate Yourself

Knowledge holds immense power, and attaining education stands as one of the most effective means of forging a brighter world.

Ensuring universal education, particularly for marginalised girls who continue to face discriminatory barriers, plays a fundamental role in reversing the decline of our planet.[6] Therefore, staying well-informed and actively contributing to the education of others becomes one of the most crucial actions we can undertake. This book serves as a tool in advancing that noble cause.

Ensuring the quality and credibility of the information we consume is an essential responsibility for each of us. By engaging with peer-reviewed articles, well-researched books, and reliable sources such as channels, podcasts, and journals, we can stay informed about the latest developments. This not only benefits us individually but also enables us to share valuable insights, enlightening articles, and encourage others to be aware of the issues crucial to our survival and the well-being of future generations.

However, it is essential to be vigilant in the face of fake news. With media biases, misinformation, and disinformation prevailing, we are inundated with a plethora of information, much of which may be useless or even misleading, posing significant risks. Navigating the ever-expanding sea of facts and staying grounded in reality can be a weighty challenge. Therefore, it is vital to remain attentive and discerning in our quest for truth.

3. Find Ways to Contribute

Across the globe, numerous influential charities and non-profit organisations are actively addressing critical issues such as climate change, biodiversity loss, women's education, hunger eradication, regenerative farming, and the restoration of nature in urban, rural, and wilderness areas. These commendable initiatives heavily rely on the support of individuals who contribute their time, energy, and financial resources.

Discovering meaningful ways to contribute that resonate with you personally is key. Take the time to research and identify the most effective initiatives aligned with your desired outcomes and lend them your support. Speaking with your wallet by donating to these causes is a powerful way to express your concerns and make a difference. If financial contributions are not feasible, consider volunteering your time to local parks, nature reserves, or community-based greening projects, as these actions can be incredibly beneficial and have a direct impact. There are numerous avenues for giving, and investing in the health and well-being of our planet earth is undoubtedly the best investment.

4. Travel Sustainably

The transportation sector contributes approximately 20% of global CO_2 emissions, with urban transport being the main contributor and showing a continuing upward trend.[7] To address this issue, it is crucial to reduce reliance on private cars and explore alternative modes of travel. Beginning with walking or cycling is a great starting point. When those options are not feasible, consider utilising public transportation such as buses, trains, underground or sky trains. Car clubs and electric vehicles present preferable alternatives to petrol-powered private cars.

The benefits of limiting automobile use while favouring alternative modes of transport are deep and wide, including:

- Mitigating climate change and enhancing air quality, leading to a decrease in greenhouse gas emissions and reducing the prevalence of respiratory illnesses.
- Promoting public health and safety through increased physical activity, such as walking or cycling, while simultaneously reducing traffic accidents and fatalities.
- Fostering equity in urban areas by catering to individuals who are unable to drive and providing accessible transportation options for all.
- Minimising the need for expansive paved roads and idle parking spaces, thereby freeing up valuable urban space that can be utilised more effectively. (In the US, for example, car parking takes up about 5 percent of urban space.)

Imagine replacing the outdated asphalt car parking spaces with vibrant urban nature spaces, ushering in a new aesthetic for our cities. By reclaiming these lands on roads and former parking lots, we can create abundant room for trees, plants, wildlife, water, and soil—a bold demonstration of inclusive coexistence with all forms of life. How remarkable would that be?

Additionally, consider reducing air travel. Opting for local business engagements and holidays can have a profound impact on your carbon footprint. Surprisingly, a single long-haul flight alone can consume an individual's entire annual carbon allocation, as defined by the agreed-upon carbon budget per person to achieve the two-degree target set in the Paris Agreement. With the global carbon budget rapidly depleting, projected to exhaust by the end of 2030, choosing to fly less becomes even more critical to stay within the 1.5 °C (35 °F) threshold of global warming.[8] The remaining carbon budget equals about 50 tonnes of CO_2 total per person. Currently, the average person globally produces 4.5 tonnes annually.[9] In higher-income countries like the US, it's much higher, at 16 tonnes on average.[10]

Embrace the power of walking, cycling, or using public transport whenever possible. Consider the necessity of each trip you take and make conscious choices. These small actions will make a world of difference.

5. Eat Well

Our food choices have a profound impact on the environment. Food production heavily influences landscapes, depletes water resources, contributes to greenhouse gas emissions, and accelerates biodiversity loss through harmful agricultural practices.[11]

Transitioning to a plant-rich diet offers extraordinary environmental benefits and promotes better human health, reducing the risk of chronic diseases. In the Western world, our high consumption of dairy and protein comes from farming practices with a significant carbon footprint. As the global population continues to grow, adopting a predominantly plant-based diet, or even a completely plant-based one, will become crucial to meet our nutritional needs. Remember the wise words of food guru Michael Pollan, "Eat food, not too much, mostly plants."[12]

You can further promote sustainability by replacing highly processed and fast foods with whole foods, preferably locally produced and organically grown. Avoid genetically modified and chemically treated produce. When consuming dairy and meat, opt for organic, free-range options sourced from pasture-raised and grass-fed animals. Supporting small-scale farmers who practice regenerative and sustainable farming methods is a pivotal choice. Many local farms now offer convenient bicycle delivery of delicious seasonal produce right to your doorstep!

6. Limit Food Waste

Every single one of us relies on the food we consume, yet the staggering reality is that it is wasted on a massive scale. Globally, nearly one in ten people lack sufficient food while approximately one-third of all produced food goes to waste.[13] This loss occurs at various stages of the supply chain, from crops rotting in fields to food languishing in storage facilities to uneaten leftovers left on our plates.

In higher-income nations, food loss tends to occur further along the supply chain. As consumers, we often reject imperfect vegetables or prepare excessive amounts of food, only to let it spoil at the back of our refrigerators. This uneaten food squanders precious resources, including seeds, water, soil, labour, and energy. Enormous amounts of carbon dioxide emissions, approximately 4.4 gigatons, are associated with this wasted food, further exacerbating global warming.[14]

Within our own homes, we have the power to make a difference. By creating weekly meal plans, purchasing only what we need, utilising and consuming leftovers, and composting organic waste, we can avoid contributing to this wasteful cycle. Let's move away from dumping it into plastic bags destined for toxic landfills and instead embrace more sustainable practices.

7. Reduce, Reuse, Recycle

Reducing household waste is an effective strategy for minimising our impact on the environment, just like addressing food waste. The accumulation of waste is an inevitable and increasingly prevalent issue. When we dispose of items such as food, paper, cardboard boxes, plastic containers, glass jars, batteries, garden waste, and appliances, the consequences for terrestrial and marine life can be catastrophic. However, much of this waste consists of materials that could be easily reused or recycled. Therefore, adopting practices of reusing and recycling presents complementary approaches to stem the continuous flow of household waste towards landfills, incinerators, and the oceans.[15]

We must take a stand against excessive consumption and waste. Prioritise purchasing products from eco-friendly companies that minimise environmental harm. Consider each item you buy and reflect on its necessity, as well as factors like its delivery, packaging, potential for reuse, and recyclability.

Refrigerators deserve special attention in this regard. Managing and safely disposing refrigerants, as highlighted in the excellent book *Drawdown: The Most Comprehensive Plan Ever Proposed to Reverse Global Warming*, is ranked as the top solution. The chemicals used, particularly hydrofluorocarbons (HFCs), have an astonishing global warming potential that is one thousand to nine thousand times greater than that of CO_2.[16] Yet, purchasing air-conditioning and refrigeration units is soaring worldwide with warming temperatures —an ironic predicament. The majority of refrigerant emissions occur at the end of their lifecycle, making proper disposal essential. Some businesses have technologies available to purify refrigerators for reuse or transform their chemicals into non-harmful substances. Ensure that your fridge, freezer, and air-conditioning units are carefully removed by a company that offers this service and recycled for purification and reuse.

8. Save Energy

Addressing the energy crisis holds immense significance in our efforts to combat climate change and halt biodiversity decline. The choice of energy sources we invest in, as well as reducing our overall energy consumption, wields substantial influence in making a positive impact.

Within our homes, opting for suppliers that prioritise renewable energy sources, such as wind, solar, geothermal, tidal, in-stream hydro, or advanced nuclear power, rather than carbon-intensive alternatives like coal and natural gas, can bring about significant change. Some individuals may even choose to adopt an off-grid approach or a combination of renewable energy systems, incorporating solar panels, wind turbines, ground source heat pumps, or hybrid systems.

Moreover, there are numerous ways to curtail our energy requirements. One of the most apparent and efficient changes we can make is transitioning to low-energy LED lighting. Additionally, improving the insulation of our homes stands out as a cost-effective and practical method to reduce energy consumption for heating and cooling. This not only helps save money but also mitigates excess emissions by regulating the heat exchange within the house. While it is most effective to incorporate insulation during new construction, retrofitting existing homes with improved insulation is also feasible. Enhancements may involve opting for "smart glass" options for windows or implementing green or "living roofs" that effectively balance thermal heat exchange while providing a cooling effect for the surrounding urban environment.[17]

9. Cultivate a Community Garden

The rapid urbanisation we have witnessed has resulted in the depletion of green spaces and local ecosystems, placing a significant burden on both the environment and human health. However, in each of our neighbourhoods, we have the power to contribute to the restoration of nature. While it may seem daunting to know where to begin, there are often local nature reserves, community parks, or allotment gardens actively seeking new members or volunteers.

You don't have to be a gardening expert or possess a green thumb to make a difference. All you need is a willingness and enthusiasm to get involved. However, knowing where to look is essential. Reach out to local wildlife or horticulture organisations, explore community notice boards either in person or online, or contact your local authority or government for guidance. In addition to more traditional garden sites, many communities are now embracing the concept of green streets. These initiatives involve integrating gardens into the urban fabric, such as roadside meadows, planted boulevards, and gardens within roundabouts or traffic circles. So, even if you don't have a personal garden, you might find a plot on a nearby street.

Apart from gardening opportunities, there are numerous ways to enhance our neighbourhoods. Engaging in activities like litter picking and participating in environmental clean-ups focused on watercourses can have a positive impact. In the event that you are unable to find existing initiatives or programs to get involved in, you have the potential to start something yourself.

Remember, by taking small steps and joining forces with others, we can collectively contribute to the restoration and preservation of nature in our own communities.

10. Tend Your Plot

Our homes and gardens serve as a potent starting point for embracing a new way of living, one that promotes health and harmony with the earth. How we care for and inhabit our own small plots reflects our beliefs about our place in the world and our connection to it. Therefore, it is a vital place to begin our journey.

In the United Kingdom, where I reside, the majority of people have gardens that cover an impressive 433,000 hectares, equivalent to over 700,000 football fields.[18] These gardens constitute approximately 50 percent of the total urban green space, providing a significant resource for wildlife to thrive. Even though larger gardens have more opportunities for creating habitat-rich spaces, postage-stamp-sized plots when considered collectively, can make a substantial difference.

Unfortunately, there is an alarming trend of losing garden habitats. More and more hard surfaces such as car parks, patios, decks, and additional buildings like sheds, garages, or greenhouses are replacing the natural ground. Even lawns are being replaced with artificial grass, causing detrimental effects on the environment.

Thankfully, there are numerous affordable and wonderful ways to support the biodiversity around us. Just imagine the urban garden created if everyone planted a tree, cultivated wildflowers to attract pollinating birds, bees, and butterflies, or created a bird bath or pond that would host a range of wildlife from frogs and newts to dragonflies. Installing nest and roost boxes for birds, bats, and invertebrates is another great option. You could also grow your own food and establish a vegetable patch with soil enriched by your kitchen compost. Even if you only have a windowsill, it is possible to grow herbs or other plants that provide nourishment for struggling pollinators.

Let's not overlook the potential of walls and roofs as vital spaces for wildlife. One study revealed that in London alone, an astounding 1000 hectares (almost 2500 acres) of roofs have the structural capacity for greening—if only we were to take the initiative and plant wildflowers. This would create an impressive habitat in the sky, compensating for the substantial ground that has been lost.[19]

It may be tempting to believe that our individual efforts in our small plots won't have a significant impact, but that notion couldn't be further from the truth. When we envision a world where each person nurtures their own plot and takes responsibility for their choices, we begin to realise the potential for radical regeneration. Echoing the wisdom of Mahatma Gandhi, "If we could change ourselves, the tendencies in the world would also change... We need not wait to see what others do."[20] In essence, be the catalyst for the change you wish to see in the world. It all starts with you.

15

Reframing Our Future

VISION TO REALITY

The biosphere, Mother Nature, Gaia, whatever name you choose to call this awe-inspiring, one-of-a-kind, living earth, is an invaluable and irreplaceable marvel. It sustains us by providing the air we breathe, the food we eat, the water we drink. It is everything to us. Our relationship with this living earth must be our utmost priority.

It is through the landscape that we can heal the divide between humanity and nature, a reconciliation long overdue. The misguided perspective of our separation from nature has caused immense suffering, wrecking landscapes, destroying habitats and extinguishing countless species. The devastation continues to escalate.

While the challenges we face may appear insurmountable—especially with the intensifying climate change, ecological decline, population growth, and other pressures outlined in the planetary boundary model—we can overcome them through a fundamental reframing of our thinking, consciousness, and vision.

To halt this destruction, we must embark on a radical paradigm shift from a portrait-centric perspective to a landscape-centric worldview, breaking free from the confinement of our limited experience. By embracing the magnificence of all of nature, we open the door wide to a new world and a new way of coexisting within it.

With this visionary landscape perspective, nature becomes an integral part of our communities, nurturing life in all its splendour. Humanity flourishes within a vibrant landscape of hope, colour and diversity. We are elevated to a transcendent realm of harmony, growth, and beauty, at one with all life.

The truth is that we are part of nature, not separate from it. We must start living that truth. The key moves set out in this book, encompassing comprehensive measures of land investment, inclusive governance structures, landscape-led development, green education, and skill-building, as well as individual and community obligation to the living world, guide us toward that truth.

The landscape framework outlined within these pages serves as a roadmap, leading us from an awakening of eco-consciousness to the realisation of community-centric values in our landscapes—a journey from vision to reality. By embracing a radical reorientation from a human-centred, economically driven world to a landscape, community-centred paradigm, we unlock boundless possibilities for joyful coexistence. This transformative path from Portrait to Landscape may be challenging, with numerous obstacles to overcome. However, choosing a different course that fosters inclusivity and regeneration for all of nature is not a mere dream—it is within our reach.

To bring this vision to life, each of us must play our part in driving global transformation. It is the choices we make, both small and significant, in the days, weeks, months, and years ahead that will shape our future. There is no one else to look to and no one else to blame. The responsibility rests solely upon our shoulders.

I began this book with one quote from Einstein, and I now conclude with another. He wisely stated, "Each of us has to do his little bit toward transforming this spirit of the times."[1] This book represents my contribution, my "bit" in this grand endeavour. I have shown you the current state of the world's landscapes, how we arrived here, the trajectory we are on, and most importantly, how we can chart a new course.

NOW, I ask you, what is your "bit"?

Appendix

Appendix A
PLANETARY BOUNDARIES

The planetary boundaries outlined in Chapter 2 are described in detail below. The text is taken directly from the Stockholm Resilience Centre website. [1]

Stratospheric ozone depletion

The stratospheric ozone layer in the atmosphere filters out ultraviolet (UV) radiation from the sun. If this layer decreases, increasing amounts of UV radiation will reach ground level. This can cause a higher incidence of skin cancer in humans as well as damage to terrestrial and marine biological systems.

The appearance of the Antarctic ozone hole was proof that increased concentrations of anthropogenic ozone-depleting chemical substances, interacting with polar stratospheric clouds, had passed a threshold and moved the Antarctic stratosphere into a new regime.

Fortunately, because of the actions taken as a result of the Montreal Protocol, we appear to be on the path that will allow us to stay within this boundary.

Loss of biosphere integrity (biodiversity loss and extinctions)

The Millennium Ecosystem Assessment of 2005 concluded that changes to ecosystems due to human activities were more rapid in the past 50 years than at any time in human history, increasing the risks of abrupt and irreversible changes.

The main drivers of change are the demand for food, water, and natural resources, causing severe biodiversity loss and leading to changes in ecosystem services. These drivers are either steady, showing no evidence of declining over time, or are increasing in intensity. The current high rates of ecosystem damage and extinction can be slowed by efforts to protect the integrity of living systems (the biosphere), enhancing habitat, and improving connectivity between ecosystems while maintaining the high agricultural productivity that humanity needs.

Further research is underway to improve the availability of reliable data for use as the 'control variables' for this boundary.

Chemical pollution and the release of novel entities

Emissions of toxic and long-lived substances such as synthetic organic pollutants, heavy metal compounds and radioactive materials represent some of the key human-driven changes to the planetary environment. These compounds can have potentially irreversible effects on living organisms and on the physical environment (by affecting atmospheric processes and climate).

Even when the uptake and bioaccumulation of chemical pollution is at sub-lethal levels for organisms, the effects of reduced fertility and the potential of permanent genetic damage can have severe effects on ecosystems far removed from the source of the pollution. For example, persistent organic compounds have caused dramatic reductions in bird populations and impaired reproduction and development in marine mammals.

There are many examples of additive and synergic effects from these compounds, but these are still poorly understood scientifically. At present, we are unable to quantify a single chemical pollution boundary, although the risk of crossing Earth system thresholds is considered sufficiently well-defined for it to be included in the list as a priority for precautionary action and for further research.

Climate change

Recent evidence suggests that the Earth, now passing 390 ppmv CO_2 in the atmosphere, has already transgressed the planetary boundary and is approaching several Earth system thresholds.

We have reached a point at which the loss of summer polar sea-ice is almost certainly irreversible. This is one example of a well-defined threshold above which rapid physical feedback mechanisms can drive the earth system into a much warmer state with sea levels metres higher than present. The weakening or reversal of terrestrial carbon sinks, for example through the on-going destruction of the world's rainforests, is another potential tipping point, where climate-carbon cycle feedbacks accelerate Earth's warming and intensify the climate impacts.

A major question is how long we can remain over this boundary before large, irreversible changes become unavoidable.

Ocean acidification

Around a quarter of the CO_2 that humanity emits into the atmosphere is ultimately dissolved in the oceans. Here it forms carbonic acid, altering ocean chemistry and decreasing the pH of the surface water. This increased acidity reduces the amount of available carbonate ions, an essential 'building block' used by many marine species for shell and skeleton formation.

Beyond a threshold concentration, this rising acidity makes it hard for organisms such as corals and some shellfish and plankton species to grow and survive. Losses of these species would change the structure and dynamics of ocean ecosystems and could potentially lead to drastic reductions in fish stocks. Compared to pre-industrial times, surface ocean acidity has already increased by 30 percent.

Unlike most other human impacts on the marine environment, which are often local in scale, the ocean acidification boundary has ramifications for the whole planet. It is also an example of how tightly interconnected the boundaries are, since atmospheric CO_2 concentration is the underlying controlling variable for both the climate and the ocean acidification boundaries, although they are defined in terms of different Earth system thresholds.

Freshwater consumption and the global hydrological cycle

The freshwater cycle is strongly affected by climate change and its boundary is closely linked to the climate boundary. Yet, human pressure is now the dominant driving force determining the functioning and distribution of global freshwater systems.

The consequences of human modification of water bodies include both global-scale river flow changes and shifts in vapour flows arising from land use change. These shifts in the hydrological system can be abrupt and irreversible. Water is becoming increasingly scarce - by 2050 about half a billion people are likely to be subject to water-stress, increasing the pressure to intervene in water systems.

A water boundary related to consumptive freshwater use and environmental flow requirements has been proposed to maintain the overall resilience of the Earth system and to avoid the risk of 'cascading' local and regional thresholds.

Land system change

Land is converted to human use all over the planet. Forests, grasslands, wetlands and other vegetation types have primarily been converted to agricultural land. This land-use change is one driving force behind the serious reductions in biodiversity, and it has impacts on water flows and on the biogeochemical cycling of carbon, nitrogen and phosphorus and other important elements.

While each incident of land cover change occurs on a local scale, the aggregated impacts can have consequences for Earth system processes on a global scale. A boundary for human changes to land systems needs to reflect not just the absolute quantity of land, but also its function, quality and spatial distribution. Forests play a particularly important role in controlling the linked dynamics of land use and climate, and is the focus of the boundary for land system change.

Nitrogen and phosphorus flows to the biosphere and oceans

The biogeochemical cycles of nitrogen and phosphorus have been radically changed by humans as a result of many industrial and agricultural processes. Nitrogen and phosphorus are both essential elements for plant growth, so fertiliser production and application is the main concern.

Human activities now convert more atmospheric nitrogen into reactive forms than all of the Earth's terrestrial processes combined. Much of this new reactive nitrogen is emitted to the atmosphere in various forms rather than taken up by crops. When it is rained out, it pollutes waterways and coastal zones or accumulates in the terrestrial biosphere. Similarly, a relatively small proportion of phosphorus fertilisers applied to food production systems is taken up by plants; much of the phosphorus mobilised by humans also ends up in aquatic systems. These can become oxygen-starved as bacteria consume the blooms of algae that grow in response to the high nutrient supply.

A significant fraction of the applied nitrogen and phosphorus makes its way to the sea, and can push marine and aquatic systems across ecological thresholds of their own. One regional-scale example of this effect is the decline in the shrimp catch in the Gulf of Mexico's 'dead zone' caused by fertiliser transported in rivers from the US Midwest.

Atmospheric aerosol loading

An atmospheric aerosol planetary boundary was proposed primarily because of the influence of aerosols on Earth's climate system. Through their interaction with water vapour, aerosols play a critically important role in the hydrological cycle affecting cloud formation and global-scale and regional patterns of atmospheric circulation, such as the monsoon systems in tropical regions. They also have a direct effect on climate, by changing how much solar radiation is reflected or absorbed in the atmosphere.

Humans change the aerosol loading by emitting atmospheric pollution (many pollutant gases condense into droplets and particles), and also through land-use change that increases the release of dust and smoke into the air. Shifts in climate regimes and monsoon systems have already been seen in highly polluted environments, giving a quantifiable regional measure for an aerosol boundary.

A further reason for an aerosol boundary is that aerosols have adverse effects on many living organisms. Inhaling highly polluted air causes roughly 800,000 people to die prematurely each year. The toxicological and ecological effects of aerosols may thus relate to other Earth system thresholds. However, the behaviour of aerosols in the atmosphere is extremely complex, depending on their chemical composition and their geographical location and height in the atmosphere.

While many relationships between aerosols, climate and ecosystems are well established, many causal links are yet to be determined.

Appendix B

UNIVERSAL DECLARATION FOR THE RIGHTS OF MOTHER EARTH

The Universal Declaration for the Rights of Mother Earth, discussed in Chapter 11, is quoted in full below. [1]

Preamble

We, the peoples and nations of Earth:

considering that we are all part of Mother Earth, an indivisible, living community of interrelated and interdependent beings with a common destiny;

gratefully acknowledging that Mother Earth is the source of life, nourishment and learning and provides everything we need to live well;

recognizing that the capitalist system and all forms of depredation, exploitation, abuse and contamination have caused great destruction, degradation and disruption of Mother Earth, putting life as we know it today at risk through phenomena such as climate change;

convinced that in an interdependent living community it is not possible to recognize the rights of only human beings without causing an imbalance within Mother Earth;

affirming that to guarantee human rights it is necessary to

recognize and defend the rights of Mother Earth and all beings in her and that there are existing cultures, practices and laws that do so;

conscious of the urgency of taking decisive, collective action to transform structures and systems that cause climate change and other threats to Mother Earth;

proclaim this Universal Declaration of the Rights of Mother Earth, and call on the General Assembly of the United Nation to adopt it, as a common standard of achievement for all peoples and all nations of the world, and to the end that every individual and institution takes responsibility for promoting through teaching, education, and consciousness raising, respect for the rights recognized in this Declaration and ensure through prompt and progressive measures and mechanisms, national and international, their universal and effective recognition and observance among all peoples and States in the world.

Article 1. Mother Earth

(1) Mother Earth is a living being.

(2) Mother Earth is a unique, indivisible, self-regulating community of interrelated beings that sustains, contains and reproduces all beings.

(3) Each being is defined by its relationships as an integral part of Mother Earth.

(4) The inherent rights of Mother Earth are inalienable in that they arise from the same source as existence.

(5) Mother Earth and all beings are entitled to all the inherent rights recognized in this Declaration without distinction of any kind, such as may be made between organic and inorganic beings, species, origin, use to human beings, or any other status.

(6) Just as human beings have human rights, all other beings also have rights which are specific to their species or kind and appropriate for their role and function within the communities within which they exist.

(7) The rights of each being are limited by the rights of other beings and any conflict between their rights must be resolved in a

way that maintains the integrity, balance and health of Mother Earth.

Article 2. Inherent Rights of Mother Earth

(1) Mother Earth and all beings of which she is composed have the following inherent rights:

(a) the right to life and to exist;

(b) the right to be respected;

(c) the right to regenerate its bio-capacity and to continue its vital cycles and processes free from human disruptions;

(d) the right to maintain its identity and integrity as a distinct, self-regulating and interrelated being;

(e) the right to water as a source of life;

(f) the right to clean air;

(g) the right to integral health;

(h) the right to be free from contamination, pollution and toxic or radioactive waste;

(i) the right to not have its genetic structure modified or disrupted in a manner that threatens its integrity or vital and healthy functioning;

(j) the right to full and prompt restoration for violation of the rights recognized in this Declaration caused by human activities;

(2) Each being has the right to a place and to play its role in Mother Earth for her harmonious functioning.

(3) Every being has the right to wellbeing and to live free from torture or cruel treatment by human beings.

Article 3. Obligations of human beings to Mother Earth

(1) Every human being is responsible for respecting and living in harmony with Mother Earth.

(2) Human beings, all States, and all public and private institutions must:

(a) act in accordance with the rights and obligations recognized in this Declaration;

(b) recognize and promote the full implementation and

enforcement of the rights and obligations recognized in this Declaration;

(c) promote and participate in learning, analysis, interpretation and communication about how to live in harmony with Mother Earth in accordance with this Declaration;

(d) ensure that the pursuit of human wellbeing contributes to the wellbeing of Mother Earth, now and in the future;

(e) establish and apply effective norms and laws for the defence, protection and conservation of the rights of Mother Earth;

(f) respect, protect, conserve and where necessary, restore the integrity, of the vital ecological cycles, processes and balances of Mother Earth;

(g) guarantee that the damages caused by human violations of the inherent rights recognized in this Declaration are rectified and that those responsible are held accountable for restoring the integrity and health of Mother Earth;

(h) empower human beings and institutions to defend the rights of Mother Earth and of all beings;

(i) establish precautionary and restrictive measures to prevent human activities from causing species extinction, the destruction of ecosystems or the disruption of ecological cycles;

(j) guarantee peace and eliminate nuclear, chemical and biological weapons;

(k) promote and support practices of respect for Mother Earth and all beings, in accordance with their own cultures, traditions and customs;

(l) promote economic systems that are in harmony with Mother Earth and in accordance with the rights recognized in this Declaration.

Article 4. Definitions

(1) The term "being" includes ecosystems, natural communities, species and all other natural entities which exist as part of Mother Earth.

(2) Nothing in this Declaration restricts the recognition of other inherent rights of all beings or specified beings.

Notes

1. Embracing Landscape

1. Albert Einstein, letter to Norman Salit, March 4, 1950. (The Hebrew University of Jerusalem).
2. Stephen Hawking and Leonard Mlodinow, "The (Elusive) Theory of Everything", *Scientific American* 303, no. 4 (2010): 70, accessed February 26, 2023, https://www.jstor.org/stable/26002214.
3. Author's own.
4. Stephen Hawking and Leonard Mlodinow, *The Grand Design* (New York: Bantam Books, 2012), 46.
5. Hawking and Mlodinow, *The Grand Design,* 46–47.
6. Daniel Kahneman, *Thinking, Fast and Slow* (London: Penguin Books, 2012), 199.
7. Kahneman, *Thinking, Fast and Slow,* 201.
8. Genesis 1:26-27, (New Revised Standard Version, Anglicised).
9. Albert Einstein, letter to Norman Salit, March 4, 1950.
10. Author's own.
11. Daniel Christian Wahl, "Ways of Knowing: Separation and Participation", *Regenerate The Future* (blog), February 24, 2017, accessed October 3, 2022, https://medium.com/activate-the-future/ways-of-knowing-separation-and-participation-6af7376a3346.
12. Richard Tarnas, *The Passion of the Western Mind: Understanding the Ideas That Have Shaped Our World View* (New York: Ballantine Books, 1991), 434.
13. Aldo Leopold, *A Sand County Almanac: And Sketches Here and There, special commemorative* (New York: Oxford University Press, 2020), 191.
14. Leopold, *A Sand County Almanac*, 191.
15. Leopold, *A Sand County Almanac*, 190.
16. Leopold, *A Sand County Almanac*, 167.
17. Leopold, *A Sand County Almanac*, 211.
18. Leopold, *A Sand County Almanac*, 208.
19. Leopold, *A Sand County Almanac*, 192.
20. Albert Einstein, letter to Norman Salit, March 4, 1950.

2. The Current Landscape

1. Rachel Carson, *Silent Spring*, 3rd ed. (London: Penguin Classics, 2000), 240.
2. Carson, *Silent Spring*, 240.
3. "Could Be Year's Most Noted Book", *The Cincinnati Enquirer*, September 29, 1962, Newspapers.com.
4. American Experience, | PBS, "Chapter 1 | Rachel Carson | American Experience | PBS", YouTube video, 8:59, posted by American Experience | PBS, January 17, 2017, accessed October 10, 2022, https://www.youtube.com/watch?v=SeJNRaE11A0.

5. Clarence Cottam and Elmer Higgins, "DDT: Its Effect on Fish and Wildlife", (Washington: Government Printing Office, 1946), 1, accessed October 20, 2022, https://spo.nmfs.noaa.gov/sites/default/files/legacy-pdfs/CIRC11.pdf.
6. Carson, *Silent Spring*, 9.
7. Cottam and Higgins, "DDT: Its Effect on Fish and Wildlife".
8. Carson, *Silent Spring*, 22.
9. Al Gore, "Introduction", in *Silent Spring*, by Rachel Carson (Boston: Houghton Mifflin Co, 1994), xviii, accessed October 20, 2022, http://eebweb.arizona.edu/courses/Ecol206/Gore1994.pdf.
10. Carson, *Silent Spring*, 30.
11. Richard P. Allan et al., "Summary for Policymakers", in IPCC, *Climate Change 2021: The Physical Science Basis. Contribution of Working Group I to the Sixth Assessment Report of the Intergovernmental Panel on Climate Change* (Cambridge, United Kingdom and New York, NY, USA: Cambridge University Press, 2021), accessed November 13, 2022, DOI:10.1017/9781009157896.001
12. "Secretary-General Calls Latest IPCC Climate Report 'Code Red for Humanity,' Stressing 'Irrefutable' Evidence of Human Influence", *United Nations Secretary-General*, August 9, 2021, accessed November 13, 2022, https://press.un.org/en/2021/sgsm20847.doc.htm.
13. Jeff Tollefson, "Climate Change Is Hitting the Planet Faster than Scientists Originally Thought", *Nature*, February 28, 2022, accessed October 15, 2022, https://doi.org/10.1038/d41586-022-00585-7. citing Hans-Otto Pörtner et al., "Climate Change 2022: Impacts, Adaptation and Vulnerability", Contribution of Working Group II to the Sixth Assessment Report of the Intergovernmental Panel on Climate Change (Cambridge: Cambridge University Press, 2022), https://doi.org/10.1017/9781009325844.
14. "Weather-Related Disasters Increase over Past 50 Years, Causing More Damage but Fewer Deaths", *World Meteorological Organization*, accessed January 24, 2023, https://public.wmo.int/en/media/press-release/weather-related-disasters-increase-over-past-50-years-causing-more-damage-fewer.
15. Martin Farrer, "Pakistan Floods: Plea for Help amid Fears Monsoon Could Put a Third of Country Underwater", *The Guardian*, August 29, 2022, accessed October 15, 2022, https://www.theguardian.com/world/2022/aug/29/pakistan-floods-plea-for-help-amid-fears-monsoon-could-put-a-third-of-country-underwater.
16. "Flooding in Pakistan: The Latest News", *British Red Cross*, accessed March 1, 2023, https://www.redcross.org.uk/stories/disasters-and-emergencies/world/climate-change-and-pakistan-flooding-affecting-millions.
17. Government of Pakistan, "Updated Nationally Determined Contributions", 2021, 12, accessed January 15, 2023, https://unfccc.int/sites/default/files/NDC/2022-06/Pakistan%20Updated%20NDC%202021.pdf.
18. "5 Natural Disasters That Beg for Climate Action", *Oxfam*, accessed January 24, 2023, https://www.oxfam.org/en/5-natural-disasters-beg-climate-action.
19. Moulid Hujale, "Somalis Abandon Their Homes in Search of Food, Water and Aid as Drought Deepens", *United Nations High Commissioner for Refugees*, September 29, 2022, accessed December 10, 2022, https://www.unhcr.org/news/stories/2022/9/633419134/somalis-abandon-homes-search-food-water-aid-drought-deepens.html.
20. "5 Natural Disasters That Beg for Climate Action".
21. Sami Adler, "How Much Would It Cost To End Climate Change?", *GlobalGiving*, March 1, 2021, accessed March 7, 2023, https://www.globalgiv-

ing.org/learn/cost-to-end-climate-change/.

22. "5 Natural Disasters That Beg for Climate Action."
23. British Columbia Coroners Service, *Extreme Heat and Human Mortality: A Review of Heat-Related Deaths in B.C. in Summer 2021*, (2022), accessed February 11, 2022, https://www2.gov.bc.ca/assets/gov/birth-adoption-death-marriage-and-divorce/deaths/coroners-service/death-review-panel/extreme_heat_death_review_panel_report.pdf.
24. Camille Labchuk, "BC Heat Waves Are a Death Sentence for Farmed Animals", *Animal Justice* (blog), July 29, 2022, accessed February 11, 2023, https://animaljustice.ca/blog/bc-heatwaves.
25. Shelby Thom, "'It's Horrible': B.C. Heat Wave Killed Birds, Some Saved by Okanagan Raptor Centre", *Global News*, July 6, 2021, accessed February 11, 2023, https://globalnews.ca/news/8006382/b-c-heat-wave-raptors-saved-lost-sorco/.
26. Justine Hunter, "Cost of rebuilding B.C. after flooding nears $9-billion", *The Globe and Mail*, Feb 19, 2022, accessed May 12, 2023, https://www.theglobeandmail.com/canada/british-columbia/article-cost-of-rebuilding-bc-after-november-storms-nears-9-billion/
27. Jonathan Watts, "Johan Rockström: 'We Need Bankers as Well as Activists... We Have 10 Years to Cut Emissions by Half'", *The Observer*, May 29, 2021, accessed April 5, 2023, https://www.theguardian.com/environment/2021/may/29/johan-rockstrom-interview-breaking-boundaries-attenborough-biden.
28. Fred Pearce, "Arctic Ice Grows Darker and Less Reflective", *New Scientist*, August 5, 2013, accessed April 5, 2023, https://www.newscientist.com/article/dn23994-arctic-ice-grows-darker-and-less-reflective/.
29. "Ain't No Sunshine When She's Gone", *National Snow and Ice Data Centre*, accessed February 1, 2023, https://nsidc.org/arcticseaicenews/2022/10/no-sunshine-when-shes-gone/.
30. Myles R. Allen et al., "Framing and Context", in *Global Warming of 1.5°C: An IPCC Special Report on the Impacts of Global Warming of 1.5°C above Pre-Industrial Levels and Related Global Greenhouse Gas Emission Pathways, in the Context of Strengthening the Global Response to the Threat of Climate Change, Sustainable Development, and Efforts to Eradicate Poverty*, ed. Valérie Masson-Delmotte et al., online (Cambridge: Cambridge University Press, 2018), 82, https://doi.org/10.1017/9781009157940.003.
31. Jeff Turrentine, "What Are the Causes of Climate Change?" *NRDC*, September 13, 2022, accessed October 5, 2022, https://www.nrdc.org/stories/what-are-causes-climate-change.
32. "The Evidence Is Clear: The Time for Action Is Now. We Can Halve Emissions by 2030", *IPCC*, April 4, 2022, accessed March 17, 2023, https://www.ipcc.ch/2022/04/04/ipcc-ar6-wgiii-pressrelease/.
33. Author's own, interpretation of "Ecosystem Land Wheel" and "Ecosystem Seas Wheel", *NatureScot*, accessed October 23, 2022, https://www.nature.scot/scotlands-biodiversity/scottish-biodiversity-strategy-and-cop15/ecosystem-approach/ecosystem-services-natures-benefits.
34. "Carbon stocks and sequestration in terrestrial and marine ecosystems: a lever for nature restoration?", *European Environment Agency*, February 7th, 2023, accessed May 29, 2023, https://www.eea.europa.eu/publications/carbon-stocks-and-sequestration-rates/carbon-stocks-and-sequestration-in.

35. Author's own, interpretation of "Have you ever asked yourself what happens to all the CO2 we generate?", *Iberdrola*, accessed November 10, 2022, https://www.iberdrola.com/sustainability/carbon-sinks.
36. "What Is a Carbon Sink?", *ClientEarth Communications*, December 22, 2020, accessed February 24, 2023, https://www.clientearth.org/latest/latest-updates/stories/what-is-a-carbon-sink/.
37. Eli Kintisch, "Amazon Rainforest Ability to Soak up Carbon Dioxide Is Falling", *Science*, March 18, 2015, accessed September 29, 2022, https://www.science.org/content/article/amazon-rainforest-ability-soak-carbon-dioxide-falling.
38. Birgitte Svennevig, "Top 5 Most Efficient Ecosystems for Carbon Storage", *SDU*, October 29, 2018, accessed December 10, 2022, https://www.sdu.dk/en/om_sdu/fakulteterne/naturvidenskab/nyheder2018/2018_10_29_eelgrass.
39. "Coastal Blue Carbon", *National Oceanic and Atmospheric Administration*, accessed March 22, 2023, https://oceanservice.noaa.gov/ecosystems/coastal-blue-carbon/.
40. "The Ocean – The World's Greatest Ally against Climate Change", *United Nations*, accessed March 13, 2023, https://www.un.org/en/climatechange/science/climate-issues/ocean.
41. Richard E. Leakey and Roger Lewin, *The Sixth Extinction: Patterns of Life and the Future of Humankind* (New York: Doubleday, 1995).
42. "What Is IPBES?", *The Intergovernmental Science-Policy Platform on Biodiversity and Ecosystem Services (IPBES)*, March 16, 2017, accessed March 13, 2023, https://www.ipbes.net/node/40.
43. Sandra Díaz et al., *IPBES: Summary for Policymakers of the Global Assessment Report on Biodiversity and Ecosystem Services of the Intergovernmental Science-Policy Platform on Biodiversity and Ecosystem Services* (Bonn, Germany: IPBES, 2019), 10, accessed January 15, 2023, https://doi.org/10.5281/zenodo.3553458.
44. Carmen Ang, "WWF: These Are the Biggest Threats to the Earth's Biodiversity", *World Economic Forum*, November 16, 2020, accessed January 25, 2023, https://www.weforum.org/agenda/2020/11/wwf-living-planet-report-2020-biodiversity-threat.
45. Author's own, based on Patrick Greenfield and Phoebe Weston, "The five biggest threats to our natural world … and how we can stop them". *The Guardian*, October 14, 2021, accessed September 29, 2022, https://www.theguardian.com/environment/2021/oct/14/five-biggest-threats-natural-world-how-we-can-stop-them-aoe.
46. WWF, *Living Planet Report 2022: Building a Naturepositive Society*, (Gland, Switzerland: WWF, 2022), 4, accessed January 25, 2023, https://wwflpr.awsassets.panda.org/downloads/lpr_2022_full_report_1.pdf.
47. Almond et al., *Living Planet Report 2022*, 34–35.
48. Mikaela Weisse and Elizabeth Goldman, "We Lost a Football Pitch of Primary Rainforest Every 6 Seconds in 2019", *World resources Institute*, June 2, 2020, accessed October 3, 2022, https://www.wri.org/insights/we-lost-football-pitch-primary-rainforest-every-6-seconds-2019. citing "Interactive World Forest Map and Tree Cover Change Data", *Global Forest Watch*, 2020, https://www.globalforestwatch.org/map/.
49. Nichole Barger et al., "Chapter 3: Direct and Indirect Drivers of Land Degradation and Restoration", in *The IPBES Assessment Report on Land Degradation and Restoration*, ed. Luca Montanarella, Robert Scholes, and Anastasia Brainich (Bonn, Germany: IPBES, 2018), 142.

50. Patricia Balvanera et al., "Chapter 2.1. Status and Trends – Drivers of Change", in *Global Assessment Report of the Intergovernmental Science-Policy Platform on Biodiversity and Ecosystem Services*, ed. Eduardo Brondizio et al. (Bonn, Germany: IPBES Secretariat, 2019), 114, accessed January 17, 2023, https://doi.org/10.5281/zenodo.3831881. citing Philip E. Hulme, "Trade, Transport and Trouble: Managing Invasive Species Pathways in an Era of Globalization," *Journal of Applied Ecology* 46, no. 1 (2009): 10–18.
51. Andrew Purvis et al., "Chapter 2.2. Status and Trends – Nature," in *Global Assessment Report of the Intergovernmental Science-Policy Platform on Biodiversity and Ecosystem Services*, ed. Eduardo Brondizio et al. (Bonn, Germany: IPBES Secretariat, 2019), 208, accessed February 8, 2023, https://doi.org/10.5281/zenodo.3832005, citing Karen R. Lips, "Overview of Chytrid Emergence and Impacts on Amphibians," *Philosophical Transactions of the Royal Society B: Biological Sciences* 371, no. 1709 (2016).
52. Purvis et al., "Chapter 2.2. Status and Trends – Nature", 2019, 263. citing Food and Agriculture Organization of the United Nations, "The Future of Food and Agriculture – Trends and Challenges", (Rome: FAO, 2017), https://www.fao.org/3/i6583e/i6583e.pdf.
53. Leakey and Lewin, *The Sixth Extinction: Patterns of Life and the Future of Humankind.*
54. "COP15: Nations Adopt Four Goals, 23 Targets for 2030 in Landmark UN Biodiversity Agreement", *Convention on Biological Diversity*, December 19, 2022, accessed February 17, 2023, https://www.cbd.int/article/cop15-cbd-press-release-final-19dec2022.
55. "FAQ 2: How will nature and the benefits it provides to people be affected by higher levels of warming?" *The Intergovernmental Panel on Climate Change*, accessed May 12, 2023, https://www.ipcc.ch/report/ar6/wg2/about/frequently-asked-questions/keyfaq2/.
56. United Nations Department of Economic and Social Affairs, *World Population Prospects 2022: Summary of Results*, (New York: UN, 2022), i–3, accessed November 10, 2023, https://www.un.org/development/desa/pd/sites/www.un.org.development.desa.pd/files/wpp2022_summary_of_results.pdf.
57. United Nations Department of Economic and Social Affairs, *World Population Prospects 2022*, i.
58. Author's own, based on previously cited data.
59. Nadja Popovich and Brad Plumer, "Who Has The Most Historical Responsibility for Climate Change?" *The New York Times*, November 12, 2021, accessed September 29, 2022, https://www.nytimes.com/interactive/2021/11/12/climate/cop26-emissions-compensation.html. citing Robbie M. Andrew and Glen P. Peters, "The Global Carbon Project's Fossil CO2 Emissions Dataset", (Zenodo, 2021), https://doi.org/10.5281/zenodo.5569235. and World Bank, "Population, Total", 2020, https://data.worldbank.org/indicator/SP.POP.TOTL.
60. Hannah Ritchie, Pablo Rosado, and Max Roser, "Meat and Dairy Production", *Our World in Data, 2019*, accessed September 29, 2022, https://ourworldindata.org/meat-production. citing "Crops and Livestock Products", *Food and Agriculture Organization of the United Nations*, 2022, https://www.fao.org/faostat/en/data/QCL.
61. Author's own, using data from Ritchie, Spooner, and Roser, "Biodiversity", citing Bar-On, Phillips, and Milo, "The Biomass Distribution on Earth".

62. Author's own, based on data from Bar-On, Phillips, and Milo, "The Biomass Distribution on Earth", 6508.
63. Hannah Ritchie, Fiona Spooner, and Max Roser, "Biodiversity", *Our World in Data*, 2022, accessed January 25, 2023, https://ourworldindata.org/biodiversity?insight=wild-mammals-make-up-only-a-few-percent-of-the-world-s-mammalsintroduction. citing Yinon M. Bar-On, Rob Phillips, and Ron Milo, "The Biomass Distribution on Earth", *PNAS* 115, no. 25 (2018): 6508, https://doi.org/10.1073/pnas.1711842115.
64. Bar-On, Phillips, and Milo, "The Biomass Distribution on Earth", 6508.
65. Kenneth V. Rosenberg et al., "Decline of the North American Avifauna", *Science* 366, no. 6461 (2019): 1, accessed January 25, 2023, https://doi.org/10.1126/science.aaw1313.
66. Johan Rockström et al., "Planetary Boundaries: Exploring the Safe Operating Space for Humanity", *Ecology and Society* 14, no. 2 (2009): 20.
67. Rockström et al., "Planetary Boundaries", 2.
68. Author's own, interpretation of "Azote for Stockholm Resilience Centre, based on analysis in Persson et al 2022 and Steffen et al 2015", *Stockholm Resilience Centre*, accessed February 12, 2023, https://www.stockholmresilience.org/research/planetary-boundaries.html.
69. "Transforming Our World: The 2030 Agenda for Sustainable Development", *United Nations Department of Economic and Social Affairs*, accessed January 26, 2023, https://sdgs.un.org/publications/transforming-our-world-2030-agenda-sustainable-development-17981.
70. "Transforming Our World".
71. António Guterres, "Remarks to High-Level Political Forum on Sustainable Development", *United Nations Secretary-General*, September 24, 2019, accessed March 5, 2023, https://www.un.org/sg/en/content/sg/speeches/2019-09-24/remarks-high-level-political-sustainable-development-forum.

3. The Cultural Landscape

1. "Transcript: Greta Thunberg's Speech At The U.N. Climate Action Summit", *NPR*, September 23, 2019, accessed February 1, 2023, https://www.npr.org/2019/09/23/763452863/transcript-greta-thunbergs-speech-at-the-u-n-climate-action-summit.
2. *I Am Greta* (BBC iPlayer, 2020), accessed December 15, 2022, https://www.bbc.co.uk/iplayer/episodes/p090xz9z/i-am-greta.
3. "Let's Hear What the World's Highest Court Has to Say about Climate Change", *World's Youth for Climate Justice*, accessed May 22, 2023, https://www.wy4cj.org.
4. Paul Crutzen and Eugene F. Stoermer, "The 'Anthropocene'", *Global Change Newsletter* 41, May 2000, 17, accessed May 22, 2023, http://www.igbp.net/download/18.316f18321323470177580001401/1376383088452/NL41.pdf.
5. Irena Borzenkova et al., "Climate Change During the Holocene (Past 12,000 Years)", in *Second Assessment of Climate Change for the Baltic Sea Basin*, ed. The BACC II Author Team, online (New York: Springer, Cham, 2015), 25, accessed February 24, 2023, https://doi.org/10.1007/978-3-319-16006-1_2.
6. Colin N. Waters et al., "Global Boundary Stratotype Section and Point (GSSP) for the Anthropocene Series: Where and How to Look For Potential Candidates",

Earth-Science Reviews 178, no. 3 (2018): 422, accessed April 24, 2023, https://doi.org/10.1016/j.earscirev.2017.12.016.

7. Kathy A. Hibbard et al., "Group Report: Decadal-Scale Interactions of Humans and the Environment", in *Sustainability or Collapse? An Integrated History and Future of People on Earth*, ed. Robert Costanza et al. (Cambridge, Massachusetts: MIT Press, 2006), 342, accessed October 5, 2022, https://doi.org/10.7551/mitpress/6572.001.0001.
8. Michael E. Mann, "Beyond the Hockey Stick: Climate Lessons from the Common Era", *PNAS* 118, no. 39 (2021): 1, accessed October 3, 2022, https://doi.org/10.1073/pnas.2112797118. Citing Raymond S. Bradley, and Malcolm K. Hughes, "Global-Scale Temperature Patterns and Climate Forcing over the Past Six Centuries", *Nature* 392, no. 4 (1998): 783, https://doi.org/10.1038/33859.
9. Author's own, interpretation of "Great Acceleration", *Anthropocene*, n.d., accessed March 8, 2023, https://www.anthropocene.info/great-acceleration.php. Citing Steffen et al., "The trajectory of the Anthropocene: The Great Acceleration", *The Anthropocene Review* 2, 1 (2015): https://doi.org/10.1177/2053019614564785.
10. Andrew Brennan and Norva Y. S. Lo, "Environmental Ethics", in *Stanford Encyclopedia of Philosophy*, ed. Edward N. Zalta, accessed March 20, 2023, https://plato.stanford.edu/archives/sum2022/entries/ethics-environmental/. Citing Aristotle, *Politics*, trans. Ernest Barker (Oxford: Oxford University Press, 1948).
11. Ian Maclean, *René Descartes: A Discourse on the Method of Correctly Conducting One's Reason and Seeking Truth in the Sciences*, trans. Ian Maclean (New York: Oxford University Press, 2006), 51, accessed 20th November 2022, https://rauterberg.employee.id.tue.nl/lecturenotes/DDM110%20CAS/Descartes-1637%20Discourse%20on%20Method.pdf.
12. Eleonora Montuschi, "Order of Man, Order of Nature: Francis Bacon's Idea of a 'Dominion' over Nature", (London: Centre for Philosophy of Natural and Social Science, London School of Economics and Political Science, 2010), accessed May 5, 2023, https://iris.unive.it/retrieve/handle/10278/24867/23441/MontuschiBacon.pdf. citing Francis Bacon, *Novum Organum*, 1620, aphorism 59.
13. Genesis 1:28 (New Revised Standard Version, Anglicised).
14. Margaret Atwood, "Margaret Atwood: Rachel Carson's Silent Spring, 50 Years On", *The Guardian*, December 7, 2012, accessed April 18, 2023, https://www.theguardian.com/books/2012/dec/07/why-rachel-carson-is-a-saint.
15. Allan Watts, *Tao: The Watercourse Way* (Pantheon, 1975), 26.
16. "Yin-yang", *Oxford Reference*, 2023, accessed June 20, 2023, https://www.oxfordreference.com/display/10.1093/oi/authority.20110803125343848
17. Carl Jung, *The Archetypes and the Collective Unconscious* (Routledge, 1968), 2nd edition.
18. Sylvain Bonhommeau et al., "Eating up the world's food web and the human trophic level", *PNAS* 110, 51 (2013): pp. 20617-20620, accessed February 16, 2023, https://doi.org/10.1073/pnas.1305827110.
19. David Attenborough, *A Life on Our Planet: My Witness Statement and a Vision for the Future*, paperback (London: Witness Books, 2022), 20.
20. Yuval Noah Harari, *Sapiens: A Brief History of Humankind*, (London: Vintage Books, 2014), 20.
21. Author's own.
22. Carl Jung, *Modern Man in Search of a Soul*, trans. W. S. Dell, 2nd ed. (Abingdon, Oxon: Routledge Classics, 2001), 146.

23. Harari, *Sapiens: A Brief History of Humankind*, 55.
24. John Ralph Nursall, "Oxygen as a Prerequisite to the Origin of the Metazoa", *Nature* 183, no. 4 (1959): 1171, accessed September 10, 2022, https://doi.org/10.1038/1831170b0.
25. Donald O. Henry, *From Foraging to Agriculture: The Levant at the End of the Ice Age* (Philadelphia: University of Pennsylvania Press, 1989), 3, accessed September 10, 2022, https://doi.org/10.9783/9781512816822.
26. Antonio Rosas et al., "The Growth Pattern of Neandertals, Reconstructed from a Juvenile Skeleton from El Sidrón (Spain)", *Science* 357, no. 6357 (2017): 1, accessed September 15, 2022, https://doi.org/10.1126/science.aan6463.
27. Abraham H. Maslow, "A Theory of Human Motivation", *Psychological Review* 50, no. 4 (1943): 372, accessed September 15, 2022, https://doi.org/10.1037/h0054346.
28. Andrey Ganopolski, Ricarda Winkelmann, and Hans Joachim Schellnhuber, "Critical Insolation–CO2 Relation for Diagnosing Past and Future Glacial Inception", *Nature* 529, no. 1 (2016): 200, accessed October 2, 2022, https://doi.org/10.1038/nature16494.
29. Tolle, *A New Earth*, xvii.
30. Kate Raworth, *Doughnut Economics: Seven Ways to Think Like a 21st-Century Economist*, 2nd ed. (London: Penguin Books, 2022).
31. Kate Raworth, "A Safe and Just Space for Humanity: Can We Live within the Doughnut?" *Oxfam Discussion Paper* February (2012), accessed March 11, 2023, http://hdl.handle.net/10546/210490.
32. Author's own, interpretation of "The Doughnut of social and planetary boundaries", *Doughnut Economics Action Lab*, n.d., accessed March 11, 2023, https://doughnuteconomics.org/about-doughnut-economics.
33. "Earth Democracy", *Navdanya International,* accessed February 21, 2023, https://navdanyainternational.org/key-issues/earth-democracy/.
34. Michael Specter, "Seeds of Doubt: An Activist's Controversial Crusade against Genetically Modified Crops", *The New Yorker*, August 18, 2014, accessed February 26, 2023, https://www.newyorker.com/magazine/2014/08/25/seeds-of-doubt.
35. Raworth, *Doughnut Economics*, 4.
36. Vandana Shiva, *Earth Democracy: Justice, Sustainability and Peace*, 2nd ed. (London: Zed Books, 2016), xiii.
37. TEDx Talks, "TEDxMasala – Dr Vandana Shiva – Solutions to the Food and Ecological Crisis Facing Us", YouTube video, 11:40, posted by TEDxTalks, September 25, 2012, accessed Jan 15, 2023, https://www.youtube.com/watch?v=ER5ZZk5atlE&t=85s&ab_channel=TEDxTalks.
38. Shiva, *Earth Democracy*, vii.
39. Credit Suisse Research Institute, *Global Wealth Databook 2015*, (Zurich: Credit Suisse AG, 2015), 3, accessed May 11, 2023, https://www.credit-suisse.com/media/assets/corporate/docs/about-us/research/publications/global-wealth-databook-2015.pdf.
40. World Bank, "Poverty and Shared Prosperity 2022: Correcting Course", (Washington, DC, 2022), xiii, accessed May 11, 2023, https://doi.org/10.1596/978-1-4648-1893-6.
41. Attenborough, *A Life on Our Planet*, 126–28.
42. Shiva, *Earth Democracy*, 2.
43. "Earth Democracy".

4. The Grandest Landscape

1. Alexander von Humboldt and Aimé Bonpland, *Essay on the Geography of Plants (1807)*, ed. Stephen T. Jackson, trans. Sylvie Romanowski (Chicago: University of Chicago Press, 2009), 79.
2. von Humboldt and Bonpland, *Essay on the Geography of Plants (1807)*, 11.
3. Andrea Wulf, *The Invention of Nature: The Adventures of Alexander von Humboldt, the Lost Hero of Science*, paperback (London: John Murray, 2016), 57–59.
4. Wulf, *The Invention of Nature*, 2.
5. "Alexander von Humboldt's vegetation of the Andes", in Patrick J. Comer, Paul Beier, and Joshua J Lawler, "Case studies of conservation plans that incorporate geodiversity: Geodiversity in Conservation Planning", *Conservation Biology* 29, 3 (2015), accessed October 15, 2022, https://www.researchgate.net/figure/Alexander-von-Humboldts-vegetation-of-the-Andes-source-Anne-Buttimer-Alexander-von_fig1_275669011.
6. "Biosphere", *National Geographic*, accessed February 3, 2023, https://education.nationalgeographic.org/resource/biosphere.
7. Author's own, incorporating artwork by William Darton and William R. Gardner, *New and Improved View of the Comparative Heights, of the Principal Mountains and Lengths of the Principal Rivers in the World*, 1823, Wikimedia Commons, accessed December 13, 2022, https://commons.wikimedia.org/wiki/File:1823_Darton_and_Gardner_Comparative_Chart_of_World_Mountains_and_Rivers_-_Geographicus_-_MountainsandRivers-darton-1823.jpg; and James S. Virtue and Co., *Bird's eye view of Lucknow and the country toward Cawnpore*, circa 1860, Wikimedia Commons, , accessed December 14, 2022, https://en.wikipedia.org/wiki/File:Lucknow-birds-eye-1860.jpg.
8. Frank White, *The Overview Effect: Space Exploration and Human Evolution* (Boston: Houghton Mifflin, 1987).
9. Caitlin Dempsey, "Overview Effect: Quotes from Astronauts", *Geography Realm* (blog), December 20, 2021, accessed January 12, 2023, https://www.geographyrealm.com/overview-effect-quotes-from-astronauts/.
10. The Blue Marble, colours converted to grayscale and rescaled by author, photograph by NASA mission AS17, edited by Deglr6328, "The Blue Marble", from Wikimedia Commons, accessed June 12, 2023, https://commons.wikimedia.org/wiki/File:The_Blue_Marble.jpg?uselang=en#filelinks.
11. James Alan Bassham and Hans Lambers, "Photosynthesis", *Encyclopædia Britannica*, December 4, 2022, accessed March 24, 2023, https://www.britannica.com/science/photosynthesis.
12. Michael Marshall, "Timeline: The Evolution of Life", *New Scientist*, July 14, 2009, accessed November 8, 2022, https://www.newscientist.com/article/dn17453-timeline-the-evolution-of-life/.
13. Marshall, "Timeline".
14. Bassham and Lambers, "Photosynthesis".
15. Wulf, *The Invention of Nature*, 5.
16. Jonn Matsen, *Eating Alive II*, (North Vancouver: Goodwin Books, 2002).
17. Matsen, *Eating Alive II*, xv.
18. Matsen, *Eating Alive II*, xv.
19. Pablo Irizar, "Da Vinci's Vitruvian Man and the Measure of All Things", *Antigone Journal*, n.d., accessed June 20th, 2023, https://antigonejournal.-

com/2021/05/da-vinci-vitruvian-man/.

20. Author's own, incorporating artwork by Leonardo da Vinci, *Vitruvian Man*, drawing, circa 1492, Wikimedia Commons, accessed March 3, 2023, https://en.wikipedia.org/wiki/File:Da_Vinci_Vitruve_Luc_Viatour.jpg, and photograph by NASA mission AS17, edited by Deglr6328, "The Blue Marble", from Wikimedia Commons, accessed June 12, 2023, https://commons.wikimedia.org/wiki/File:The_Blue_Marble.jpg?uselang=en#filelinks.
21. Matsen, *Eating Alive II*, xv–xvi.
22. IPBES and IPCC, *IPBES-IPCC Co-sponsored Workshop Report on Biodiversity and Climate* Change (Bonn, Germany: IPBES, 2021), accessed May 24, 2023, https://www.ipbes.net/sites/default/files/2021-06/20210609_workshop_report_embargo_3pm_CEST_10_june_0.pdf.
23. Margaret Atwood, "Margaret Atwood on Literature and the Environment", *Penguin Books*, April 18, 2022, accessed February 6, 2023, https://www.penguin.co.uk/articles/2022/04/margaret-atwood-extract-literature-environment-essay. citing Margaret Atwood, *Burning Questions* (New York: Vintage Publishing, 2022).
24. Alexander von Humboldt, *Views of Nature: Or Contemplations on the Sublime Phenomena of Creation*. Translated by Mark W.Person (Chicago: University of Chicago Press, 2014).

5. Defining Landscape

1. Alexander Pope, "Of the Use of Riches", Epistle to Bathurst (addressed to Allen, Lord Bathurst, 1733).
2. Albert Einstein, letter to Norman Salit, March 4, 1950.
3. Pope, "Of the Use of Riches".
4. Council of Europe, *European Landscape Convention*, (Strasbourg: Council of Europe, 2000), 9, accessed November 8, 2022, https://rm.coe.int/european-landscape-convention-book-text-feb-2008-en/16802f80c6.
5. Claire L. Wicks et al., "The Impact of the Coronavirus Pandemic on the Contribution of Local Green Space and Nature Connection to Mental Health", *Int J Environ Res Public Health* 20, 6 (2023): May 21, 2023, doi: 10.3390/ijerph20065083.
6. Roger S. Ulrich, "View through a Window May Influence Recovery from Surgery", *Science* 224, no. 4647 (1984): 420, accessed April 17, 2023, https://doi.org/10.1126/science.6143402.
7. Omid Kardan et al., "Neighborhood Greenspace and Health in a Large Urban Center", *Scientific Reports* 5, no. 11610 (2015): 1, accessed April 17, 2023, https://doi.org/10.1038/srep11610.
8. Bum Jin Park et al., "The Physiological Effects of Shinrin-Yoku (Taking in the Forest Atmosphere or Forest Bathing): Evidence from Field Experiments in 24 Forests across Japan", *Environmental Health and Preventive Medicine* 15, no. 1 (2010): 25, accessed 17, 2023, https://doi.org/10.1007/s12199-009-0086-9.
9. FIG.23 Opportunity Wheel in Alexandra Steed URBAN, *Vol. 1 South Essex Strategic Green and Blue Infrastructure Study: Resilient by Nature* (2020), 29.
10. Appleseed, *The Central Park Effect: Assessing the Value of Central Park's Contribution to New York City's Economy*, (New York: Central Park Conservancy, 2015), accessed November 13, 2023, https://assets.centralparknyc.org/pdfs/about/The_Central_Park_Effect.pdf.

11. Photograph by Andrew Bertuleit, "Aerial shot of Central Park, Manhattan, New York", converted to grayscale by author.
12. Appleseed, *The Central Park Effect*, 9.
13. Daniel Pecoraro, "Analyzing Central Park as a Source of Biodiversity", *Exploring Central Park*, accessed March 22, 2023, https://eportfolios.macaulay.cuny.edu/themanhattanproject/field-lab-8/analyzing-central-park-as-a-source-of-biodiversity/.
14. John L. Crompton, "The Impact of Parks on Property Values: A Review of the Empirical Research", *Journal of Leisure Research* 33, no. 1 (2001): 8.
15. Crompton, "The Impact of Parks on Property Values", 1.
16. Appleseed, *The Central Park Effect*, 9.
17. "History", *High Line*, accessed March 22, 2023, https://www.thehighline.org/history/.
18. "Coulée Verte René-Dumont", *Paris Tourist Office*, accessed March 22, 2023, https://en.parisinfo.com/paris-museum-monument/71237/Coulee-verte-Rene-Dumont.
19. "History".
20. Photograph by Ferrantraite, "The High Line Park New York", converted to grayscale by author.
21. Suzanne A.G. Leroy, "Natural Hazards, Landscapes and Civilizations", *Reference Module in Earth Systems and Environmental Sciences* B978-0-12-818234-5.00003-1 (2020): accessed May 29, 2023, doi: 10.1016/B978-0-12-818234-5.00003-1.
22. Pope, "Of the Use of Riches". Italicised by author.

6. Urban Landscapes

1. Kim Wilkie, *Led by the Land: Landscapes by Kim Wilkie*, revised (London: Pimpernel Press Ltd, 2019), 28.
2. Dorota Węziak-Białowolska, "Quality of life in cities – Empirical evidence in comparative European perspective", *Cities* 58, (2016): pp. 87-96, accessed May 29, 2023, https://doi.org/10.1016/j.cities.2016.05.016.
3. Wilkie, *Led by the Land*, 29.
4. Terry Farrell, *Shaping London: The Patterns and Forms That Make the Metropolis* (Hoboken, New Jersey: John Wiley & Sons Ltd, 2010), 40.
5. GB Historical GIS, University of Portsmouth, and London GovOf, "London GovOf through Time | Population Statistics | Total Population," *A Vision of Britain through Time*, accessed March 13, 2023, https://www.visionofbritain.org.uk/data_cube_page.jsp?data_theme=T_POP&data_cube=N_TOT_POP&u_id=10097836&c_id=10001043&add=N.
6. Henry Letheby, *Report on the Sanitary Condition of the City of London, for the Year 1866-1867; With a Report on the Cholera Epidemic of 1866*, (London: M. Lownds, 1868), 18, accessed March 3, 2023, https://wellcomelibrary.org/moh/report/b20056485?c=0&m=0&s=0&cv=0.
7. Bill Luckin, *Pollution and Control: A Social History of the Thames in the Nineteenth Century* (Bristol: A. Hilger, 1986).
8. "Major £70million upgrade to Stratford's Victorian sewer system", *Thames Water*, January 17, 2023, accessed February 26, 2023, https://www.thameswater.co.uk/about-us/newsroom/latest-news/2023/jan/70million-stratford-sewer-upgrade.

9. "River Thames: More than 2bn Litres of Raw Sewage Discharged Over Two Days", *BBC News*, January 18 2022, accessed February 10, 2023, https://www.bbc.co.uk/news/uk-england-london-60046320.
10. Author's own, based on map by Nicholas Barton, in *The Lost Rivers of London* by Nicholas Barton (London: Phoenix House, 1962); and data from OS data © Crown copyright OS Open Greenspace and OS Open Rivers 2022.
11. Zhifeng Liu et al., "How Much of the World's Land Has Been Urbanized, Really? A Hierarchical Framework for Avoiding Confusion", *Landscape Ecology* 29, no. 5 (2014): 766, accessed January 23, 2023, https://doi.org/10.1007/s10980-014-0034-y.
12. "Urban Development", *World Bank*, accessed 26 January 26, 2023, https://www.worldbank.org/en/topic/urbandevelopment/overview1.
13. United Nations Department of Economic and Social Affairs, *World Urbanisation Prospects 2018: Key Facts*, Synthesised Report (New York: UN, 2019), 1, accessed October 18, 2023, https://population.un.org/wup/Publications/Files/WUP2018-Highlights.pdf.
14. "World Urbanisation Prospects: The 2018 Revision, 2018", *United Nations Department of Economic and Social Affairs*, accessed March 24, 2023, https://population.un.org/wup/download/.
15. United Nations Department of Economic and Social Affairs, *World Urbanisation Prospects 2018: Key Facts*, 1.
16. Author's own.
17. United Nations Human Settlements Programme, *Streets as Public Spaces and Drivers of Urban Prosperity*, (Nairobi: UN-Habitat 2013), vii, accessed September 20, 2022, https://unhabitat.org/sites/default/files/2020/08/streets_as_public_spaces_and_drivers_of_urban_prosperity.pdf.
18. Photograph by Linda Bair, "Underground utility repairs", converted to grayscale by author.
19. Damian Carrington, "Britain Flouting Duty to Protect Citizens from Toxic Air Pollution – UN," *The Guardian*, September 10, 2017, accessed November 18, 2022, https://www.theguardian.com/environment/2017/sep/10/uk-flouting-duty-to-cut-air-pollution-deaths-says-un-human-rights-report.
20. "Cleaning Up London's Toxic Air", *Talk London*, accessed March 13, 2023, https://www.london.gov.uk/talk-london/cleaning-londons-toxic-air.
21. Hannah Ritchie, "Cars, Planes, Trains: Where Do CO2 Emissions from Transport Come From?", *Our World in Data*, October 6, 2020, accessed March 3, 2023, https://ourworldindata.org/co2-emissions-from-transport. citing "Transport Sector CO2 Emissions by Mode in the Sustainable Development Scenario, 2000-2030", *International Energy Agency*, October 26, 2022, https://www.iea.org/data-and-statistics/charts/transport-sector-co2-emissions-by-mode-in-the-sustainable-development-scenario-2000-2030.
22. Greater London Authority, *The London Plan 2021: The Spatial Development Strategy for Greater London*, (London: Greater London Authority, 2021), sec. 3.8.1, accessed December 5, 2022, https://www.london.gov.uk/sites/default/files/the_london_plan_2021.pdf.
23. Greater London Authority, *The London Plan 2021*, sec. 10.2.1.
24. Author's own.
25. Author's own.
26. Including information from Lancaster City Council, *A Local Plan for Lancaster District 2020 – 2031, Green & Blue Infrastructure Strategy*, (Lancaster: Lancaster City

Council, 2021), accessed October 10, 2022, https://www.lancaster.gov.uk/assets/attach/10486/GBI-Strategy.pdf.

27. Photograph by Terry Farrell, *Shaping London,* 240.
28. Photograph by _ultraforma_, "Panoramic view of Canary Wharf, City of London, The Shard, BT Tower and London Eye at day", converted to grayscale by author.
29. Nick Mathiason, "Man with blueprint - and lofty vision", *The Guardian*, Feb 8, 2004, accessed May 12, 2023, https://www.theguardian.com/business/2004/feb/08/greaterlondonauthority.olympics2012
30. "London 2012 Olympic and Paralympic Games Legacy", *AECOM*, accessed March 22, 2023, https://publications.aecom.com/social-infrastructure/projects/london-2012-olympic-and-paralympic-games-sustainable-legacy-communities-1.
31. Photograph by Dynasoar, "The London 2012 Olympics Park", converted to grayscale by author.
32. "Looking To Get More Involved with the London National Park City?", *London National Park City*, accessed March 22, 2023, https://www.nationalparkcity.london/getinvolved.
33. Vivid Economics, *Natural Capital Accounts for Public Green Space in London*, (London: Vivid Economics, 2017), 3, accessed May 22, 2023, https://www.london.gov.uk/sites/default/files/11015viv_natural_capital_account_for_london_v7_full_vis.pdf.
34. Azila Ahmad Sarkawi, Alias Abdullah, and Norimah M. D. Dali, "A Critical Review on the Worldwide Economist Intelligence Unit, Mercer and Monocle Quality of Life Indicators", *Journal of Business and Economics* 8, no. 7 (2017): 584, accessed May 22, 2023, http://www.academicstar.us/UploadFile/Picture/2017-12/201712422542525.pdf.
35. Damien Gayle, Niamh McIntyre, and Karl Martinsson, "Funding for England's Parks Down £330M a Year in Real Terms since 2010", *The Guardian*, August 23, 2022, accessed October 8, 2022, https://www.theguardian.com/environment/2022/aug/23/funding-for-englands-parks-down-330m-a-year-in-real-terms-since-2010.
36. Andy Pratt, "The Rise of the Quasi-Public Space and Its Consequences for Cities and Culture", *Palgrave Communications* 3, no. 36 (2017): 2, accessed October 15, 2022, https://doi.org/10.1057/s41599-017-0048-6.

7. Peri-Urban Landscapes

1. Mathis Wackernagel and William Rees, *Our Ecological Footprint: Reducing Human Impact on the Earth* (Philadelphia: New Society Publishers, 1996), 4.
2. Wackernagel and Rees, *Our Ecological Footprint*, 1.
3. Wackernagel and Rees, *Our Ecological Footprint*, 4.
4. Wackernagel and Rees, *Our Ecological Footprint*, 5
5. Wackernagel and Rees, *Our Ecological Footprint*, 7
6. Wackernagel and Rees, *Our Ecological Footprint*, 4
7. Author's own, interpretation of "Figure 1.1: We are part of nature", in Wackernagel and Rees, *Our Ecological Footprint*, 8. Artwork incorporated from Caspar David Friedrich, *Der Wanderer über dem Nebelmeer*, painting, 1817, Wikimedia Commons, accessed May 24, 2023, https://en.wikipedia.org/wiki/File:Caspar_-

David_Friedrich_-_Wanderer_above_the_sea_of_fog.jpg; Joseph Constantine Stadler, *Geology: comparative heights of mountains. Coloured aquatint*, etching, 1817, Wikimedia Commons, https://commons.wikimedia.org/wiki/File:Geology;_comparative_heights_of_mountains._Coloured_aquatint_Wellcome_V0025140.jpg; Alexander Francis Lydon, *Wild Deer*, illustration, circa 1860, Pixels, accessed May 24, 2023, https://pixels.com/featured/wild-deer-alexander-francis-lydon.html; Greenock, Scotland, from T. Nelson and Sons, *Souvenir of Scotland: its Cities, Lakes, and Mountains*, (London, Edinburgh and New York: T. Nelson and Sons, 1889; unknown artist, *Factory Smoke At Dowlais, South Wales*, drawing, 1875, Fine Art America, accessed May 24, 2023, https://fineartamerica.com/featured/factory-smoke-at-dowlais-south-wales-mary-evans-picture-library.html; and F. Gleason, *Saw-mills on the Penobscot River, at Oldtown, Maine*, drawing, circa 1854, Maine Memory Network, accessed May 24, 2023, https://www.mainememory.net/artifact/1488.

8. International Institute for Environment and Development, *Citizen Action to Lighten Britain's Ecological Footprints*, (London: International Institute for Environment and Development, 1995), 148, accessed December 10, 2022, https://www.gdrc.org/uem/footprints/IIED-UK_footprints.pdf.
9. George Orwell, *The Road to Wigan Pier* (London: Victor Gollancz, 1937), 9.
10. International Institute for Environment and Development, *Citizen Action to Lighten Britain's Ecological Footprints*, 72.
11. Tim Burrows, "The Only Grave Is Essex: How the County Became London's Dumping Ground", *The Guardian*, October 25, 2016, accessed December 5, 2022, https://www.theguardian.com/cities/2016/oct/25/london-dumping-ground-essex-skeleton-crossrail-closet.
12. Staff Reporter, "Thurrock named one of the most polluted areas in the country", *Your Thurrock*, Dec 12, 2019, accessed May 12, 2023, https://www.yourthurrock.com/2019/12/12/thurrock-named-one-polluted-areas-country/.
13. Nigel Williams, "Sea-Change Riches", *Current Biology* 17, no. 21 (2007): R901, accessed April 17, 2023, https://doi.org/10.1016/j.cub.2007.10.023.
14. Environment Agency, *TE2100 Plan: Managing Flood Risk through London and the Thames Estuary*, (London: Thames Estuary 2100, 2012), 28, https://assets.publishing.service.gov.uk/government/uploads/system/uploads/attachment_data/file/322061/LIT7540_43858f.pdf.
15. Author's own, based on data from Climate Central, *Land Projected to be Below Annual Flood Level in 2100*, accessed April 11, 2023, https://coastal.climatecentral.org/map/10/0.2134/51.5318/?theme=sea_level_rise&map_type=coastal_dem_comparison&basemap=roadmap&contiguous=true&elevation_model=best_available&forecast_year=2100&pathway=rcp45&percentile=p50&refresh=true&return_level=return_level_1&rl_model=gtsr&slr_model=kopp_2014
16. Photograph by Nigel Stripe, "Thames flood barrier with blue sky and white clouds", converted to grayscale by author.
17. David A. Ross, *Introduction to Oceanography*, (New York: Harper Collins College Publishers, 1995).
18. Allan et al., "Summary for Policymakers".
19. Wackernagel and Rees, *Our Ecological Footprint*, 4.
20. Environment Agency, *TE2100 Plan.*
21. Author's own.

22. Alexandra Steed URBAN, *Vol. 1 South Essex Strategic Green and Blue Infrastructure Study: Resilient by Nature* (2020).
23. Pierre Bélanger, *Landscape as Infrastructure* (Routledge, 2016).
24. Carl Steinitz, *A Framework for Geodesign: Changing Geography by Design* (Redlands, Calf: Esri, 2012).
25. Ian McHarg, *Design with Nature* (Hoboken, New Jersey: John Wiley & Sons, Inc., 1992), 25th Anniversary Edition.
26. FIG.26 GBI Strategy Conceptual Diagram in Alexandra Steed URBAN, *Vol. 1 South Essex Strategic Green and Blue Infrastructure Study: Resilient by Nature* (2020), 34.
27. TAB.4 Objectives and SEE Park Key Moves, in Alexandra Steed URBAN, *Vol. 1 South Essex Strategic Green and Blue Infrastructure Study: Resilient by Nature* (2020), 33.
28. FIG.30 Key Moves: Proposed Regional Parkland - overlaid on the existing park and open spaces network, in Alexandra Steed URBAN, *Vol. 1 South Essex Strategic Green and Blue Infrastructure Study: Resilient by Nature* (2020), 36.
29. FIG.51 Public Connectors and FIG.72 Wildlife Railway Connector with Green Bridge in Alexandra Steed URBAN, *Vol. 1 South Essex Strategic Green and Blue Infrastructure Study: Resilient by Nature* (2020), 52-54.
30. FIG. 67 Wildlife Connector and FIG.59 Blue Connectors in Alexandra Steed URBAN, *Vol. 1 South Essex Strategic Green and Blue Infrastructure Study: Resilient by Nature* (2020), 50-52.
31. FIG.83 Shoreline: in areas of agriculture in Alexandra Steed URBAN, *Vol. 1 South Essex Strategic Green and Blue Infrastructure Study: Resilient by Nature* (2020), 58.

8. Rural and Wilderness Landscapes

1. Attenborough, *A Life on Our Planet*, 100.
2. Attenborough, *A Life on Our Planet*, 100.
3. Attenborough, *A Life on Our Planet*, 7.
4. James E. M. Watson et al., "Protect the Last of the Wild", *Nature* 563, no. 11 (2018): 27, accessed October 4, 2022, https://doi.org/10.1038/d41586-018-07183-6.
5. Watson et al., "Protect the Last of the Wild", 29.
6. Intergovernmental Science-Policy Platform on Biodiversity and Ecosystem Services, *The Global Assessment Report on Biodiversity and Ecosystem Services* (Bonn, Germany: IPBES secretariat, 2019), 206-209.
7. Author's own, based on map by James R. Allan, Oscar Venter, and James E.M. Watson, "Figure 1: Workflow of our approach to mapping pressure free lands and the Last of the Wild", in Allan, Venter, and Watson, "Temporally inter-comparable maps of terrestrial wilderness and the Last of the Wild", *Scientific Data* 4, (2017), accessed February 17, 2023, https://www.nature.com/articles/sdata2017187.
8. "Food systems account for more than one third of global greenhouse gas emissions", *The Food and Agriculture Organization of the United Nations*, Mar 9, 2021, accessed May 12, 2023, https://www.fao.org/news/story/en/item/1379373/icode/.
9. Author's own, based on graph by Hannah Ritchie, Pablo Rosado and Max Roser, "The environmental impacts of food and agriculture", from Ritchie, Rosaso, and Roser, "Environmental Impacts of Food Production", *Our World in Data*, 2022,

accessed May 12, 2023, https://ourworldindata.org/environmental-impacts-of-food.

10. "Land Use in Agriculture by the Numbers", *Food and Agriculture Organization of the United Nations*, accessed January 27, 2023, https://www.fao.org/sustainability/news/detail/en/c/1274219/.
11. Max Roser, "Employment in Agriculture", *Our World in Data*, April 26, 2013, accessed February 11, 2023, https://ourworldindata.org/employment-in-agriculture. citing "Employment In Agriculture (% Of Total Employment) (Modeled ILO Estimate)", International Labor Organization, 2023, https://databank.worldbank.org/reports.aspx?dsid=2&series=SL.AGR.EMPL.ZS.
12. Discover Permaculture with Geoff Lawton, "Green is the New Silver (Lining): Crisis, Hope and Permaculture", YouTube video, 2:48, posted by Discover Permaculture with Geoff Lawton, Jan 27, 2019, accessed May 12, 2023, https://www.youtube.com/watch?v=ejMHuRzYlmE.
13. Balvanera et al., "Chapter 2.1. Status and Trends – Drivers of Change", 121.
14. Díaz et al., *IPBES: Summary for Policymakers of the Global Assessment Report on Biodiversity and Ecosystem Services of the Intergovernmental Science-Policy Platform on Biodiversity and Ecosystem Services*, xlvi.
15. WWAP (United Nations World Water Assessment Programme), *The United Nations World Water Development Report 2017. Wastewater: The Untapped Resource*, (Paris: UNESCO, 2017), 2, accessed February 25, 2023, https://unesdoc.unesco.org/ark:/48223/pf0000247153.
16. "AQUASTAT - FAO's Global Information System on Water and Agriculture", *Food and Agriculture Organization of the United Nations*, 2010, accessed March 24, 2023, https://www.fao.org/aquastat/en/overview/methodology/water-use.
17. Food and Agriculture Organization of the United Nations, *The State of the World's Land and Water Resources for Food and Agriculture – Systems at Breaking Point (SOLAW 2021)*, (Rome: FAO, 2021), xi, accessed March 12, 2023, https://www.fao.org/documents/card/en/c/cb7654en.
18. Balvanera et al., "Chapter 2.1. Status and Trends – Drivers of Change", 121. Citing Alexandra S. Richey et al., 'Quantifying Renewable Groundwater Stress with GRACE', *Water Resources Research* 51, no. 7 (2015): 5217–38, https://doi.org/10.1002/2015WR017349.
19. Office of Assistant Director-General (Natural Resources Management and Environment Department), *Livestock and Landscapes* (FAO, 2012), 1, accessed February 8, 2023, https://www.fao.org/3/ar591e/ar591e.pdf.
20. Greenpeace, *Feeding the Problem: The Dangerous Intensification of Animal Farming in Europe*, (Greenpeace: Brussels, 2019), 5, accessed May 22, 2023, https://www.greenpeace.org/static/planet4-eu-unit-stateless/2019/02/83254ee1-190212-feeding-the-problem-dangerous-intensification-of-animal-farming-in-europe.pdf.
21. Greenpeace, *False Sense of Security: Why European Food Systems Lack Resilience, (Greenpeace: Brussels, 2020)*, 12, accessed May 22, 2023, https://www.greenpeace.org/static/planet4-eu-unit-stateless/2020/10/85cc908b-false-sense-of-security_final_en.pdf.
22. Vincent Chatellier, "Review: International Trade In Animal Products and the Place of the European Union: Main Trends over the Last 20 Years," *Animal* 15, no. 1 (2021): 1, accessed May 17, 2023, https://doi.org/10.1016/j.animal.2021.100289.
23. Chatellier, "Review: International Trade In Animal Products and the Place of the European Union", 3.

24. Xiaoming Xu et al., "Global Greenhouse Gas Emissions from Animal-Based Foods Are Twice Those of Plant-Based Foods", *Nature Food* 2, no. 9 (2021): 724, accessed November 24, 2023, https://doi.org/10.1038/s43016-021-00358-x.
25. Stone Barns Center for Food and Agriculture, Armonia LLC, Bonterra Partners and SLM

    Partners, *Back to Grass: The Market Potential for U.S. Grassfed Beef* (2017), 5, accessed October 14, 2022, https://www.stonebarnscenter.org/wp-content/uploads/2017/10/Grassfed_Full_v2.pdf.
26. "Our global food system is the primary driver of biodiversity loss", *UN environment programme*, February 3, 2021, accessed May 12, 2023, https://www.un-ep.org/news-and-stories/press-release/our-global-food-system-primary-driver-biodiversity-loss.
27. Food and Agriculture Organization of the United Nations, *The State of the World's Forests 2022: Forest Pathways for Green Recovery and Building Inclusive, Resilient And Sustainable Economies*, (Rome: FAO, 2022), xiii, accessed May 12, 2023, https://www.fao.org/3/cb9360en/cb9360en.pdf.
28. Hannah Ritchie, "The World Has Lost One-Third of Its Forest, but an End of Deforestation Is Possible", *Our World in Data*, February 9, 2021, accessed January 27, 2023, https://ourworldindata.org/world-lost-one-third-forests. citing Michael Williams, *Deforesting the Earth: From Prehistory to Global Crisis* (Chicago: University of Chicago Press, 2003), https://www.vlebooks.com/Product/Index/468509?page=0.
29. Food and Agriculture Organization of the United Nations, *The State of the World's Forests 2022*, xiii.
30. Food and Agriculture Organization of the United Nations, *The State of the World's Forests 2022*, vi.
31. Karina Winkler, Richard Fuchs, Mark Rounsevell & Martin Herold, "Global land use changes are four times greater than previously estimated", *Nature Communications* 12, (2021), accessed May 12, 2023, https://www.nature.com/articles/s41467-021-22702-2#citeas.
32. Rajeev Pillay et al., "Tropical Forests Are Home to over Half of the World's Vertebrate Species", *Frontiers in Ecology and the Environment* 20, no. 1 (2021): 12, accessed May 12, 2023, https://doi.org/10.1002/fee.2420.
33. Pillay et al., "Tropical Forests Are Home to over Half of the World's Vertebrate Species", 10.
34. Pillay et al., "Tropical Forests Are Home to over Half of the World's Vertebrate Species", 12.
35. Matthew C. Hansen et al., "High-Resolution Global Maps of 21st-Century Forest Cover Change", *Science* 342, no. 6160 (2013): 850, accessed May 12, 2023, https://doi.org/10.1126/science.1244693.
36. Rachel E. Gallery, "Ecology of Tropical Rain Forests", in *Ecology and the Environment*, ed. Russell K. Monson, The Plant Sciences (New York: Springer, 2014), 249, accessed April 17, 2023, https://doi.org/10.1007/978-1-4614-7501-9_4.
37. Anders Krogh, *State of the Tropical Rainforest: The Complete Overview of the Tropical Rainforest, Past and Present*, (Oslo: Rainforest Foundation Norway, 2021), 3, accessed March 30, 2023, https://d5i6is0eze552.cloudfront.net/documents/Publikasjoner/Andre-rapporter/RF_StateOfTheRainforest_2020.pdf?mtime=20210505115205.

38. Hansen et al., "High-Resolution Global Maps of 21st-Century Forest Cover Change", 850.
39. "Palm Oil: Deforestation for Everyday Products", *Rainforest Rescue*, accessed January 30, 2023, https://www.rainforest-rescue.org/topics/palm-oil.
40. Photograph by Luoman, "Deforestation in the Amazon", converted to grayscale by author.
41. Dayton Duncan and Ken Burns, *The Dust Bowl: An Illustrated History* (San Francisco: Chronicle Books, 2012), 65.
42. Tyler J. Lark et al., "Cropland Expansion in the United States Produces Marginal Yields at High Costs to Wildlife", *Nature Communications* 11, no. 9 (2020): 1, accessed February 12, 2023, https://doi.org/10.1038/s41467-020-18045-z.
43. Author's own, based on illustration by Heidi Natura, "Root Systems of Prairie Plants", from Scott Vogt, "Roots of Native Plants", *Dyck Arboretum*, May 24, 2022, accessed on April 17, 2023, https://dyckarboretum.org/roots-of-native-plants/.
44. Author's own, based on infographic by Soil Association, "The Seven Ways to Save Our Soils" from Louise Payton, *Saving Our Soils: Healthy soils for our climate, nature and health* (Bristol: Soil Association, 2021), 18-19, accessed May 3, 2023, https://www.soilassociation.org/media/24941/saving-our-soils-report-dec21.pdf.
45. Díaz et al., *IPBES: Summary for Policymakers of the Global Assessment Report on Biodiversity and Ecosystem Services of the Intergovernmental Science-Policy Platform on Biodiversity and Ecosystem Services*, 24.
46. Nick C. Davidson, "How Much Wetland Has the World Lost? Long-Term and Recent Trends in Global Wetland Area", *Marine and Freshwater Research* 65, no. 10 (2014): G, accessed December 13, 2023, https://doi.org/10.1071/MF14173.
47. Ramsar Convention on Wetlands, *Global Wetland Outlook: State of the World's Wetlands and Their Services to People*, (Gland, Switzerland, 2018), 61, accessed January 15, 2023, https://www.ramsar.org/sites/default/files/documents/library/gwo_e.pdf.
48. Tyler D. Eddy et al., "Global Decline in Capacity of Coral Reefs to Provide Ecosystem Services", *One Earth* 4, no. 9 (2021): 1277, accessed January 15, 2023, https://doi.org/10.1016/j.oneear.2021.08.016.
49. Renee O. Setter, Erik C. Franklin, and Camilo Mora, "Co-Occurring Anthropogenic Stressors Reduce the Timeframe of Environmental Viability for the World's Coral Reefs", *PLOS Biology* 20, no. 10 (2022): 1, accessed January 15, 2023, https://doi.org/10.1371/journal.pbio.3001821.
50. Setter, Franklin, and Mora, "Co-Occurring Anthropogenic Stressors Reduce the Timeframe of Environmental Viability for the World's Coral Reefs", 1.
51. Ove Hoegh-Guldberg et al., "Coral Reef Ecosystems under Climate Change and Ocean Acidification", *Frontiers in Marine Science* 4, no. 5 (2017): 2, accessed February 25, 2023, https://doi.org/10.3389/fmars.2017.00158. Citing Rebecca Fisher et al., "Species Richness on Coral Reefs and the Pursuit of Convergent Global Estimates", *Current Biology* 25, no. 4 (2015), https://doi.org/10.1016/j.cub.2014.12.022.
52. Zoe T. Richards and Jon C. Day, "Biodiversity of the Great Barrier Reef – How Adequately Is It Protected?" *PeerJ* 6, no. 5 (2018): 5, accessed February 6, 2023, https://doi.org/10.7717/peerj.4747. Citing Pat Hutchings, Michael Kingsford, and Ove Hoegh-Guldberg, eds., *The Great Barrier Reef: Biology, Environment and Management* (Boca Raton: CRC Press, 2019), https://www.routledge.com/The-Great-Barrier-Reef-Biology-Environment-and-Management-Second-Edition/Hutchings-Kingsford-Hoegh-Guldberg/p/book/9780367174286.

53. Andreas Dietzel et al., "Long-Term Shifts in the Colony Size Structure of Coral Populations along the Great Barrier Reef", *Proceedings of the Royal Society B: Biological Sciences* 287, no. 1936 (2020): 1, accesses February 6, 2023, https://doi.org/10.1098/rspb.2020.1432.
54. Dietzel et al., "Long-Term Shifts in the Colony Size Structure", 2.
55. Dietzel et al., "Long-Term Shifts in the Colony Size Structure", 4.
56. Dietzel et al., "Long-Term Shifts in the Colony Size Structure", 1.
57. Davy Vanham et al., "The Water Footprint of Different Diets within European Sub-National Geographical Entities", *Nature Sustainability* 1, no. 9 (2018): 518, accessed March 5, 2023, https://doi.org/10.1038/s41893-018-0133-x.
58. Joan Sabaté et al., "The Environmental Cost of Protein Food Choices", *Public Health Nutrition* 18, no. 11 (2014): 2067, accessed March 5, 2023, https://doi.org/10.1017/S1368980014002377.
59. Lan Wang-Erlandsson et al., "A Planetary Boundary for Green Water", *Nature* 3, no. 6 (2022): 380, accessed March 24, 2023, https://doi.org/10.1038/s43017-022-00287-8.
60. Paul Withers and Phil Haygarth, "Agriculture, Phosphorus and Eutrophication: A European Perspective," *Soil Use and Management* 23, no. s1 (2007): 1, accessed March 21, 2023, https://doi.org/10.1111/j.1475-2743.2007.00116.x.
61. Balvanera et al., "Chapter 2.1. Status and Trends – Drivers of Change", 60.
62. Purvis et al., "Chapter 2.2. Status and Trends – Nature", 208.
63. David A. Kroodsma et al., "Tracking the Global Footprint of Fisheries", *Science* 359, no. 6378 (2018): 1, accessed January 28, 2023, https://www.science.org/doi/10.1126/science.aao5646.
64. Food and Agriculture Organization of the United Nations, *The State of World Fisheries and Aquaculture 2020: Sustainability in Action*, (Rome: FAO, 2020), 47, accessed January 27, 2023, https://www.fao.org/3/ca9229en/ca9229en.pdf.
65. Hannah Ritchie and Max Roser, "Fish and Overfishing", *Our World in Data*, October, 2021, accessed March 7, 2023, https://ourworldindata.org/fish-and-overfishing.
66. Douglas J. McCauley et al., "Wealthy Countries Dominate Industrial Fishing", *Science Advances* 4, no. 8 (2018): 4, accessed January 12, 2023, https://doi.org/10.1126/sciadv.aau2161.
67. "NEW RESEARCH: Fishing Gear Accounts for an Alarming Amount of Plastic Pollution in Oceans", *The Nature Conservancy*, September 16, 2021, accessed May 12, 2023, https://www.nature.org/en-us/newsroom/ca-ocean-plastic/.
68. Madeleine M. Jones, "Fishing Debris in the Australian Marine Environment", *Marine Pollution Bulletin* 30, no. 1 (1995): 27, accessed October 20, 2022, https://doi.org/10.1016/0025-326X(94)00108-L.
69. Chelsea M. Rochman et al., "Early Warning Signs of Endocrine Disruption in Adult Fish from the Ingestion of Polyethylene with and without Sorbed Chemical Pollutants from the Marine Environment", *Science of The Total Environment* 493, no. 9 (2014): 660, accessed March 10, 2023, https://doi.org/10.1016/j.scitotenv.2014.06.051.
70. Rochman et al., "Early Warning Signs of Endocrine Disruption in Adult Fish from the Ingestion of Polyethylene with and without Sorbed Chemical Pollutants from the Marine Environment", 660.
71. Bernhard, "The Nitrogen Cycle".
72. James N. Galloway and Ellis B. Cowling, "Reactive Nitrogen and The World: 200 Years of Change", *AMBIO: A Journal of the Human Environment* 31, 2 (2002), 64,

accessed April 10, 2023, https://doi.org/10.1579/0044-7447-31.2.64
73. Robert W. Howarth, "Coastal Nitrogen Pollution: A Review of Sources and Trends Globally and Regionally," *Harmful Algae*, HABs and Eutrophication, 8, no. 12 (2008): 15, accessed March 24, 2023, https://doi.org/10.1016/j.hal.2008.08.015.
74. Julio A Camargo and Alvaro Alonso, "Ecological and Toxicological Effects of Inorganic Nitrogen Pollution in Aquatic Ecosystems: A global assessment", *Environ Int.* 32, 6 (2006): 831.
75. Camargo and Alonso, "Ecological and Toxicological Effects of Inorganic Nitrogen Pollution in Aquatic Ecosystems", 831.
76. "What Is a Dead Zone?", *National Oceanic and Atmospheric Administration*, January 20, 2023, March 20, 2023, https://oceanservice.noaa.gov/facts/deadzone.html.
77. Robert J. Diaz and Rutger Rosenberg, "Spreading Dead Zones and Consequences for Marine Ecosystems", *Science* 321, no. 5891 (2008): 926, accessed November 18, 2022, https://doi.org/10.1126/science.1156401.
78. Attenborough, *A Life on Our Planet*, 216.

9. Design for Life

1. Leopold, *A Sand County Almanac*, xxii.
2. Elizabeth Howell, "How Did Earth Get Its Name?", *Live Science*, May 31, 2022, accessed February 6, 2023, https://www.livescience.com/32274-how-did-earth-get-its-name.html.
3. The Episcopal Church in the United States of America, *The (Online)Book of Common Prayer*, (New York: Church Publishing Incorporated, 2007), 485, accessed March 24, 2023, https://www.bcponline.org/PastoralOffices/BurialI.html.
4. Wendell Berry, *The Unsettling of America*, (San Francisco: Sierra Club Books, 1977).
5. Author's own, using data from Figure 1: Typical Components of Soil, chart by Gurpal S. Toor in Gurpal S Toor, and Amy Shober, "Soils & Fertilizers for Master Gardeners: Soil Organic Matter and Organic Amendments1", *EDIS* 1, (2009), accessed May 9, 2023, DOI:10.32473/edis-mg454-2009.
6. Laurie J. Schmidt, "From the Dust Bowl to the Sahel", *Earthdata*, March 5, 2001, accessed November 13, 2022, https://www.earthdata.nasa.gov/learn/sensing-our-planet/from-the-dust-bowl-to-the-sahel.
7. Jim Morrison, "The 'Great Green Wall' Didn't Stop Desertification, but It Evolved into Something That Might", *Smithsonian Magazine*, August 23, 2016. Accessed May 22, 2023, https://www.smithsonianmag.com/science-nature/great-green-wall-stop-desertification-not-so-much-180960171/.
8. Photograph by FAO/Giulio Napolitano, "22 June 2016, Kaya, Burkina Faso - Women at work in a rice field", converted to grayscale by author.
9. McKinley Corbley, "Dozens of Countries Are Working Together to Plant 'Great Green Wall' across Africa – And It Is Holding Back Poverty", *Good News Network*, March 31, 2023. Accessed May 22, 2023, https://www.goodnewsnetwork.org/dozens-of-countries-have-been-working-to-plant-great-green-wall-and-its-producing-results/.
10. "What Is Permaculture?", *Permaculture Research Institute*, accessed February 28, 2023, https://www.permaculturenews.org/what-is-permaculture/.
11. "Greening The Desert Project", *Greening The Desert Project*, accessed February 28, 2023, https://www.greeningthedesertproject.org/.

12. Author's own, interpretation of "What Is Permaculture?", *Permaculture Research Institute*, accessed February 28, 2023, https://www.permaculturenews.org/what-is-permaculture/, base artwork copyright of Alexandra Steed, *untitled*, woodcut, 1996.
13. Photograph by Greening the Desert Project, from "Home", *Greening the Desert Project*, n.d., accessed March 29, 2023, https://www.greeningthedesert-project.org/, colours converted to grayscale by author.
14. Alexandra Steed, *Naturalized Streescapes: A Case Study of Crown Street, Vancouver* (Vancouver: City of Vancouver, 2002), accessed October 13, 2022, https://sustainabilitynow.com/Docs/Naturalized%20Streetscapes-AS.pdf.
15. Figure 3.2.3 Finished Product, from City of Vancouver, *Crown Street: Sustainable Streetscapes: and Fish Habitat Enhancement Project*, (Vancouver: Engineering Services, City of Vancouver, no date), accessed October 13, 2022, https://www.waterbuck-et.ca/gi/sites/wbcgi/documents/media/39.pdf, converted to grayscale by author.
16. "Water & Energy Cycles" *NASA Goddard Earth Sciences (GES) Data and Information Services Center (DISC)*, accessed November 13, 2022, https://disc.gsfc.nasa.gov/in-formation/documents?title=Water%20%26%20Energy%20Cycles
17. Author's own, interpretation of diagram by US Geological Service, "The Water Cycle", from "Precipitation Education", *NASA*, n.d., accessed May 9th, 2023, https://gpm.nasa.gov/education/images/usgs-water-cycle-diagram. Artwork incorporated from by William Darton and William R. Gardner, *New and Improved View of the Comparative Heights, of the Principal Mountains and Lengths of the Principal Rivers in the World*, 1823, Wikimedia Commons, accessed December 13, 2022, https://commons.wikimedia.org/wiki/File:1823_Darton_and_Gardner_Com-parative_Chart_of_World_Mountains_and_Rivers_-_Geographicus_-_MountainsandRivers-darton-1823.jpg; and Greenock, Scotland, from T. Nelson and Sons, Souvenir of Scotland: its Cities, Lakes, and Mountains, (London, Edinburgh and New York: T. Nelson and Sons, 1889.
18. "Explore All Countries – World", *Central Intelligence Agency*, accessed September 20, 2022, https://www.cia.gov/the-world-factbook/countries/world/.
19. Igor A. Shiklomanov, "Appraisal and Assessment of World Water Resources", *Water International* 25, no. 1 (2000): 11, https://doi.org/10.1080/02508060008686794.
20. "Watershed", National Geographic, accessed February 8, 2023, https://educa-tion.nationalgeographic.org/resource/watershed.
21. Maeve Campbell, "What Are Sponge Cities and Could They Solve China's Water Crisis?", *Euronews*, October 22, 2022, accessed January 12, 2023, https://www.eu-ronews.com/green/2022/10/22/china-s-sponge-cities-are-a-revolutionary-rethink-to-prevent-flooding.
22. Sarah O'Meara, "CITYLAB: Why China Wants to Build Something Called 'sponge Cities'", *Turenscape*, Nov 25, 2015, accessed May 12, 2023, https://www.-turenscape.com/en/news/detail/341.html.
23. Maeve Campbell, "What Are Sponge Cities and Could They Solve China's Water Crisis?".
24. Daisy Gill, "Sponge City Concepts Could Be the Answer to China's Impending Water Crisis", *Earth.Org*, August 30, 2021, accessed January 12, 2023, https://earth.org/sponge-cities-could-be-the-answer-to-impending-water-crisis-in-china/.
25. Tessa Wong, "The Man Turning Cities into Giant Sponges to Embrace Floods", *BBC News*, November 11, 2021, accessed January 12, 2023, https://www.bbc.-

com/news/world-asia-china-59115753.

26. Photographs by Turenscape, from "Yanweizhou Park in Jinhua City", *Landezine*, March 24, 2015, accessed March 29, 2023, https://landezine.com/a-resilient-landscape-yanweizhou-park-in-jinhua-city-by-turenscape/, converted to grayscale by author.
27. Landezine, "A Resilient Landscape: Yanweizhou Park in Jinhua City by Turenscape", March 24, 2015, accessed December 22, 2022, https://landezine.com/a-resilient-landscape-yanweizhou-park-in-jinhua-city-by-turenscape/.
28. Kate Orff, *Toward an Urban Ecology*, (New York: Monacelli Press, Inc, 2016), 89.
29. Eric Klinenberg, "The Seas Are Rising. Could Oysters Help?", *The New Yorker*, Aug 9, 2021, accessed May 12, 2023, https://www.newyorker.com/magazine/2021/08/09/the-seas-are-rising-could-oysters-protect-us.
30. Klinenberg, "The Seas Are Rising. Could Oysters Help?"
31. Klinenberg, "The Seas Are Rising. Could Oysters Help?"
32. Kate Orff, interviewed by Anne Rieselbach, "SCAPE / Landscape Architecture interview", *The Architectural League NY*, March 9, 2012, accessed May 25, 2023, https://archleague.org/article/scape-landscape-interview/.
33. Orff, interview.
34. "Atmosphere", National Geographic, accessed February 8, 2023, https://education.nationalgeographic.org/resource/atmosphere.
35. Spinalcord.com Team, "What You Need to Know About Brain Oxygen Deprivation" *Spinalcord.com*, April 26, 2021, accessed December 22, 2022, https://www.spinalcord.com/blog/what-happens-after-a-lack-of-oxygen-to-the-brain.
36. "The Nine Planetary Boundaries", Stockholm Resilience Centre, accessed February 8, 2023, https://www.stockholmresilience.org/research/planetary-boundaries.html.
37. "Billions of People Still Breathe Unhealthy Air: New WHO Data", *World Health Organization*, April 4, 2022, accessed January 12, 2023, https://www.who.int/news/item/04-04-2022-billions-of-people-still-breathe-unhealthy-air-new-who-data.
38. Nada Osseiran and Christian Lindmeier, "9 Out of 10 People Worldwide Breathe Polluted Air, but More Countries Are Taking Action", *World Health Organisation*, May 2, 2018, accessed January 12, 2023, https://www.who.int/news/item/02-05-2018-9-out-of-10-people-worldwide-breathe-polluted-air-but-more-countries-are-taking-action.
39. "Results from the 2022 Global Green Economy Index™ (GGEI)", *Dual Citizen*, April 18, 2022, accessed November 13, 2022, https://dualcitizeninc.com/results-from-the-2022-global-green-economy-index-ggei/.
40. "The Man-Made History of Stanley Park", *Vancouver Magazine*, August 21, 2013, accessed September 20, 2022, https://www.vanmag.com/city/general/the-man-made-history-of-stanley-park/.
41. Photograph by Edgar Bullon, "Beautiful Aerial View of Lions Gate Bridge, Stanley Park and Vancouver Downtown", converted to grayscale by author.
42. Engineering Services Greenways Program, "City Greenways: Improving Connections across Vancouver", *City of Vancouver*, accessed March 22, 2023, https://vancouver.ca/streets-transportation/city-greenways.aspx.
43. Cheryl Ng Hui Ting, *Natural Capital Valuation of Vancouver's Parks*, (Vancouver: Vancouver Board of Parks & Recreation, 2020), https://sustain.ubc.ca/sites/de-

fault/files/2020-53_Natural%20Capital%20Valuation%20Vancouver%20Parks_Ng.pdf.
44. Ng Hui Ting, *Natural Capital Valuation of Vancouver's Parks*, 5.
45. Marthe de Ferrer, "Singapore: The City That Learned How to Blend Nature with Urban Living", *Euronews*, November 11, 2021, accessed September 20, 2022, https://www.euronews.com/green/2021/11/11/how-has-singapore-learned-to-blend-nature-with-urban-living.
46. "A City of Green Possibilities", *Singapore Green Plan 2030*, accessed March 23, 2023, https://www.greenplan.gov.sg/.
47. "Singapore", *Biophilic Cities*, accessed March 23, 2023, https://www.biophiliccities.org/singapore.
48. "Air Pollution", *National Environment Agency*, accessed March 23, 2023, https://www.nea.gov.sg/our-services/pollution-control/air-pollution/air-quality.
49. Photograph by Patrick Bingham Hall, from "Gardens by the Bay", *Grant Associates*, n.d., accessed May 5, 2023, https://grant-associates.uk.com/projects/gardens-by-the-bay.

10. True Investment

1. Nick Estes, "Bill Gates Is the Biggest Private Owner of Farmland in the United States. Why?" *The Guardian – Opinion*, April 5, 2021, accessed March 23, 2023, https://www.theguardian.com/commentisfree/2021/apr/05/bill-gates-climate-crisis-farmland.
2. Eric O'Keefe, "Farmer Bill", *The Land Report*, January 11, 2021, accessed March 23, 2023, https://landreport.com/2021/01/farmer-bill/.
3. Estes, "Bill Gates Is the Biggest Private Owner of Farmland in the United States. Why?"
4. Jon Bernstein, "Preview: Who Owns the World?", *New Statesman*, March 10, 2011, accessed March 23, 2023, https://www.newstatesman.com/politics/2011/03/queen-state-territories.
5. Kevin Cahill, *Who Owns the World*, 2nd ed. (Edinburgh: Mainstream Publishing Company Ltd, 2007), 21.
6. Guy Shrubsole, *Who Owns England?*, paperback (London: William Collins, 2020), 2.
7. Shrubsole, *Who Owns England?*, 2–3.
8. Cahill, *Who Owns the World*, 156.
9. Cahill, *Who Owns the World*, 17.
10. Kevin Cahill, "Who Owns the World?", *New Statesman*, March 11, 2017, accessed September 20, 2022, https://www.newstatesman.com/politics/2017/03/land-queen-world-australia.
11. "How Big Is a Football Pitch in Acres UK?", *Ibaworldtour*, November 23, 2021, accessed March 16, 2023, https://ibaworldtour.com/how-big-is-a-football-pitch-in-acres-uk/.
12. Martin-Brehm Christensen et al., "Survival of the Richest: How We Must Tax the Super-Rich Now to Fight Inequality" (Oxfam, 2023), 7, accessed October 24, 2022, https://doi.org/10.21201/2023.621477.
13. Tim Gore, "Confronting Carbon Inequality: Putting Climate Justice at the Heart of the COVID-19 Recovery", media briefing (Oxford: Oxfam, 2020), 2, accessed

October 24, 2022, https://oxfamilibrary.openrepository.com/bitstream/handle/10546/621052/mb-confronting-carbon-inequality-210920-en.pdf.

14. Author's own, interpretation of illustration from Gabrielle Merite, "Data Doodles #2020", *Behance*, January 1, 2021, accessed March 29, 2023, https://www.behance.net/gallery/110510317/Data-Doodles-2020.
15. "Richest 1% Bag Nearly Twice as Much Wealth as the Rest of the World Put Together over the Past Two Years", *Oxfam*, January 16, 2023, accessed September 20, 2022, https://www.oxfam.org/en/press-releases/richest-1-bag-nearly-twice-much-wealth-rest-world-put-together-over-past-two-years.
16. Oxfam, *Survival of the Richest: Methodology Note*, (Oxford: Oxfam, 2023), 2, accessed September 20, 2022, https://oxfamilibrary.openrepository.com/bitstream/handle/10546/621477/mn-survival-of-the-richest-methodology-160123-en.pdf
17. Jonathan Woetzel et al., "The Rise and Rise of the Global Balance Sheet: How Productively Are We Using Our Wealth?", *McKinsey & Company*, November 15, 2021, accessed March 23, 2023, https://www.mckinsey.com/industries/financial-services/our-insights/the-rise-and-rise-of-the-global-balance-sheet-how-productively-are-we-using-our-wealth
18. Christensen et al., "Survival of the Richest: How We Must Tax the Super-Rich Now to Fight Inequality", 9.
19. Estes, "Bill Gates Is the Biggest Private Owner of Farmland in the United States. Why?"
20. "Richest 1% Bag Nearly Twice as Much Wealth as the Rest of the World Put Together over the Past Two Years"
21. Jesse Eisinger, Jeff Ernsthausen, and Paul Kiel, "The Secret IRS Files: Trove of Never-Before-Seen Records Reveal How the Wealthiest Avoid Income Tax", *ProPublica*, June 8, 2021, accessed March 23, 2023, https://www.propublica.org/article/the-secret-irs-files-trove-of-never-before-seen-records-reveal-how-the-wealthiest-avoid-income-tax.
22. Christensen et al., "Survival of the Richest: How We Must Tax the Super-Rich Now to Fight Inequality", 11.
23. Yvon Chouinard, "Earth Is Now Our Only Shareholder", *Patagonia Inc.*, September 14, 2022, accessed January 12, 2023, https://eu.patagonia.com/gb/en/ownership/.
24. Oxfam, "Richest 1% Bag Nearly Twice as Much Wealth as the Rest of the World Put Together over the Past Two Years", citing Christensen et al., "Survival of the Richest: How We Must Tax the Super-Rich Now to Fight Inequality".
25. "What You Need to Know about the COP27 Loss and Damage Fund", *United Nations Environment Programme*, November 29, 2022, accessed March 23, 2023, https://www.unep.org/news-and-stories/story/what-you-need-know-about-cop27-loss-and-damage-fund.
26. Anil Markandya and Mikel González-Eguino, "Integrated Assessment for Identifying Climate Finance Needs for Loss and Damage: A Critical Review" in *Loss and Damage from Climate Change: Climate Risk Management, Policy and Governance*, ed. Reinhard Mechler et al. (New York: Springer, Cham, 2019), 349, https://doi.org/10.1007/978-3-319-72026-5_14.
27. Mohamed Adow, "Here's the Exciting COP27 Breakthrough No One Is Talking About", *Context*, December 6, 2022, accessed March 23, 2023, https://www.context.news/net-zero/opinion/heres-the-exciting-cop27-breakthrough-no-one-is-talking-about.

28. Avinash Persaud, "Opinion: The Bridgetown Initiative", *UN Climate Summit*, November 15, 2022, accessed March 23, 2023, https://unclimatesummit.org/opinion-the-bridgetown-initiative/.
29. United Nations Secretary-General, "Secretary-General's Address to the General Assembly", press release, September 20, 2022, accessed January 12, 2023, https://www.un.org/sg/en/content/sg/statement/2022-09-20/secretary-generals-address-the-general-assembly-trilingual-delivered-follows-scroll-further-down-for-all-english-and-all-french.
30. "True Cost of Big Oil's Profits: Trillions in Unpaid Health and Environmental Costs", Transport and Environment, April 28, 2022, accessed November 12, 2022, https://www.transportenvironment.org/discover/true-cost-of-big-oils-profits-trillions-in-unpaid-health-and-environmental-costs/. Citing Léa Pham Van and Gerard Rijk, 'European Big Oil: Big Liability in Carbon, Pollution and Health Care Costs' (Amsterdam, 2022), https://www.transportenvironment.org/wp-content/uploads/2022/04/ReportBigOil25April2022Def.pdf.
31. "The Polluters Pay Climate Fund" *Make Polluters Pay*, accessed March 16, 2023, https://www.makepolluterspaybill.com/the-plan.
32. "2% More: The Extra Step to Save Our Future", *Sapienship*, accessed February 21, 2023, https://www.sapienship.co/decision-makers/2-percent-more.
33. TED, "Yuval Noah Harari: The Actual Cost of Preventing Climate Breakdown | TED", YouTube video, 10:25, posted by TED, Jun 17, 2022, accessed Sep 20, 2022. https://www.youtube.com/watch?app=desktop&v=SiCvGQn-weAg&ab_channel=TED.
34. TED, "Yuval Noah Harari", 2022.
35. TED, "Yuval Noah Harari", 2022.
36. TED, "Yuval Noah Harari", 2022.
37. TED, "Yuval Noah Harari", 2022.
38. TED, "Yuval Noah Harari", 2022.

11. Humble Governance

1. Meenakshi Ganguly, "Seeds of Self-Reliance", *Time*, August 18, 2002, accessed September 20, 2022, https://content.time.com/time/magazine/article/0,9171,338625,00.html.
2. Albert Einstein, letter to Norman Salit, March 4, 1950.
3. "Universal Declaration for the Rights of Mother Earth", *GARN*, April 22, 2010, accessed March 22, 2023, https://www.garn.org/universal-declaration-for-the-rights-of-mother-earth/.
4. "Who We Are", *GARN*, accessed 22 March 2023, https://www.garn.org/about-garn/.
5. Author's own, influenced by Studio Céline Baumann, *Parliament of Plants*, collage, 2019, accessed March 29, 2023, https://studiocelinebaumann.com/works/parliament-of-plants/.
6. "GARN Global Alliance for the Rights of Nature", *GARN*, accessed March 22, 2023, https://www.garn.org/.
7. "Who We Are"
8. Tim Gibbins, "An American Original: Aldo Leopold in the Gila Wilderness", *National Forest Foundation*, Summer/Fall 2014, accessed February 21, 2023,

https://www.nationalforests.org/our-forests/your-national-forests-magazine/aldo-leopold-in-the-gila-wilderness.

9. U.S. Geological Survey (USGS) Gap Analysis Project (GAP), *Protected Areas Database of the United States (PAD-US) 2.1 Summary Statistics by GAP Status Code: U.S. Geological Survey Data Release*, 2021, accessed February 21, 2023, https://doi.org/10.5066/P9KJLB3Q.
10. Heather C. Bingham et al., eds., "Executive Summary," in *Protected Planet Report 2020* (Cambridge: UNEP-WCMC and IUCN, 2020), accessed February 15, 2023, https://livereport.protectedplanet.net/chapter-1.
11. Heather C. Bingham et al., eds., "Chapter 5", in *Protected Planet Report 2020* (Cambridge: UNEP-WCMC and IUCN, 2020), accessed February 15, 2023 https://livereport.protectedplanet.net/chapter-5.
12. Convention on Biological Diversity, "Joint Statement on Post-2020 Global Biodiversity Framework", press release, January 30, 2019, accessed November 13, 2022, https://presspage-production-content.s3.amazonaws.com/uploads/1763/jointstatement-905923.pdf?10000.
13. Nigel Dudley, *Guidelines for Applying Protected Area Management Categories*, (Gland, Switzerland: IUCN, 2008), 2.
14. Using data from Nigel Dudley, *Guidelines for Applying Protected Area Management Categories*, 13-22.
15. Nigel Dudley, *Guidelines for Applying Protected Area Management Categories,* 26.
16. Eric Dinerstein et al., "A Global Deal for Nature: Guiding Principles, Milestones, and Targets," *Science Advances* 5, no. 4 (2019): eaaw2869, accessed September 20, 2022, https://doi.org/10.1126/sciadv.aaw2869.
17. "Indigenous Peoples: 6 Ways Indigenous Peoples Are Helping the World Achieve #ZeroHunger," *Food and Agriculture Organization of the United Nations*, August 9, 2017, accessed September 20, 2022, https://www.fao.org/indigenous-peoples/news-article/en/c/1029002.
18. "Government of Canada Announces $340 Million to Support Indigenous-Led Conservation," press release, *Environment and Climate Change Canada*, August 12, 2021, accessed February 17, 2023, https://www.canada.ca/en/environment-climate-change/news/2021/08/government-of-canada-announces-340-million-to-support-indigenous-led-conservation.html.
19. Jim Robbins, "How Returning Lands to Native Tribes Is Helping Protect Nature," *Yale Environment 360*, June 3, 2021, accessed February 24, 2023, https://e360.yale.edu/features/how-returning-lands-to-native-tribes-is-helping-protect-nature.
20. Ben Smee, "Indigenous Traditional Owners Win Back Daintree Rainforest in Historic Deal," *The Guardian*, September 28, 2021, accessed February 24, 2023, https://www.theguardian.com/australia-news/2021/sep/29/indigenous-traditional-owners-win-back-daintree-rainforest-in-historic-deal.
21. Alicia Guzmán León and Gregorio Mirabal, "Building Global Support for Indigenous-Led Efforts to Protect 80% of Amazonia by 2025," *IUCN: Crossroads Blog* (blog), November 25, 2021, accessed February 12, 2021, https://www.iucn.org/crossroads-blog/202111/building-global-support-indigenous-led-efforts-protect-80-amazonia-2025.
22. Organisation for Economic Co-operation and Development, *OECD Environmental Performance Reviews: Denmark 1999*, (OECD, 1999), 1, accessed November 13, 2022, https://www.oecd.org/env/country-reviews/2447500.pdf.

23. Rosie Frost, 'The End of Fossil Fuels: Which Countries Have Banned Exploration and Extraction?', *Euronews Green*, January 14, 2022, accessed November 29, 2022, https://www.euronews.com/green/2021/08/12/the-end-of-fossil-fuels-which-countries-have-banned-exploration-and-extraction.
24. World Future Council, "Forest Policies from Six Countries Shortlisted for Future Policy Award", press release, July 5, 2011, accessed September 20, 2022, https://www.worldfuturecouncil.org/forest-policies-six-countries-shortlisted-future-policy-award/.
25. Environment Act, 2021, c. 30 (The Government of the United Kingdom).
26. Ursula Quill, "Ireland's Citizens' Assembly on Biodiversity Loss: Potential and Limitations for Deliberative Democracy," *ConstitutionNet*, January 31, 2023, accessed March 24, 2023, https://constitutionnet.org/news/irelands-citizens-assembly-biodiversity-loss.
27. United Nations Environment Programme, *Environmental Rule of Law: First Global Report*, (Nairobi: United Nations Environment Programme, 2019), viii, accessed November 13, 2023, https://wedocs.unep.org/bitstream/handle/20.500.11822/27279/Environmental_rule_of_law.pdf?sequence=1&isAllowed=y.
28. "Agricultural Land Use in England at 1 June 2022", *Department for Environment Food & Rural Affairs*, September 29, 2022, accessed April 15, 2023, https://www.gov.uk/government/statistics/agricultural-land-use-in-england/agricultural-land-use-in-england-at-1-june-2022.
29. Jonathan Watts, "1% Of Farms Operate 70% of World's Farmland," *The Guardian*, November 24, 2020, accessed September 20, 2022, https://www.theguardian.com/environment/2020/nov/24/farmland-inequality-is-rising-around-the-world-finds-report.
30. Alice Calder, "Agricultural Subsidies: Everyone's Doing It", *Hinrich Foundation*, October 15, 2020, accessed November 13, 2022, https://www.hinrichfoundation.com/research/article/protectionism/agricultural-subsidies/. Citing Organisation for Economic Co-operation and Development, *Agricultural Policy Monitoring and Evaluation 2022: Reforming Agricultural Policies for Climate Change Mitigation*, (Paris: OECD Publishing, 2022), https://doi.org/10.1787/7f4542bf-en.
31. Food and Agriculture Organization of the United Nations, United Nations Development Programme, and United Nations Environment Programme, *A Multi-Billion-Dollar Opportunity: Repurposing Agricultural Support to Transform Food Systems*, (Rome: FAO, 2021), vii.
32. Food and Agriculture Organization of the United Nations, United Nations Development Programme, and United Nations Environment Programme, *A Multi-Billion-Dollar Opportunity*, xvii.
33. Author's own.
34. Food and Agriculture Organization of the United Nations, *Building a Common Vision for Sustainable Food and Agriculture: Principles and Approaches* (Rome: FAO, 2014), 12, accessed March 24, 2023, https://www.fao.org/3/i3940e/i3940e.pdf.
35. Food and Agriculture Organization of the United Nations, *Building a Common Vision for Sustainable Food and Agriculture*, 18.
36. International Union for Conservation of Nature, "Agriculture and Land Health Initiative," initiation note, April 28, 2021, accessed November 13, 2022, https://www.iucn.org/sites/default/files/2022-06/in_agric_dialogue_28042021_for_sharing-20210805.pdf.

37. Food and Agriculture Organization of the United Nations, United Nations Development Programme, and United Nations Environment Programme, *A Multi-Billion-Dollar Opportunity*, xiii.
38. "Key Reforms in the New Cap," *European Commission*, January 26, 2023, accessed March 24, 2023, https://agriculture.ec.europa.eu/common-agricultural-policy/cap-overview/new-cap-2023-27/key-reforms-new-cap_en.
39. Department for Environment Food & Rural Affairs, "Environmental Land Management Schemes: Overview", *GOV.UK*, March 15, 2021, accessed February 23, 2023, https://www.gov.uk/government/publications/environmental-land-management-schemes-overview/environmental-land-management-scheme-overview.
40. Food and Agriculture Organization of the United Nations, United Nations Development Programme, and United Nations Environment Programme, *A Multi-Billion-Dollar Opportunity*, 96.
41. Shaik Galab et al., *Impact Assessment of Zero Budget Natural Farming in Andhra Pradesh – Consolidated Report 2018-19: A Comprehensive Approach Using Crop Cutting Experiments*, (Hyderabad: Centre for Economic and Social Studies, 2020), accessed September 20, 2023, https://idsap.in/assets/reports/3%20Consolidated%20Report%202018-19.pdf.
42. Food and Agriculture Organization of the United Nations, United Nations Development Programme, and United Nations Environment Programme, *A Multi-Billion-Dollar Opportunity*, 97. Citing Galab et al., "Impact Assessment of Zero Budget Natural Farming in Andhra Pradesh—Consolidated Report 2018-19: A Comprehensive Approach Using Crop Cutting Experiments".
43. "Empowering Women Farmers to End Hunger and Poverty", *Oxfam*, May 25, 2022, accessed November 13, 2023, https://www.oxfam.org/en/empowering-women-farmers-end-hunger-and-poverty.
44. "Empowering Women Farmers to End Hunger and Poverty".
45. "Women in Agriculture", *Global Agriculture*, accessed February 23, 2023, https://www.globalagriculture.org/report-topics/women-in-agriculture.html.
46. "Women Hold the Key to Building a World Free from Hunger and Poverty", *Food and Agriculture Organization of the United Nations*, December 16, 2016, accessed February 23, 2023, https://www.fao.org/news/story/en/item/460267/icode/.
47. "Women Hold the Key to Building a World Free from Hunger and Poverty".
48. The SDG Land Momentum Group, *5 Years Later: Progress Towards the SDG Land Rights Commitments*, (The Land Portal Foundation, 2020), 3, accessed October 18, 2022, https://landportal.org/library/resources/progress-towards-sdg-land-rights-commitments.
49. "The 17 Goals", *United Nations*, n.d., accessed May 12, 2023, https://sdgs.un.org/goals, converted to black and white by author.
50. "Her Rights. Her Land. A Better Future for All", *Stand For Her Land Campaign*, accessed February 23, 2023, https://stand4herland.org/.
51. "New Chinese Land Laws Will Help Strengthen Land Rights of 240 Million Families", *Landesa*, March 24, 2019, accessed October 17, 2022, https://www.landesa.org/press-and-media/new-chinese-land-laws-will-help-strengthen-land-rights-of-240-million-families/.
52. "Three Organizations. One Vision", *Friends Of Navdanya*, accessed February 21, 2023, https://www.friendsofnavdanya.org/about-us.
53. "Friends of Navdanya", *Friends of Navdanya*, accessed February 21, 2023, https://www.friendsofnavdanya.org/.

54. Vandana Shiva, "The Takeover of Democracy by Corporations and Billionaires", *Navdanya International* (blog), July 15, 2021, accessed February 21, 2023, https://navdanyainternational.org/the-takeover-of-democracy-by-corporations-and-billionaires/.
55. Vandana Shiva and Vaibhav Singh, "Health per Acre: Organic Solutions to Hunger and Malnutrition", accessed March 22, 2023, https://navdanyainternational.org/wp-content/uploads/2017/07/Health-Per-Acre.pdf.

12. Landscape-Led Development

1. McHarg, *Design with Nature*, 5.
2. Lynn Margulis, James Corner, and Brian Hawthorne, *Ian McHarg: Conversations with Students: Dwelling in Nature* (New York: Princeton Architectural Press, 2007).
3. McHarg, *Design with Nature,* vii.
4. Margulis, Corner, and Hawthorne, *Ian McHarg: Conversations with Students: Dwelling in Nature.*
5. McHarg, *Design with Nature*, 7.
6. Author's own, based on FIG.14 Inspirational Section for SEEPark, in Alexandra Steed URBAN, *Vol. 1 South Essex Strategic Green and Blue Infrastructure Study: Resilient by Nature* (2020), 18.
7. McHarg, *Design with Nature*, 57-61.
8. *Breaking Boundaries: The Science Of Our Planet*, Netflix, 2021, streaming broadcast, https://www.netflix.com/gb/title/81336476.
9. "What Is GIS?", *Esri*, accessed February 24, 2023, https://www.esri.com/en-us/what-is-gis/overview.
10. Tom Turner, "Ian McHarg's Legacy to Landscape Architecture and Landscape Urbanism", *Landscape Architecture Association*, December 11, 2017, accessed November 18, 2022, http://www.landscapearchitecture.org.uk/ian-mchargs-legacy-landscape-architecture-landscape-urbanism/.
11. Jaqueline Tyrwhitt, "Surveys for Planning", in *Town and Country Planning Textbook*, ed. Association for Planning and Regional Reconstruction (London: Architectural Press, 1950), 146–96.
12. Paola Zanotto, "Planning Education by Post: Jaqueline Tyrwhitt's War Correspondence Course", in *MOMOWO: Women Designers, Craftswomen, Architects and Engineers between 1918 and 1945*, ed. Marjan Groot et al. (Ljubljana: ZRC Publishing House, 2017), 152, accessed February 24, 2023, https://omp.zrc-sazu.si/zalozba/catalog/download/1141/4844/680-1?inline=1.
13. Carl Steinitz, Paul Parker, and Lawrie Jordan, "Hand-Drawn Overlays: Their History and Prospective Uses," *Landscape Architecture Magazine* 66, no. 5 (1976): 446, accessed April 15, 2023, https://www.jstor.org/stable/44664237.
14. Tyrwhitt, "Surveys for Planning".
15. FIG.15 A Layered Approach to South Essex Mapping and Analysis in Alexandra Steed URBAN, *Vol. 1 South Essex Strategic Green and Blue Infrastructure Study: Resilient by Nature* (2020), 21.
16. Pope, "Of the Use of Riches".
17. Irizar, "Da Vinci's Vitruvian Man and the Measure of All Things".
18. FIG.25 SEE Park digital information in Alexandra Steed URBAN, *Vol. 1 South Essex Strategic Green and Blue Infrastructure Study: Resilient by Nature* (2020), 31-32.

19. Table 3 Themes - Challenges, Objectives - Opportunities, and GBI Functions in Alexandra Steed URBAN, *Vol. 1 South Essex Strategic Green and Blue Infrastructure Study: Resilient by Nature* (2020), 19-20.
20. FIG.146 Proposed GBI Layout: South Essex in Alexandra Steed URBAN, *Vol. 1 South Essex Strategic Green and Blue Infrastructure Study: Resilient by Nature* (2020), 90.
21. Gayle, McIntyre, and Martinsson, "Funding for England's Parks Down £330M a Year in Real Terms since 2010".
22. Pratt, "The Rise of the Quasi-Public Space and Its Consequences for Cities and Culture", 2.
23. Alexander Wandl and Marcello Magoni, "Sustainable Planning of Peri-Urban Areas: Introduction to the Special Issue", *Planning Practice & Research* 32, no. 1 (2017): 2, https://doi.org/10.1080/02697459.2017.1264191.
24. Photograph by Manfred Thuerig, "View towards Al Ula, an oasis in the middle of the mountainous landscape of Saudi Arabia".
25. Author's own.
26. Author's own.
27. UNWTO and the G20 Tourism Working Group, *AlUla Framework for Inclusive Community Development through Tourism* (Madrid: World Tourism Organization, 2020).
28. Nadine V. Gerner et al., "Large-Scale River Restoration Pays Off: A Case Study of Ecosystem Service Valuation for the Emscher Restoration Generation Project," *Ecosystem Services* 30, no. Part B (2018): 327, https://doi.org/10.1016/j.ecoser.2018.03.020.
29. "NODU: Landschaftspark Duisburg Nord, DE", *Latz + Partner*, accessed March 23, 2023, https://www.latzundpartner.de/de/projekte/postindustrielle-landschaften/landschaftspark-duisburg-nord-de/.
30. Emscher Landschafts Park, *Emscher Landscape Park: Visitor's Guide*, (Salzhausen: Werbedruck GmbH, 2013), 3–4, accessed March 23, 2023, https://climate-adapt.eea.europa.eu/en/metadata/case-studies/a-flood-and-heat-proof-green-emscher-valley-germany/11305605.pdf.
31. Photograph by Diadis, "Landschaftspark Duisburg Nord Industrial Culture Germany", converted to grayscale by author.
32. Arancha Muñoz Criado, "Green Infrastructure: A New Landscape Strategy for Valencia, Spain: Policies, Plans and Actions, 2007-2010," (Valencia: Generalitat Valenciana, 2009).
33. Photograph by Joaquin Corbalan, "Valencia, Spain - November 24, 2022: View of the Cabezera de Valencia park with panoramic views of the northern area of the city", converted to grayscale by author.
34. "Room for the River Programme", *Dutch Water Sector*, 2019, accessed February 23, 2023, https://www.dutchwatersector.com/news/room-for-the-river-programme.
35. Photograph by Donald Böing, "Aerial of Deventer and the IJssel river, part of the room for the river high water protection program", converted to grayscale by author.

13. Green Education and Skills

1. Darius Radkevicius, "My Green School. Future of School and or Happiness. Education and Bhutan", YouTube video, 44:36, posted by Darius Radkevicius,

September 25, 2018, accessed March 23, 2023, https://www.youtube.com/watch?v=Mg-EmqkAYP8.

2. Hammad Gilani et al., "Decadal Land Cover Change Dynamics in Bhutan", *Journal of Environmental Management, Land Cover/Land Use Change (LC/LUC) and Environmental Impacts in South Asia* 148, no. 1 (2015): 91, https://doi.org/10.1016/j.jenvman.2014.02.014.
3. Aparna Banerjee and Rajib Bandopadhyay, "Biodiversity Hotspot of Bhutan and Its Sustainability," *Current Science* 110, no. 4 (2016): 521.
4. John Elliott, "The King of Bhutan's Hopes in 1987 for Gross National Happiness," *Riding the Elephant* (blog), November 27, 2015, accessed September 20, 2022, https://ridingtheelephant.wordpress.com/2015/11/27/the-king-of-bhutans-hopes-in-1987-for-gross-national-happiness/.
5. Royal Government of Bhutan, *Bhutan: In Pursuit of Sustainable Development,* (Thimphu: National Environment Commission Secretariat, 2012), ii, accessed February 23, 2023, https://sustainabledevelopment.un.org/content/documents/798bhutanreport.pdf.
6. Darius Radkevicius. "My Green School", 2018.
7. Annie Kelly, "'Let Nature Be Your Teacher': Bhutan Takes Conservation into the Classroom", *The Guardian,* January 2, 2013, accessed March 24, 2023, https://www.theguardian.com/global-development/2013/jan/02/nature-teacher-bhutan-conservation-classroom.
8. *An Inconvenient Truth,* (Lawrence Bender Productions, 2006), documentary.
9. John hardy, "My Green School Dream", TED talk, 2010, accessed September 20, 2022, https://www.ted.com/talks/john_hardy_my_green_school_dream/transcript?language=en.
10. "Green School International", *Green School,* accessed February 28, 2023, https://www.greenschool.org/.
11. "Green Bronx Machine," *Green Bronx Machine,* accessed February 28 2023, https://greenbronxmachine.org/.
12. Stephen Ritz, "Stephen Ritz: A Teacher Growing Green in the South Bronx", YouTube video, 13:42, posted by "TED", July 31, 2012, accessed April 17, 2023, https://www.youtube.com/watch?v=RF6qTlgtHU0.
13. Stephen Ritz, "Stephen Ritz: A Teacher Growing Green in the South Bronx", 2012.
14. "Eco-Schools History," *Eco Schools*, accessed February 28, 2023, https://www.ecoschools.global/our-history.
15. "What Is the Permaculture Research Institute," *Permaculture Research Institute,* accessed February 28, 2023, https://www.permaculturenews.org/permaculture-research-institute/what-is-the-permaculture-research-institute/.
16. "What Is the Permaculture Research Institute".
17. Photograph by Bjmcse, "Spring farmland on mountain", converted to grayscale by author.
18. VPRO Documentary, "Regreening the Desert with John D. Liu | VPRO Documentary | 2012", YouTube video, 47:30, posted by VPRO Documentary, May 7, 2017, accessed October 2, 2023, https://www.youtube.com/watch?v=IDgDWbQtlKI.
19. "Vision, Mission & Foundation", *Ecosystem Restoration Camps*, August 24, 2017, accessed November 12, 2022, https://ecosystemrestorationcamps.org/foundation/.

20. "How It Works", *Ecosystem Restoration Camps*, February 17, 2020, accessed November 12, 2022, https://ecosystemrestorationcamps.org/how-it-works/.
21. Landscape Institute, *Skills for Greener Places: A Review of the UK's Landscape Workforce*, (London: Landscape Institute, 2022), 17, accessed January 12, 2023, https://landscapewpstorage01.blob.core.windows.net/www-landscapeinstitute-org/2022/12/773450-Landscape-Institute_INTERACTIVE.pdf.
22. Author's own, interpretation of "Figure 2 Definition of the landscape economy" and "Figure 3 A coalition of landscape activities", in Landscape Institute, 17-18.
23. Landscape Institute, 10.
24. Mike Appleton, *A Global Register of Competences for Protected Area Practitioners*, (Gland: IUCN, 2016), vii, accessed February 23, 2023, https://portals.iucn.org/library/sites/library/files/documents/PATRS-002.pdf.
25. Landscape Institute, 51.
26. Juhohn Lee, "Here's Why the Ultra-Wealthy like Bill Gates and Thomas Peterffy Are Investing in U.S. Farmland," *CNBC*, August 20, 2021, accessed on March 24, 2023, https://www.cnbc.com/2021/08/20/heres-why-the-ultra-wealthy-like-bill-gates-investing-to-farmland.html.
27. Author's own.
28. Author's own.

14. Tend Your Plot

1. Voltaire, *Candide* (Geneva: Cramer, 1759), 2006 eBook edition by Project Gutenberg, 167, accessed March 24, 2023, https://www.gutenberg.org/files/19942/19942-h/19942-h.htm.
2. Josh Jones, "What Voltaire Meant When He Said That 'We Must Cultivate Our Garden': An Animated Introduction," *Open Culture*, September 24, 2020, accessed February 23, 2023, https://www.openculture.com/2020/09/what-voltaire-meant-when-he-said-that-we-must-cultivate-our-garden.html.
3. Author's own.
4. "Climate Plans Remain Insufficient: More Ambitious Action Needed Now", *United Nations Framework Convention on Climate Change*, October 26, 2022, accessed on December 5, 2022, https://unfccc.int/news/climate-plans-remain-insufficient-more-ambitious-action-needed-now.
5. United Nations Department of Economic and Social Affairs, *The Sustainable Development Goals Report 2022*, (New York: UN, 2022), accessed on March 24, 2023, https://unstats.un.org/sdgs/report/2022/The-Sustainable-Development-Goals-Report-2022.pdf.
6. UN Women, *Progress on the Sustainable Development Goals: The Gender Snapshot 2022*, (New York: UN, 2022), 18, accessed March 24, 2023, https://data.unwomen.org/sites/default/files/documents/Publications/GenderSnapshot_2022.pdf.
7. Ritchie, "Cars, Planes, Trains: Where Do CO2 Emissions from Transport Come From?". Citing "Historical Emissions", *Climate Watch*, 2019, https://www.climatewatchdata.org/data-explorer/historical-emissions?historical-emissions-data-sources=cait&historical-emissions-gases=co2&historical-emissions-regions=All%20Selected&historical-emissions-sectors=total-including-lucf%2Ctransportation&page=1&sort_col=country&sort_dir=ASC.
8. Díaz et al., *IPBES: Summary for Policymakers of the Global Assessment Report on Biodiversity and Ecosystem Services of the Intergovernmental Science-Policy Platform on*

Biodiversity and Ecosystem Services, 4.

9. "Should You Be Thinking about Your Personal Carbon Budget?" *Flightnook*, accessed March 7, 2023, https://www.flightnook.com/should-you-be-thinking-about-your-personal-carbon-budget.
10. "How to Help: Calculate Your Carbon Footprint," *The Nature Conservancy*, accessed March 7, 2023, https://www.nature.org/en-us/get-involved/how-to-help/carbon-footprint-calculator/.
11. Ritchie, Rosado, and Roser, "Environmental Impacts of Food Production,".
12. Michael Pollan, "In Defense of Food Reader's Guide," Penguin Random House, accessed 22 March 2023, https://www.penguinrandomhouse.-com/books/301692/in-defense-of-food-by-michael-pollan/9780143114963.
13. "5 Facts about Food Waste and Hunger", *World Food Programme*, June 2, 2020, accessed September 20, 2022, https://www.wfp.org/stories/5-facts-about-food-waste-and-hunger.
14. Paul Hawken, ed., *Drawdown: The Most Comprehensive Plan Ever Proposed to Reverse Global Warming* (London: Penguin Books, 2018), 42.
15. Hawken, *Drawdown*, 159.
16. Hawken, *Drawdown*, 164–65.
17. Hawken, *Drawdown*, 1.
18. "Garden as a Resource for Wildlife", *Wildlife Gardening Forum*, February 8, 2020, accessed February 23, 2023, http://www.wlgf.org/garden_resource.html.
19. Dusty Gedge, "How London Could Become the Green Capital of the World," *Livingroofs* (blog), accessed March 7, 2023, https://livingroofs.org/how-london-could-becoming-the-green-roof-capital-of-the-world/.
20. "Be the Change You Wish To See in the World", *Quote Investigator*, October 23, 2017, accessed March 7, 2023, https://quoteinvestigator.com/2017/10/23/be-change/.

15. Reframing Our Future

1. Albert Einstein, *The World as I See It*, abridged (Texas: Snowball Publishing, 2014), 17.

Appendix A

1. "The nine planetary boundaries", *Stockholm Resilience Centre*, n.d., accessed October 13, 2022, https://www.stockholmresilience.org/research/planetary-boundaries/the-nine-planetary-boundaries.html.

Appendix B

1. "Universal Declaration for the Rights of Mother Earth", *GARN*, April 22, 2010, accessed March 22, 2023, https://www.garn.org/universal-declaration-for-the-rights-of-mother-earth/.

errors or omissions in the above list and would be grateful if notified of any corrections that should be incorporated in future reprints or editions of this book.

Acknowledgments

This book is the culmination of a lifetime of learning and experience, and I am grateful to the many individuals who have supported and encouraged me along the way. First and foremost, I would like to express my gratitude to the exceptional educators who introduced me to the world of landscape architecture during my university studies. Don Luymes, Patrick Condon, Susan Herrington, Moura Quayle, Alan Duncan, Liz Watts and Illarion Gallant gave me generous instruction. Along with colleagues Joanne Proft, Derek Masselink, Angela Gonyea Morin, and Dale Mikkelsen, they created an inspirational learning environment that nurtured my passion for landscape architecture.

I am indebted to the countless experts, practitioners, and visionaries who have generously shared their wisdom over the past two decades. Through enlightening conversations and collaborations, both locally and internationally, with work colleagues, corporate executives, community groups, policymakers, university students, and academics, my understanding of the intricate interplay between landscapes, people, and the environment has been greatly enriched. Each interaction has left an indelible mark on my journey, and I extend my heartfelt appreciation to all those who have contributed to the vibrant tapestry of knowledge and insight that has shaped this book.

I would like to extend my sincere thanks to the individuals who provided support and guidance throughout the process of writing this book. Scott Allan at SPS offered invaluable coaching, helping me navigate the challenges and complexities of the writing journey. Audrey Tang provided encouragement and insightful feedback. I am also deeply grateful to my dear friend Kim Segel, whose editing skills and keen eye for detail enhanced the clarity and coherence of the manuscript.

I am also profoundly thankful for my dedicated team at Urban, including Lei Jiao, Poppy Main, Rhys Jones, Mei-Ling Schmid, Warren Osborne, and Vera Patricio. Their beautiful graphic contributions, as well as their feedback on draft versions, have been instrumental. Special thanks go to John Goldwyn, Susanna Abse and Roger Jeffs for their encouragement in embarking on this book project.

Throughout my career, I have had the privilege of collaborating with exceptional colleagues who have enriched my professional journey and become friends. Kim Wilkie, Jason Prior, Arancha Munoz, Martha Schwartz, Julian Gitsham, Edward Denison, and Guang Yu Ren have significantly shaped my thinking, challenged me to push boundaries, and provided support and guidance.

I am immensely grateful for the opportunities afforded me through my involvement with the Office for Place, Design Council, and The Bartlett. These organisations have provided enrichment to both my life and career.

To my dear friends and family, including Jemima Hoadley, Joanna Dawes, Vanessa Muscara, Juliet Bingham, Jenny Higham, Charlotte Lamont, Ellen Nassiri, Sarah Fenton, Fouzia Stanley, Kirree Jenkings, Gorana Shepherd, Olga Gomez, and Wendy Fitzgerald in Vancouver, I am forever grateful.

Countless inspirational thinkers, philosophers, and visionaries have shaped my worldview. From the profound ecological insights of Rachel Carson and Aldo Leopold to the urban wisdom of Jane Jacobs, the scientific brilliance of Albert Einstein and Stephen Hawking, the spiritual teachings of Carl Jung, Eckhart Tolle and Mark Nepo, the environmental activism of Vandana Shiva and Johan Rockstrom, and the forward-thinking perspectives of Yuval Harari and Kate Raworth, among countless others, each has left an indelible impression on my thinking and inspired me to envision a more sustainable, harmonious, and inclusive world.

Finally, I must express my deepest gratitude to my parents, Joan and Derek, who instilled in me a love for nature and beauty and a quest for truth from an early age. I extend my appreciation to all my family in Vancouver, notably Shauna Seiler, Anna Hoffmann, Lexi Kleaman, and Deb Traub for their love and support. And last but certainly not least, I am immensely grateful to my children, Johnny and Angus, whose inspiration has driven me to strive for a better world. Their patience and support during the countless hours I spent writing in the kitchen, with fewer homemade muffins for breakfast, are truly appreciated.

About the Author

Alexandra Steed is a passionate landscape architect with a deep commitment to art, sustainability, and the transformative power of landscapes. As a Fellow of the Landscape Institute (FLI) and the Royal Society of Arts (FRSA), she has made a lasting impact on urban environments globally over her two-decade career.

In 2013, she founded URBAN with a vision to create landscapes that bring joy and enhance well-being. Steed's designs aim to foster meaningful connections with the natural environment and enrich people's lives.

Beyond her practice, Steed actively advises and serves on expert panels for organisations such as the Design Council UK and the Government's Office for Place. She shares her knowledge as a lecturer at The Bartlett, UCL, and volunteers her time to empower communities and develop inclusive public spaces through neighbourhood plans and landscape visions.

Steed's exceptional contributions to landscape architecture have earned her prestigious awards, including the WAFX Award for innovative solutions to global challenges. She has also received The LI Award for Excellence in Tackling Climate Change and won the Best Landscape Architecture Project in the UK. Additionally, she was shortlisted for the Sir David Attenborough Award, highlighting her dedication to preserving and enhancing biodiversity and ecosystems.

With valuable experience as Principal of Design for AECOM London and Director of Martha Schwartz Partners' London office, Steed is dedicated to integrating natural processes and systems into her designs. Her work and advocacy strive to combat climate change, protect ecosystems, and inspire others to appreciate and engage with the natural world.

info@alexandrasteedurban.com

www.alexandrasteedurban.com

x.com/@ASUrbanLondon

instagram.com/alexandrasteedurban

Manufactured by Amazon.ca
Acheson, AB

11961854R00188